communications graphics

communications
graphics

Matthew P. Murgio

VAN NOSTRAND REINHOLD COMPANY
New York   Cincinnati   Toronto   London   Melbourne

Designed by Klaus Burg
Type set by H. O. Bullard
Printed by The Guinn Company
Bound by Van Rees Book Binding Corp.
Published by Van Nostrand Reinhold Company
450 West 33 Street, New York, N.Y. 10001
Published simultaneously in Canada by
D. Van Nostrand Company (Canada), Ltd.

16 15 14 13 12 11 10 9 8 7 6 5 4 3 2 1

Acknowledgments

To produce a book such as this one, singlehandedly, is indeed rare, and this book is not one of those rarities. A number of people have made valuable and significant contributions, without which the book would have been considerably less than it is.

Without exception, each person I called upon for help gave freely of his time, talents, and moral support — accordingly, I extend my gratitude to them all. There are, however, a few on whom I leaned most heavily, who I feel should be pointed out.

The overall design, as well as a number of illustrations, are the work of Klaus Burg, who is truly the Design Editor of the book. Klaus also deserves the credit for bringing this book to the attention of the Reinhold Book Corporation, where he is a consulting editor.

The bulk of the preparation of artwork — a meticulously demanding job — was done by my wife, Riff. The illustrations are immeasurably enriched by her craftsmanship.

The many charts provided by the courtesy of Lybrand, Ross Bros. & Montgomery were done by the firm's Graphics Group, and in particular by Joan Vilató, who is the Art Director.

My gratitude is also extended to William Metzig and Ib Ohlsson for the magnificent and excellent illustrations with which they provided me. Also, I wish to thank the organizations that cooperated so graciously in allowing me to use their illustrations and photographs.

Editorially, I was helped immensely by Beatrice Burg, who kept me on the straight and narrow, and brought a sense of order and clarity to my work.

I am also extremely grateful to Robert Muir, and to my brother Joseph Murgio, for their help in the technical aspects of the book. Bob's ability in this area, which he exercised in his editorial reviews for the technical soundness of the material, was truly most invaluable to me. Joe is credited particularly with the mathematical work and computer programming he did for the material on facilities planning. His knowledge and review in this and other areas were indeed indispensable.

Special thanks go to Margaret DiBerardino, who not only found time to type the whole manuscript, but also did an outstanding job of copy-editing.

Finally, I would like to express my thanks to James J. Mahon, a partner of Lybrand, for his enthusiasm and encouragement.

Contents

Introduction

In the City of London, at the head of Ludgate Hill, stands Saint Paul's Cathedral — the Baroque masterpiece of Sir Christopher Wren. Its construction began in 1675 and continued for some thirty-five years. When the masterly edifice was completed, King George I told Wren that his work was "amusing, awful, and artificial." The King's words would mortally crush a modern architect, but inasmuch as 300 years ago amusing meant amazing, awful meant awe-inspiring, and artificial meant artistic, Sir Christopher was indeed delighted with the royal compliment.

Words, like styles, have vogues. Every generation introduces new words into our vocabulary. Some words, like radio, were invented to fill an identification void, and some words, like automation, were coined to express broader concepts. But by and large the meanings of existing words are expanded to take on additional connotations, or, through the mysterious evolution of usage, are changed altogether.

For example, in contemporary usage the word sophisticated connotes someone who (or, wrongly used, something which) is smoothly polished, urbanely knowledgeable, professionally proficient, incredulously worldly-wise, and so forth. In short, it has a positive connotation, and, when used to describe someone (or something), it assumes a laudatory meaning. Moreover, it can be considered an "in" word — in being semantic shorthand for on the inside . . . in the know . . . in the province of the sophisticate — which brings us around the full circle.

In fourteenth-century Middle English, however, the word was introduced as "an adulteration of the truth"; the fifteenth century held it to mean "a fallacious argument"; the sixteenth century saw it as a "corruption or perversion of a statement"; while the seventeenth century said it was "primitive simplicity"; and the eighteenth century construed it as "made artificial" — none of which is a positive or laudatory connotation.

Actually, the word came into our language to describe the characteristics attributed to the Sophists, a school of Greek philosophers of the fifth century B.C., who were adroitly specious in their reasoning. Regardless of the world's philological origin and evolution, it has changed in meaning, and may continue to change because we have a living language that responds to our needs and desires to communicate with each other.

Meaning is indeed elusive. Not only is a living language continually changing, but also hardly any word has the identical meaning in any two different contexts. Take the verb "strike," which has over 100 different meanings attached to it. You can strike up a band, or strike down a foe; strike out a word, or strike in an opinion; strike off a name, or strike on a color; strike over an issue, or strike below the belt. You can strike a balance, a bargain, a flag, a fish, a match, or a coin. Sometimes, you strike hands, or terror into hearts, or even strike it rich. If a batter strikes out that's bad, but if a bowler makes a strike that's good. Lightning strikes, predators strike, clocks strike, and sometimes workers strike. The example may strike you as funny, but it is intended to strike home the point that the meaning is subject to the words around it.

Yet context doesn't always provide the clue to the meaning of words. Meaning as it is transmitted, and as it is received, are often worlds apart. An absurd example of this point is *Stengelese,* a loosely strung conglomeration of words and phrases concocted by Casey Stengel, and delivered somewhat like a stream of consciousness to describe the antics of his baseball world. He might have said, for instance, something like this:

"The big feller didn't see any of them good kind since last time, what with a bum flipper, pretty soon he ain't gonna be green . . ."

When liberally translated, this would mean that his team didn't win because Mickey Mantle was in a batting slump, Whitey Ford had an injured elbow, and Joe Pepitone was a rookie first baseman. Casey was an eccentric and his venial jargon was part of his colorful image, which delighted his audience.

Some jargon obscures its meanings in other ways — by being restrictive for example. Cant, cloaked in the legitimacy of being technical, forms shells that allow the various worlds of specialization to remain exclusive. Invariably the idiom used within these microcosms is comprehensible only to a small group of participating technicians.

Take the specialty of medicine as an example: if your doctor is foolish enough to tell you that you are suffering from "Coryza with rhinitis causing laryngitis and hyperpyrexia; thus your cephilgia and anorexia are producing malaise," you can rest assured that you have only a common cold. So take two aspirins and go to bed.

We can afford to smile at these and other humorous examples of extremes. We can afford to overlook the idiosyncrasies of the odd instances because they are unique and have little bearing on our lives. But the failure to understand does not stop with the oddities. Indeed, it is with us everywhere.

The vast majority of us communicates in a common ordinary everyday language (if there is such a thing!) that uses a limited number of words to express a limitless number of things. And, while we are willing to acknowledge that "other people" may have difficulty in communicating, most of us reason that we are not part of that unfortunate group. Yet we know from experience that no matter how well we think we are communicating, people do misunderstand!

What are the barriers that impede understanding? The science of linguistics, which studies the many facets of language, attempts to identify these barriers, and, while linguistics is not within the province of this book, some of the barriers to understanding are. The process of getting ideas from one mind to another is not a simple matter.

Let there be no mistake: language is (as it will always be) our main channel of communication. With all its snares and vagaries it serves us well. There is nothing that cannot be communicated in words, but there is some information that can be communicated more quickly, clearly, and memorably if words are supplemented, or replaced, by graphic representations.

That is the premise of this book; it is especially apropos because we are living in an era in which human knowledge is fast becoming the most important capital resource in our economy — and we must find ways to utilize it to the fullest. It is also the contention of this book that words alone are not sufficient to meet today's communication demands: more information, about more things, is being generated more rapidly, and it just takes too many words to do the job.

While only a relative few of the countless billions of words that are generated concern the particular work each of us does, there is so much information in each specialty that we cannot afford the time required to sift through the mountains of words for the specific information we need. Nor can we afford the misunderstandings arising from semantic differences in what the transmitter depicts and the receiver perceives.

Never before in the history of man has so much been happening so rapidly. We are, in fact, experiencing an information explosion (a recurring theme in this book), which is inundating us with so many facts, figures, and ideas that its volume threatens to diminish our capacity to absorb the essential information necessary to conduct our work in a purposeful manner.

Not only is the amount of information increasing significantly, but the speed at which it is produced has reached measures beyond ordinary comprehension. We are, therefore, faced with the serious problem of sorting out the essential from the superfluous, the important from the trivial. Moreover, the rate of obsolescence of information is a factor that denies us the luxury of time. We must comprehend and digest vast amounts of information quickly and at the right moment.

Communicating through graphic means can quicken the process of transmitting and receiving information; it validates the adage that "a picture is worth a thousand words." Moreover, graphic representations help overcome many of the bar-

riers to understanding that result from the transmitter's improper use of words and the receiver's indifference in translating them.

Although visual presentation is not a new concept, and has been used effectively for a long time, its potential as a communication device has not as yet been fully exploited — partially because the need has not, until now, really been acute, and partially because its methods and techniques have not been fully accepted by many people.

The purpose of this book, therefore, is to point up the growing necessity and increasing demand for visual presentations—a demand that will multiply with increasing rapidity in the next decade or two — and, equally important, to demonstrate that there is no mystique to visual presentations, no inflexible set of rules to learn painfully and follow slavishly, and no great artistic talent required to conceive competent visual material.

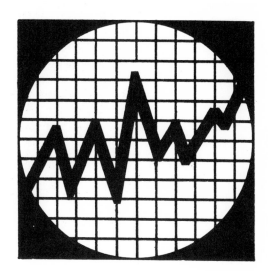

1-1 "A" is for Apple

1

We Live in a Visual World

Look about you, and you will see a multitude of objects: big objects, small objects, colored objects, shaped objects — an infinite variety of objects that we identify through given names.

We notice these things before we can identify them. Identification is accomplished through naming or labeling — which is one of the first learning processes we go through. As we label individual objects in our immediate environment, and then learn of other, similar objects not actually seen by us, we begin the process of generalization. So the word "table" grows to mean not only our table, the one in our dining room, but all three- or four-legged objects with a flat surface upon which things are set, in a wide variety of appearances. From visual objects we advance to abstractions, to non-visual things — to ideas. Through this process of generalizing from the particular we arrive at concepts, which constitute our body of knowledge. Since concepts are generalizations, however, their exact meaning is often not identical for different people — what one means and what another understands are frequently not the same thing. To reconcile these differences, people strive (sometimes desperately) to exchange their ideas — and that's what communication is all about.

Yet, in order to arrive at or receive a concept it must first be perceived through our senses. The debate among psychologists as to whether perception is sensation plus experience, or whether perceptions occurs before sensation, or whether there are really more than the five classic senses, is happily none of our affair here. It is sufficient to know (and none will disagree) that we perceive the world about us mostly through our eyes.

The mind, like a sensitive photographic plate, records everything we see and enters the images of these concepts into the most fantastic data-retrieval system ever created: the human brain. Hence, our orientation is "visual"; the communication of our thoughts and the understanding of what we hear are accomplished largely through visualization.

For instance, in order to talk about a cat, we usually first form a mental picture of a cat, then, using the language label we have learned, we pronounce the word "cat" with great clarity. The listener's brain accepts the sound and, with a speed that puts any computer to shame, retrieves and converts the word into its own mental picture of a cat. Although the listener's visualization may not be identical to our image of "cat," he has, nevertheless, arrived at the conceptual classification of "cat"; thus, he has understood the message.

Illustrations like this are strong evidence for the claim that our minds do not think in terms of words, but rather in pictures. Hence, the process of thought, the mental mechanism (or chemistry, as biochemists prefer to call it), uses pictures or images as the vehicle of conceptualization.

In fact, the sense of seeing is so important to us that we commonly use the verb *to see* to imply understanding. For instance, when someone talks about "the way he sees" something, he is really referring to the extent and nature of his understanding. When someone "gets the picture," he is indicating that he grasps the thought. And when someone speaks of his "viewpoint," it represents his conceptualization of the issue at hand.

The phenomenon of visualization has been observed and recorded from the earliest times. Men

13

of learning have long known that percepts must be translated into concepts before they can be transmitted. The fact that we don't know the *how* and *why* of the phenomenon does not preclude us from using it to our best advantage. After all, how much do we really know about electricity?

So while we know empirically that without visualization learning is almost impossible, the actual process remains open to controversy. Throughout the years, rival schools of belief have advanced explanations which have both denigrated and superseded each other. The argument remains unsettled, and new ideas are continually being presented. The "new biology," for instance, has successfully tumbled concepts of learning from pedestals on which they have roosted, inviolately, for generations.

Nevertheless, a basic theory of learning does exist, and can be utilized to demonstrate the necessity of visualization for our way of experiencing. We will just have to ignore the accusations of scientific inexactness.

The Theory of Learning

Basically, the theory of learning supposes that new concepts are learned in terms of concepts already known — knowledge being a series of building blocks. To explain this rudiment let us subject Mr. Smith to the learning process by presenting him with an unknown object. And let us suppose this object is a cougar (snarling or otherwise).

Smith's first instinct, upon seeing the cougar, is to set his data-retrieval system into action and try to come up with a concept of what he is looking at — or at least something very close to this creature glaring at him. While he draws a blank in labeling exactly what it is, he almost simultaneously does draw out something — within his realm of experience — that closely resembles it.

From the broad classification of animal, vegetable or mineral his mind has selected "animal." So far, so good. Once having decided the new object is of the animal class, his mind instantly attempts a more refined generic isolation: canine? . . . bovine? . . . ovine? . . . feline? FELINE! That's it! The cougar reminds Smith of his cat. Ergo, Mr. Smith concludes that this creature staring menacingly at him is nothing but a big cat — but

if he is prudent, he dare not pet it.

Later, when he describes the big cat to others he will be told that it was a cougar. At this point the miraculous step of learning will have taken place — the point of comprehension reached: a cougar is a big (and ferocious) cat. If he bothers to consult the dictionary he will find that he has also learned what a puma, panther, catamount, and mountain lion are, for these are different names for a cougar.

This is how learning occurs — at least in theory; a new idea is classified, identified, labeled, and assimilated. Of course, the instant of recognition takes milli-, if not microseconds. (With some of us, unfortunately, it takes ages; abstract ideas, especially, are assimilated slowly.) But no matter how thought is perceived, visualization plays a key role in the learning process.

How We Learn

In 1670 the English Philosopher John Locke posed a question in his *Essay Concerning Human Understanding*, which echoed the puzzlement of times before, and which haunts us yet today. He wrote: "Let us suppose the mind to be, as we say, a white paper void of all characters, without ideas. How comes it to be furnished . . . ?" That is the question: *How comes it to be furnished?* How do we learn? We don't really know for sure.

We observe, however, that some people learn more quickly than others do; some people learn some things more quickly than they do other things; and some people remember what they learn longer than others do — all for inexplicable reasons. Psychologists, the people who have designated themselves to explain learning, are apparently split into two major camps: the Behaviorists and the Cognitive Psychologists, whose opposing views this book intends neither to explain, side with, nor contradict with its own hypotheses. The communicator's concern with "how we learn" is a broad quantitative measure of the avenues of perception; i.e. by which sensory device do we learn the most, the fastest, the most efficiently — if indeed they are measurable?

The possibility, however, that some things may or may not be measurable — including sensory organs — has never stood in the way of the indomitable researcher. Reseach has been cited to substantiate any point made by anybody about

1-2 Photo by Robert Muir

and all other senses that no adjustment for error or incidents of exception could lessen the impact of sight on the process of learning. So it is vision that is the main avenue of perception, the eyes that carry the burden of learning.

Yet for all their persuasiveness, the studies have a serious chink in them. The trouble is that seeing does not always lead to learning. And more provocatively, seeing is not necessarily perceiving, because to perceive, something must register on the brain — a sophistry justified by pointing to the chronic television viewer, who with a glassy stare sees all, but perceives virtually nothing!

To perceive, that is to learn, the quantity of what is seen must be tempered by the quality of what is shown — in terms of perception, 100 per cent of nothing is less than 1 per cent of something. This is of the highest significance for visual communication. Of equal concern to learning is the retention of what we learn; a sieve cannot be used for drinking.

How Much Learning Do We Retain

The same (anonymous) sources of Research that studied how we learn also turned their attention to what we retain from our learning. Accordingly, "studies indicate that people generally remember:

10% of what they read
20% of what they hear
30% of what they see
50% of what they hear and see
70% of what they say
90% of what they say as they do a thing."

Again the statistics are impressive. And it is not unreasonable to suppose that they represent a good indication of what actually happens. The 70% and 90% levels, however, involve the person as a transmitter, rather than as a recipient, of a communication. But it is the recipient — the member of an audience—that interests the communicator. To him the most significant figure is the 50% that represents the approximate rate of retention of what is simultaneously heard (or read) and seen.

This is the aim, the optimum. For if members of an audience can retain — as part of their reservoirs of knowledge — as much as half of everything they are presented with, the communication will have been a smashing success.

anything. And so in awe are we of scientific jargon that we swallow it hook, line, and sinker. Research says this, or that, or the opposite, converse, inverse, or really anything else its quoter deems it to be.

In the case of quantifying perceptual learning, however, Research, that factual or fanciful IT, becomes a benefactor, which we call upon, without looking that gift horse in the mouth.

Research has purportedly produced some indications to confirm practical observations that we learn mostly through our eyes. Many reputable communications practitioners and educators cite these "studies," probably because their experiences in practice have tended to corroborate them. However, no authoritative documentation can be found (by this author) to support them. With this understanding in mind, it is alleged that:

"We learn approximately
1% through taste
2% through touch
4% through smell
10% through hearing
83% through sight."

The meaning is obvious: learning through sight so much overshadows learning through any

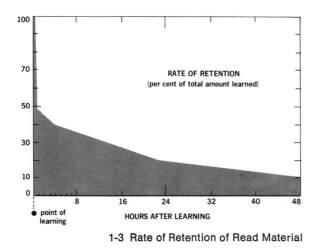

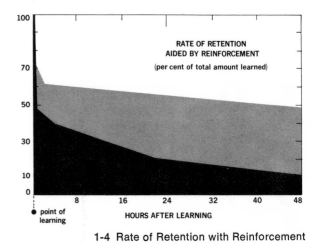

1-3 Rate of Retention of Read Material
                1-4 Rate of Retention with Reinforcement

Figure 1-3, the work of a contemporary psychologist, indicates that students retain roughly 10% of what they learn. Figure 1-4 adds the results of a study by another psychologist. In this chart the term "reinforcement" in the title refers to a relearning of original learning, in which the student spent additional time rereading what he had originally read. The result was that the student's rate of retention was raised to about 50%. But if the conceptual reinforcement was accomplished by the addition of visuals rather than by the repetition of reading, the retention rate of 50% could very well be more than coincidental.

In view of the probability that the reader has retained only 10 per cent of the foregoing pages it is best at this point to recapitulate:

The mind is passive, what it perceives it cannot avoid perceiving, and it perceives mostly through sight. Furthermore, we do not think in words; rather, our minds think in pictures—in other words we visualize. Through this process of visualization we learn. It is said that we learn some 83 per cent through our eyes, and retain some 30 per cent of what we see. If we also hear what we see, retention could be as much as 50 per cent.

At this point the late Clarence Darrow would probably rest his case, for no strong case is improved by overstatement. The conclusion is obvious: to communicate facts, figures, and ideas most effectively, a visual presentation should be employed.

A visual presentation is based on the use of symbols, forms, colors, and pictures. To varying degrees it uses abstractions, and to varying extents the conversion of data into visual form gives rise to generalizations. Because of these characteristics the graphic visual presentation requires considerable thought on the part of the user, and an intellectual understanding on the part of the viewer.

Yet, while there are a number of persuasive arguments to support the use of visual aids, it is well to bear in mind that there are also some instances in which a visual presentation is totally unnecessary. And this is really the first consideration of the communicator in formulating a presentation.

16

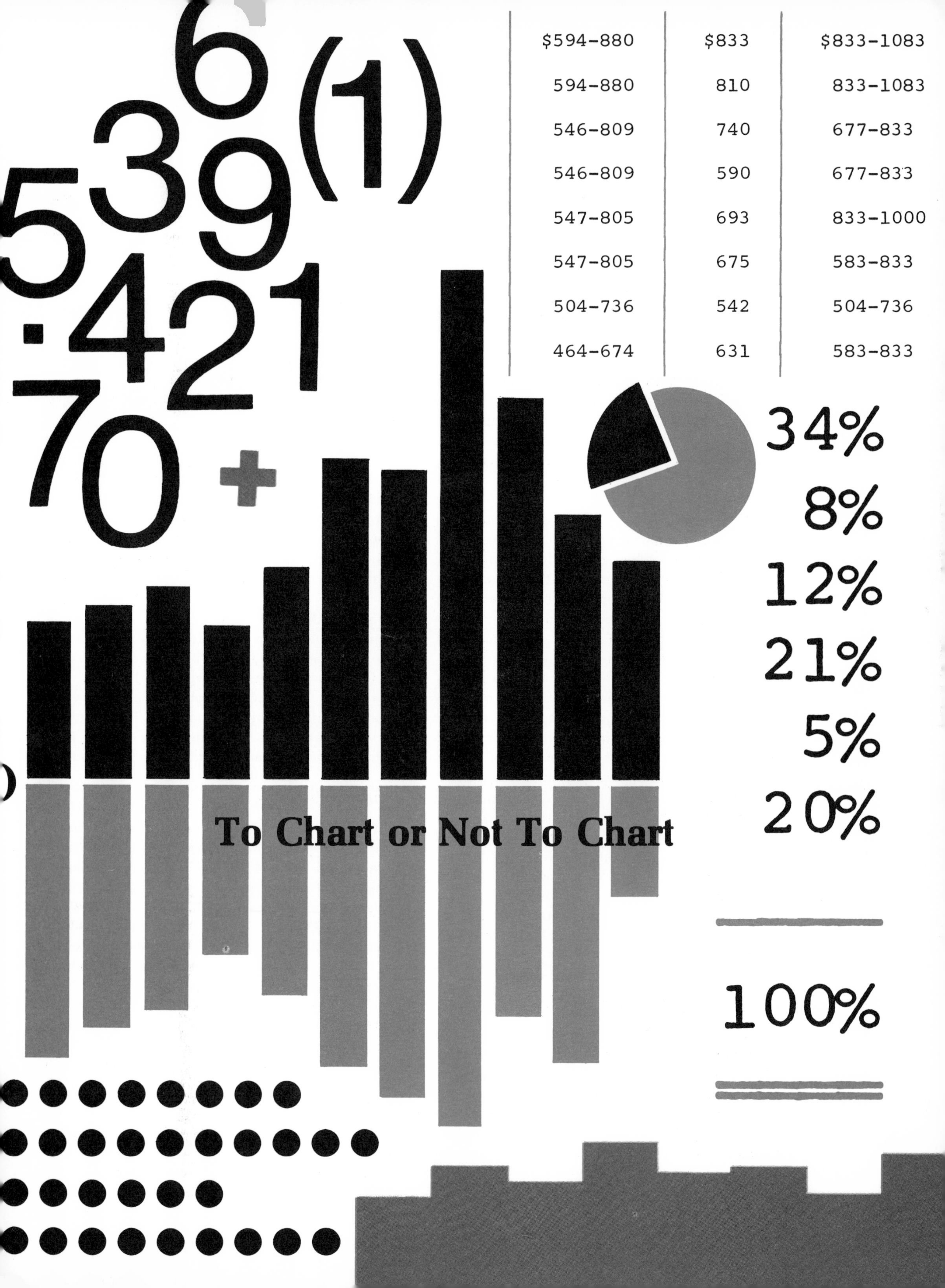

6
(1)
539
·421
70+

$594–880	$833	$833–1083
594–880	810	833–1083
546–809	740	677–833
546–809	590	677–833
547–805	693	833–1000
547–805	675	583–833
504–736	542	504–736
464–674	631	583–833

34%

8%

12%

21%

5%

20%

To Chart or Not To Chart

100%

To Chart or Not To Chart

Charting techniques are effective communication devices — but they are by no means a panacea for all the problems inherent in communicating. At the outset, we should remember that in certain instances plain text, as well as some tabular data, do a better job of communicating in their original form.

Not everything must, or should be, translated into symbols, forms, or pictures — a tortured symbolization or far-fetched graphic formulation may become a liability to a presentation. It may, in fact, bias an audience against the presentation, and even against future presentations.

Also, as a practical matter, the production of charts requires expenditures—some involve a considerable amount. And though it may be nice to have all data in graphic form, some data may not warrant the time and cost necessary to convert them. In fact, even when virtually unlimited resources are available the communicator should refrain from becoming "chart-happy." The graphic mode has a saturation point; once reached, it will tend to lessen the impact of the material that should be presented in chart form. In short, too many charts spoil the message.

Therefore, the very first decision the communicator must make is whether to chart the data at all. Actually this is not a terribly difficult choice if he possesses a reasonable understanding of what *should* be charted, what *can* be charted, and what *needs* to be charted.

The Purpose Served by Visualization

A communicator was once asked, "Why do you chart data?" He thought a while, and with a slow grin replied, "Because it's there." This communicator, typical of countless others, charted without rhyme or reason. But what motivates the mountain climber should not likewise motivate the communicator. The latter's reasons need to be founded on a clearer purpose: the inquisitive

"why" requires a definitive answer.

Charts are used primarily to amplify and to reinforce the written or verbal text of a communication. Of course, there are many, many other "whys" in charting, but they are subsidiary ones that will be treated elsewhere in this book, as their pertinence arises. Amplification and reinforcement, however, are the roots, the bedrock, the primacies of charting, and, as such, become the groundwork for all other considerations of whether to chart or not to chart.

VISUAL AMPLIFICATION   As its name implies, visual amplification is used to expand or extend the ideas being expressed by the communicator. It is necessary when text alone is likely to lack the clarity and comprehensibility necessary for easy assimilation by the audience. The following extract, from a paper explaining the use of charitable trusts in planning an individual's estate, is a good example of text requiring visual amplification.

An individual in the 60% tax bracket owns $50,000 worth of stock having a projected average annual yield of 1½%. The ten-year accumulation or fund created by investing the annual after-tax amount from the annual dividends ($750 dividend, $300 after-tax benefit) compounded annually at 3½% (tax-exempt income) will equal $3,500. In comparison, the ten-year accumulated fund resulting from the after-tax benefits of the contributions to charity of the annual income ($15,000 charitable deduction, immediate tax savings of $9,000) and compounded annually at 3½% (tax-exempt income) will equal $12,300. This is $8,800 or 250% more than without a charitable trust.

The same text, when amplified by the chart shown in Figure 2-2, is easier to follow and, hence, easier to understand (see page 20).

VISUAL REINFORCEMENT The purpose of reinforcement is to strengthen the visualization of an abstract idea. It is necessary when an explanation would require a considerable amount of text to convey a thought that would be made clearer and comparatively easier to explain in visual form.

Take, as an example, the concept of a "model," as used by the management scientist to study (by computer simulation) the reactions of an industrial plant's operation to certain stimuli, e.g. different production volumes, under or over capacity, strikes, and so forth.

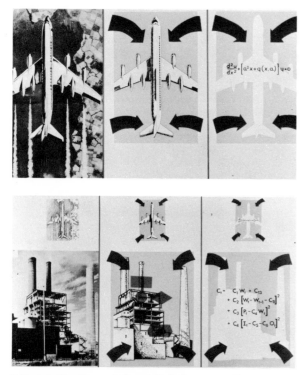

2-3, 2-4 The Use of Visual Reinforcement To Illustrate the Concept of a Model (Courtesy of Lybrand)

To explain the term model, some simple analogies are made. The first panel in Figure 2-3 is a picture of a real airplane in flight. In order to determine its behavior under actual flight conditions (without the danger of crashing it) an exact-scale replica is built and tested in a wind tunnel. The replica is a model, shown in the second panel. The third panel makes the point that identical testing can be made without a wind tunnel or a replica, by translating the object—its environment and conditions—into mathematical formulas. These formulas now become the model, which can be tested by computer simulation.

Figure 2-4 parallels the conversion of an object into a model, using an industrial plant rather than an airplane as its subject. Panel one is the real plant. Panel two shows the model represented by various systems used to describe the plant's operations. And Panel three shows a further abstraction, represented by a mathematical formula, which becomes the model. By using this mathematical model it is possible for an operations researcher to manipulate it, thereby simulating (in a computer) what would happen in real life if the plant were exposed to certain stimuli. Above each panel in Figure 2-4, the parallel analogy of the airplane is shown as visual reinforcement.

While the use of visualization to amplify and reinforce establishes the purpose of charting, this purpose is not the only consideration in determining whether to chart or not. Some kinds of material should almost never be charted.

Kinds of Material That Should Not Be Charted

All quantitative material and almost all abstract ideas can be converted into some graphic form or other — an almost irresistible temptation. But no communicator can afford to be so naïve as to believe that it is physically possible to chart everything. Nor should any communicator become so misled as to believe that charting anything and everything would be of benefit to him.

While such cautions obviously lack specificity, it must be realized that any attempt to catalogue all situations in which material should not be charted would indeed be a quixotic exercise — no listing could ever be comprehensive or avoid being riddled with exceptions.

On the other hand, it is entirely possible to describe, at least in general terms, kinds of material that should not be charted. So this broad-brush approach is taken here, with full awareness of its vulnerability to the caviling gaggle.

MATERIAL THAT IS TOO ABSTRACT Normally, material dealing in "pure" abstractions —

19

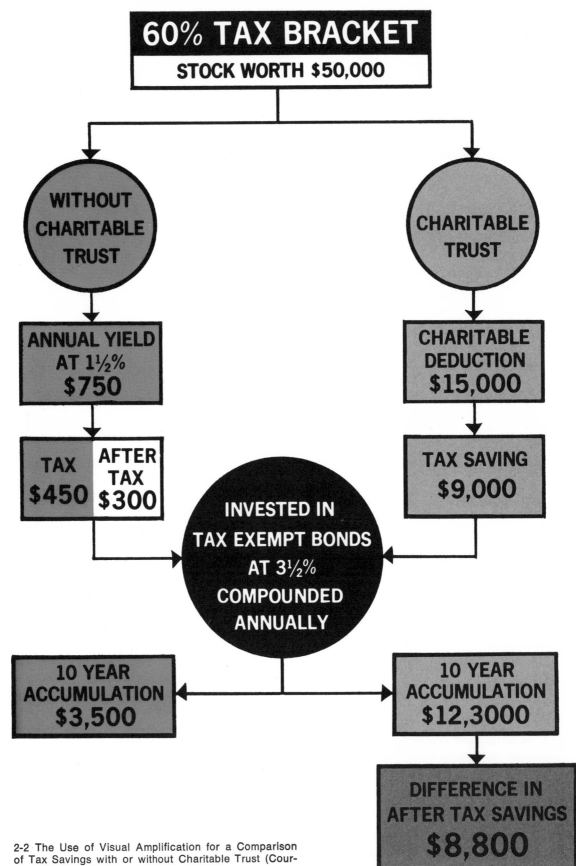

20

2-2 The Use of Visual Amplification for a Comparison of Tax Savings with or without Charitable Trust (Courtesy of Lybrand)

i.e. general ideas perceptible intellectually — is not adaptable to charting. A discourse on philosophy is an example, however absurd the thought of charting it. Almost invariably, purely abstract material is neither expressed quantitatively, nor is it explanatory of a functional concept (like the theory of random sampling).

Consequently, it has no visual handle. Would you chart, for example, your company's policy manual, or legal contracts, or even any of your own memoranda dealing with general expository subjects? Probably no more so than you would consider charting the Lord's Prayer, or a poem by Shelley, or the Gettysburg Address. The parallel is not altogether ridiculous; the inappropriateness of charting the latter examples is obvious, but the former are less obviously inappropriate and, therefore, potentially more apt to be attempted.

Unfortunately it is sometimes tried, much to the embarrassment of the audience and the communicator. Since abstract material generally provides no basis for quantitative comparisons or procedural explanations, the inevitable approach to charting is a pictorial one — and somehow the pictures always turn out to be cartoons. The communicator overlooks the fact that this is using charts as illustrations, which may relieve the visual monotony of printed text but neither expands, explains, nor fulfills any of the other functions that charts are meant for. Furthermore, cartoons — the "can't we have a little man..." type — are, nine out of ten times, deadly. It is often all too obvious that they are forced, out of place — charting for charting's sake. Moreover, the visual material is invariably irrelevant to the text.

Visual irrelevancy, a not uncommon pitfall, is the use, or inclusion, of extraneous pictorial material that has little, and sometimes nothing whatsoever, to do with the subject being visualized. These irrelevancies are typified by the use of an illustration that more often than not adds little to the communication of the material — like the ubiquitous cartoon of the sad little man, hobbling on crutches, representing "Sickness and Death Benefits" in so many insurance booklets. This is not to say that cartoons cannot be dynamic graphic devices. They can, but not with hard-to-grasp abstract material, which, by and large, does not lend itself to charting.

MATERIAL THAT IS TOO SIMPLE To consider charting material that is simple in its original form would be to carry charting to an extreme. When materials contain relationships, comparisons, or explanations so obvious that they need no further embellishment, it is a waste to put them in graphic form (and often it even amounts to poor judgment).

Charting is used to clarify complex textual and tabular details so that they are made clear, easy to read, and readily understood. But if these ends already exist in a communication, the charting of the material can be only, at the very best, a redundancy.

The use of charts where charts are not needed, and the use of excessive visual images to convey a simple thought, are *visual redundancies* — both types offend the intelligence of the viewer.

Figure 2-5 is an example of the latter, in which visual redundancy is particularly apparent. The message is "Sales went down," and is conveyed (1) by the oral or written text that states: "Sales Went Down!"; (2) the title on the chart that reads: "Sales Went Down"; (3) the sales curve that plunges dramatically, symbolizing forcefully that: "Sales Went Down"; (4) the curve that is often in red (subtly) connoting a negative movement, and the curve capped with an arrow showing its directional thrust: "Sales Went Down!"; and (5) the chart that (audaciously) shows an

2-5 An Example of Visual Redundancy

SALES WENT DOWN

illustration of a melancholy little man, grieving that "Sales Went Down."

The message is hammered home five times, at least three of which are superfluous. And while it may be argued that repetition is the root of learning, a rebuttal is that redundancy is the root of boredom.

MATERIAL THAT IS TOO SPECIFIC Even data that are wholly quantitative, thus seeming ideally suited to charting, are sometimes not suitable at all. Accounting records, inventory stock activity, and cash transactions are examples of data much too specific to lend themselves to the interpolations necessary in reading charted material. Operating figures must remain precisely labeled to be of value. Certainly they can be charted, but normally it would be almost ridiculous to do so. In situations where the exactness of double-entry bookkeeping is required and zero sums are important, charting is usually uncalled for.

The communicator should be especially wary of material having specificity because, per se, it is highly adaptable to charting. It is a thin grey line that separates specific from too specific. In some contexts (say to show trends or rates of change) charting may be just right. But when specific material is used as operating data, the inexactness of charting is not desirable.

MATERIAL THAT IS TOO FAMILIAR Within any particular sphere of interest, much of the ordinary information disseminated is basically familiar to its recipients. It is the kind of information that is generally exchanged between the initiated — people of similar backgrounds and interests who do not need generalizations to understand, and who often prefer all the details to muse upon. As a rule, they are so conversant with the subject matter that to chart it would be superfluous — the proverbial gilding of the lily.

This kind of information is usually communicated merely to keep members of the group informed as to what is going on. Much of it is found in the innumerable "information" copies that find their way into the hands of countless people, many of whom, after reading the memoranda, can't quite decide exactly what to do with them, so they file them (unfortunately not often enough in the "round file").

Typically, this kind of information involves projects or reports in their preliminary or development stage, and, though the final products of these efforts may require charting — so that others may also understand — the interim progress reports can often do just as well without it.

Thus, if data are purely abstract, extremely simple, too specific, or inherently familiar, the advisability of charting is open to doubt. This does not mean that charting should be automatically ruled out. It is entirely possible for any one of these types of material to be involved in a specific situation where it would be desirable to chart it. The reader must remember that these guideposts are just that — not ironclad rules or irrevocable proscriptions.

Once the communicator has decided that his material is not subject to the above limitations, there are still certain characteristics that should be present, in order to consider charting it. These characteristics can be viewed as criteria.

Criteria for Charting

In brief, to chart any material its subject must be important, its information timely, and its figures meaningful. These are broad statements, and some elaboration is necessary.

THE SUBJECT MUST BE IMPORTANT ENOUGH TO CHART A subject's importance is a highly relative thing that can only be subjectively determined. What is important to A may not be to B; C may disregard both A and B. People are funny that way. It is often the case that the same bit of information may not be equally important to different people of the same company, or even the same division, department, or function.

Also, in the abstract sense, the importance of a subject is gauged differently from its "practical" importance. One wag, for instance, tells the story about a housewife who, when being interviewed by a consumer researcher bent on exploring how "importance" is determined, stated (with a straight face) that she had an arrangement with her husband: she would decide the trivial things, like what car, or house, or furniture they would buy; he would decide the important things like whether we should go to war, or drop the atom bomb, or exonerate Benedict Arnold posthumously. (The researcher dutifully recorded the information—on the special form provided.)

The point is that importance, as far as charting is concerned, must be determined as a relative functional importance; the subject need not necessarily be important in the large abstract sense, but it must be of interest and concern to those who will receive its communication.

THE INFORMATION MUST BE TIMELY ENOUGH TO CHART

Timeliness, like importance, is an open-ended subject. What is timely in some circumstances is obsolete in others. Judgments on whether information is timely mostly depend upon the end purposes that the charting will serve. For instance, if we were charting the market activity of selected stocks on a daily basis, Monday's activity would be old hat on Tuesday. But if our purpose were to chart these stocks on a weekly basis, Monday's activity would be timely through Friday. So, timeliness is a function of purpose.

On the other hand, the requirements which make information timely in some circumstances may at the same time not render it conducive to charting. For instance, data handled by real-time systems (wherein information is fed directly into a computer from on-line stations—untouched by human hands, so to speak) is processed in a fraction of a second (probably too fast be be charted in the conventional manner).

Thus, at a minimum, the timeliness of information must be of sufficient duration to allow time for analysis and charting before it becomes obsolete, and yet not be so out-of-date as to be of little use in the decision-making process.

Charting, even rough operating work charts, has production lead time that must be taken into consideration before it is begun. Timeliness, like importance, requires a mental checkpoint that asks: will the information still be timely, given the necessary time to produce it? If the answer is yes!—then you are ready to chart away. But before you do, you must establish one more checkpoint: are the figures to be charted meaningful?

THE FIGURES MUST BE MEANINGFUL ENOUGH TO CHART

Obviously, within any body of data that is important and timely, not all of its figures can be charted. The communicator must be able to select the most salient features of the data and convert these into clear, simple, and meaningful charts. Accordingly, the value of the ensuing charts is nothing more than a reflection of the worth of the figures selected. Therefore, figures taken as meaningful must truly be meaningful—a profundity worthy of further examination. The meaningfulness of figures is determined by the attitude of the communicator. To explain: in every body of data there are a number of relationships between the figures constituting the statistics. Take this body of data as an example:

Product	Sales	Gross Margin
A	$ 5.1	$ 0.88 (in millions)
B	3.2	0.63
C	1.7	0.49
	$10.0	$ 2.00

Now, there are a number of "meaningful" relationships here, depending on the "attitude" one takes. Suppose our burning interest were gross margin as a per cent of sales: then, both the sales and gross margin figures would be meaningful. Or, suppose we could not rest until we knew the contribution that each product made to total sales: then only the sales figures would be meaningful; gross margin figures would be disregarded. Conversely, if gross margin were the object of our concern, sales would not be particularly meaningful.

Although an oversimplification, this little example is intended to demonstrate that meaningful figures are not necessarily meaningful per se, but only in the eyes of the selector, who may have diverse reasons for so concluding.

Thus, the criteria for charting—importance of the subject, timeliness of the information, and meaningfulness of the figures—are key checkpoints in determining whether or not to chart the data. To fulfill the criteria, the communicator need only know his job or question the chart requestor. A negative response at any of the checkpoints should cause the communicator to pause and reflect—and most likely put the data aside uncharted.

On the other hand, material that meets these criteria and that is also not too abstract, too simple, too specific, or too familiar is still not out of the woods — not by a long shot. There is still another point the communicator must check before he decides to chart: will a chart tell the story better than text or tabular presentations?

Fortunately, this evaluation is not quite so general in nature as it appears; some specific classes of subject matter lend themselves ideally to charting, and will tell their stories better in chart form.

Subjects That Lend Themselves to Charting

The essence of charting is the depiction of comparative data in a manner that reveals their relationships to each other. Of course, not all information has built-in comparisons, but those that do can be described rather briefly.

QUANTITATIVE RELATIONSHIPS This kind of information is classed as statistical data, and it forms by far the largest body of charted material. Its subjects are myriad: sales versus profits, supply and demand, many dollars compared to few dollars, exports in relation to imports, births as opposed to deaths, and on and on — countless examples can be given.

Most quantitative relationships employ basic graphic devices in their charting.

As a rule, whenever a numerical difference exists, quantitative relationships can be made.

METHODOLOGICAL EXPLANATIONS Obviously, not all information is quantitative, and some material that is not also lends itself to charting. Methodological explanations are one kind; they are perhaps more familiar as "how to" subjects. Some of these familiar explanations, however, do not require charting; cooking recipes, for instance, are "how to" information that rarely require visualization. But many others do — take the "do-it-yourself" building craze as an example. The weekend craftsman and the perennial Santa Claus, who desperately toils and blasphemes into the early hours of Christmas morning putting together a bicycle, train set, or a doll house from a set of written instructions, can attest to the value of step-by-step pictorialized instructions.

Thus, charting in many cases is an indispensable part of the methodological explanation.

FUNCTIONAL EXPLANATIONS Similar to the "how to" methodological explanations are functional explanations. The latter explain how something works — an operation, a machine, a system, or something in the physical or natural world. A good example is shown in Figure 2-6.

Functional explanations play an important role in training. Visualization techniques like Process and Flow charting help immeasurably in the understanding of the function of a subject. It is a special favorite of the Annual Report, which uses functional explanations to inform stockholders just what their company makes, and how it makes it.

Thus, this type of subject matter — because it lends itself so well to pictorial charting — is often used in situations where the function of something needs to be explained.

STRUCTURAL RELATIONSHIPS Most structures contain multirelationships: of the parts to the whole and to each other. The conventional organization chart is a prime example of this kind of subject. There are many similar relationships that can be depicted graphically, for instance, the structure of our Federal Government, the makeup of the United Nations, the composition of a baseball team, the analysis of a military command, and many more.

Thus, whenever an interaction exists in an organized structure, the relationship of its parts and their interaction can be shown by charting.

In the pages that follow, many more examples of quantitative and structural relationships and methodological and functional explanations will be shown, because almost all the material worth charting can be found in these classifications.

To Chart or Not To Chart

After thoroughly evaluating his material in light of the many factors discussed above, the communicator should have arrived at his decision to chart or not to chart. If he decides to chart he will have to face one more decision: what kind of chart?

Throughout this book almost all of the charts shown and discussed are *presentation* charts, as differentiated from *operating* charts. The former are works characterized by their graphic elaborateness, and by the fact that they are designed to be formally shown to an audience. Operating charts, in contrast, are work charts, using a minimum amount of graphic effort and/or techniques. However, it is important to note that, while a distinction is made between these two chart types, the communication objectives and most charting techniques apply to both. Hence, what is said will not necessarily exclude operating charts, but is primarily (and sometimes only) suitable for presentation charts.

Operating charts, by and large, take a minimum amount of effort to produce, and, except for the kinds of material which should not otherwise be charted (as discussed above), they can often be used to supplement or replace written reports. Monthly sales movements, absenteeism trends, price fluctuations, and other data of this nature can be effectively shown by what is commonly referred to as "quick and dirty" charting. Actually, these charts are not that quickly produced, and certainly are not that dirty. Proper mechanics must still be employed and charting principles must be observed. By and large, there is a considerable amount of data that warrants the time and effort to make it into operating charts, but would definitely not merit being made into presentation charts.

Because of the considerably higher preparation cost for presentation charts, the anticipated return on investment—be it either in profit, productivity, or satisfaction—must be carefully and realistically weighed before the project is begun. There are some clues to look for when deciding whether the data should be put into presentation-chart form.

For instance, charts that will have a one-time use hardly ever warrant presentation treatment. Charts that are aimed at audiences that are not decision-making bodies (or advisors to decision-makers) seldom require elaborate preparation. And subjects whose content is not of sufficient consequence to an audience virtually never rate presentation charts.

Perhaps it can all be summed up by noting: you must have something worth saying to some-

2-6 An Explanation of a Function (Illustrated by Ted Hanke. Courtesy of *Business Week* © September 2, 1967)

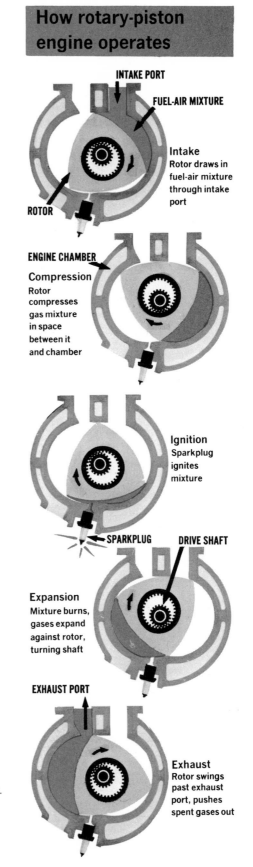

How rotary-piston engine operates

INTAKE PORT

FUEL-AIR MIXTURE

Intake
Rotor draws in fuel-air mixture through intake port

ROTOR

ENGINE CHAMBER

Compression
Rotor compresses gas mixture in space between it and chamber

Ignition
Sparkplug ignites mixture

SPARKPLUG   DRIVE SHAFT

Expansion
Mixture burns, gases expand against rotor, turning shaft

EXHAUST PORT

Exhaust
Rotor swings past exhaust port, pushes spent gases out

one worthy of hearing it to warrant the time and effort required to chart. Material, however, that is not worthy of a presentation-chart treatment could very well be useful as operating charts. But material not worthy of operating charting is not worthy of charting at all.

The question of whether to chart or not, however, becomes an academic one in an environment where the concept of charting itself is not accepted as a means of communication. Although the technique of charting has been with us for some time, its use still meets pockets of resistance — often for reasons that are far from being objective.

Naturally, charting done poorly or inappropriately, or used when it should not have been used, contributes substantially to this resistance. But even more important is the dissenter's attitude toward the charting function — an attitude that prevents him from properly understanding and evaluating the functions, advantages, and disadvantages of charting.

Cornerstones, Pillars, and Pitfalls of Charting

3

Cornerstones, Pillars, and Pitfalls of Charting

An unfortunate legacy of generations of adherence to the Protestant Ethic is the businessman who still finds it difficult to put aside the preconceived notion that "that arty stuff" interferes with the plain facts necessary to run an operation. He views graphics with suspicion and somewhat reluctantly accepts the imposition of aesthetics on his material. "Sure," he says, "advertising is a must, and packaging is needed to compete, but charts — why do we need them?"

In our everyday business world, where each function has a practical raison d'être, the occupation of chartist holds a curious position. In the eyes of the conventional businessman it is an art, because it involves artistic judgments and unfamiliar methods to accomplish some aesthetic result. In the eyes of the traditional artist, however, it is not an art, but a craft, because it denigrates talent to achieve some practical end. Consequently, the chartist and his work are alien to both camps.

The merits of these points of view can be left to debate on long winter nights. The real issue is not how a chartist is categorized, but what he does. A chartist prepares visual material that is used to communicate facts, figures, and ideas. And as such he performs an important service that has no parallel in the business organization. This chapter attempts to establish the importance of the visual medium as a vehicle of communication by examining the functions, advantages, and disadvantages of charting.

Cornerstones of Charting

The substance of communications graphics lies in charting. And to appraise properly the role of charts in communications we must first consider

their use, and, second, identify the cardinal functions by which this role is exercised.

To begin with, charts are used to *transmit information in a lucid, rapid, and memorable manner.* The criterion of lucidity is of primary importance. If charts are clear and easily understood they automatically communicate rapidly, and will be memorable.

Functionally, charting rests on certain cornerstones that the communicator must be aware of when employing the graphic technique. Categorically, these cornerstones are: emphasis, the expansion of perception, summarization, and the addition of variety.

A CHART IS USED TO EMPHASIZE One of the main functions of a visual is to add emphasis: to emphasize the main thoughts of the communicator, the significance of relationships, and the most important points of the data. Thus, if you wish (or need) to focus attention on something, you emphasize it, because the eyes, as gateways to the mind, involuntarily register emphasis before anything else.

In charting, emphasis is created both unintentionally and intentionally. For the most part, points of emphasis inherent in the data are mired in obscurity when the material is presented in text or tabular form. But once the data are translated into visual form the relationships are underscored, bringing the points of emphasis into sharper focus. Moreover, the mere act of committing the data to visual form automatically produces emphasis, regardless of the communicator's intention.

Take, for example, the statement that the postwar boom has increased holdings of Mutual Funds

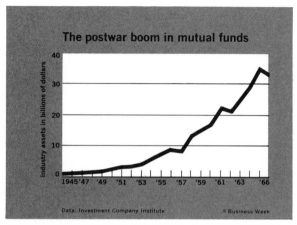

The postwar boom in mutual funds

Data: Investment Company Institute   © Business Week

3-2 A Chart Producing Unintentional Emphasis (Courtesy of *Business Week* © December 10, 1966)

from a few billion dollars to almost forty billion dollars of industry assets over the last twenty years. As a statement, this fact has little impact because the conceptualization of a "few billion dollars" as opposed to "almost forty billion dollars" over a span of twenty years is difficult to make. But, as a chart (Fig. 3-2), this fantastic upsurge is emphasized and becomes meaningful.

Intentional emphasis uses a contrived frame of reference that helps conceptualize the point the communicator wishes to make. As an example, suppose we were emphasizing the phenomenon of size reduction in electronics made possible by micro-miniaturization. Micro-miniaturization has revolutionized the electronics industry. Because of it, computer technology, for one, has taken a giant stride forward, and doubtless its application to familiar electronic devices will soon follow. The nub of micro-miniaturation is a tiny silicon chip (whose circuitry cannot be seen with the naked eye), which has replaced the vacuum tube and the transistor.

The introduction of this technological achievement has excited the imagination of all who have come in contact with it. The phenomenon of its size is startling. When discussing the silicon chip, people emphasize its size. Invariably they say that it is small — very small; in fact, it is tiny. But how small is very small? How small is tiny? This can be answered by providing a frame of reference which will intentionally emphasize the size of the silicon chip.

In Figure 3-3, the pencil was chosen as a frame

of reference because it is common. The vacuum tube, transistor, and silicon chip have been compared to the pencil, in order to establish the relative sizes of the three power sources. The major point of emphasis is achieved by relating the chip to the pencil's eraser. Now we have a good idea of just how small a silicon chip is.

A CHART IS USED TO EXPAND PERCEPTION
The human mind is a wonderful instrument. As science delves deeper into its mysteries, trying to parallel its functions and copy its operation, our appreciation of its magnificent complexities and efficiency grows ever greater. The mind, however, for all its intricacy and incredible circuitry, works sequentially. That is to say, one event at a time occurs. The transmission time between the stimulus of occurrence and reaction by the brain virtually defies measurement.

3-3 A Chart Producing Intentional Emphasis (Courtesy of Lybrand)

Third Generation Equipment is Smaller, Cheaper, and More Powerful

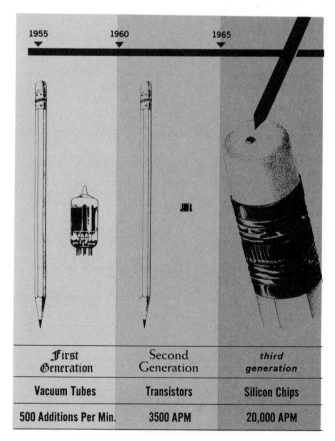

First Generation	Second Generation	third generation
Vacuum Tubes	Transistors	Silicon Chips
500 Additions Per Min.	3500 APM	20,000 APM

29

Perception is like a strip of movie film — what is seen is translated into mental images and held for a split second in our minds. If we were to close our eyes and concentrate on something it would flicker on and off, and be impossible to hold firm. At the same time little "bits" of associated information would dance in and out of this mental picture.

Because the mind works in this manner the number of mental steps we are capable of making at any one moment is limited. However, once an already formed "picture" is placed before us, the mind is relieved of the burden of holding an image still, and it can concentrate on relating the parts of the picture to the whole. Sequentially, one by one, the image elements are perceived and translated into understanding. Moreover, multiple relationships, which were not recognized in our mental abstraction process, are now uncovered.

An important function of the visual aid is to provide the mind with an already formed picture. And the more numerous the interrelationships of the picture elements are, the more valuable the visual aid is.

A simple demonstration of this claim can be made by Figure 3-4. The chart is divided into two parts: its top portion is a common job ticket, the kind used in almost every kind of manufacturing business; the bottom portion is a matrix that relates the source of information provided by the job ticket to the function that will utilize it. The purpose of the job ticket is to provide information for the various record-keeping functions of a company, e.g. Production Control and Cost Control. Since each of the record-keeping functions is in some manner interrelated, that is, their independent operations are part of an integrated system that controls the process of producing an end product, the information contained on the job ticket is useful for more than one function. Each type of information provided by the job ticket has been coded with a number, to facilitate its identification. For example, "Order Number" is assigned number 1, "Quantity" is assigned number 3, and so on.

The bottom portion of the chart is a matrix on which the numbers identifying the kinds of information provided by the job ticket are placed on the horizontal axis, and the record-keeping functions that use the information are placed on the vertical axis. Where the information is pertinent to the function's records it is so indicated by a dot. In this manner the many existing relationships between data and user are established.

Thus, with the chart before you, it is easy to establish that Production Control uses all the information except "Clock Number and Employee Name." Just as easily, it can be established that the Production Scheduling, Production Control, and Cost Control functions are the only ones using the information "Order Number" on the job ticket.

To try to establish these relationships in the mind's eye would be folly. (Test this thesis by covering the chart, trying to recall it, and establishing all the possible multiple relationships.) Even the simplest set of relationships has more permutations than the mind can cope with at any one time. Take for example, the incredible num-

JOB TIME CARD

ORDER NO. 1	PART NO. 2	QUANTITY 3	DATE ISSUED 4
			DATE SCHEDULED
MATERIAL	PART DESCRIPTION 2		
MACH. NO. 5	OPERATION 5 SHIFT	DEPT. NO. 6	DATE PRODUCED 7	IN
CLOCK NO. 8	EMPLOYEE NAME	QUANTITY GOOD 9	OUT 10 / IN
REMARKS		QUANTITY REJECT	OUT

	1	2	3	4	5	6	7	8	9	10
PRODUCTION SCHEDULE	●	●	●	●	●	●	●		●	●
PRODUCTION CONTROL	●	●	●	●	●	●			●	●
QUALITY CONTROL		●			●	●			●	
INVENTORY CONTROL		●					●			
COST CONTROL	●	●			●	●			●	●
PAYROLL					●	●	●	●	●	●

3-4 A Chart Explaining How Relationships Expand Perception (Courtesy of Lybrand)

ber of combinations possible in this simple matrix:

$$
\begin{array}{ccc}
 & 1 \quad 2 \quad 3 \\
A & \\
B & \\
C &
\end{array}
$$

It is hard to believe that it contains 511 permutations (2^9-1), but it does.

Only a visual aid holds the image in place firmly so that the mind can move from one element to another while always having the remaining elements as a constant frame of reference. In this manner a chart is used to expand perception.

A CHART IS USED TO SUMMARIZE   A very practical function of a visual is to summarize. In essence, every chart is a summary. The need for summarization has never been greater — tomorrow it will be even greater. In every walk of life we are deluged by a flood of paper. Data-processing techniques, for one, are spewing an unbelievable amount of information onto the desks of the managers of the many systems and committees required to operate an organization. Granted this may be an old saw; the literature on the subject almost rivals the output of the computers themselves. But just stop to think a moment. The data output (i.e. hard copy) that is inundating management has been already abstracted (in some coded or symbolic form) from the original data. And yet, we have all seen reports of thin — very thin — hard-copy printouts, reports that would take an incredible number of hours to read, digest, and understand. How can an operating manager possibly pour through all this garbage (an affectionate euphemism) and gain a clear picture* of what is happening now?

To summarize this cumbersome mass of tabular data we must resort to more expedient means, and charting is certainly one of those means. Figure 3-5 is an example of a computer printout

---

* While the decision-maker needs a "picture" from the mounting statistics, operating personnel still require the data in their original form. For instance, a stock-status report or an accounts-receivable report must remain in precise absolute numbers to be processed.

1263	324	256	258	1	1.55	1961	225	97	312	411	538	570
164	271	257	260	1	1.63	1902	225	84	250	343	431	510
264	163	249	244	-2	2.72	1819	222	86	262	354	453	506
364	229	248	242	-2	3.30	1752	221	76	212	298	367	454
464	205	235	220	-7	4.11	1593	215	70	190	270	337	410
564	175	217	192	-13	5.02	1405	207	66	178	255	318	370
664	189	209	188	-11	5.92	1332	203	57	139	206	267	327
764	133	203	172	-9	6.92	1238	200	56	140	206	266	311
864	161	199	175	-7	4.15	1219	198	50	113	172	229	288
964	200	199	182	-5	1.69	1246	198	46	101	153	209	283
1064	216	201	190	-3	0.98	1284	199	44	94	144	199	284
1164	303	209	209	0	-1.28	1452	203	54	131	195	255	340
1264	382	223	237	4	-3.36	1707	210	72	204	285	351	441
165	193	220	228	2	-2.92	1631	209	68	185	263	328	413
265	249	223	230	2	-3.60	1607	210	61	154	226	289	384
365	147	217	216	-0	-2.12	1540	207	64	170	245	308	386
465	137	210	203	-2	-0.86	1478	204	66	181	258	321	385
565	134	204	193	-3	0.18	1421	201	67	185	261	324	378
665	218	205	199	-2	-0.21	1420	201	61	157	228	289	355
765	103	197	184	-4	1.26	1363	197	66	182	257	319	367
865	273	203	200	-1	-0.08	1476	200	69	196	274	337	396
965	174	201	196	-1	0.33	1419	199	63	168	241	302	364
1065	216	202	200	-1	0.02	1407	200	56	140	206	266	340
1165	296	210	216	2	-1.52	1530	203	62	163	236	298	379

3-5 A Computer Printout in Tabular Form

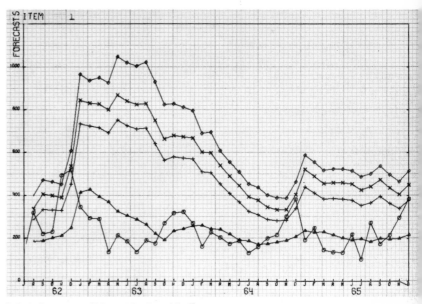

3-6 A Computer Printout in Graphic Form

in a tabular form. It is a formidable-looking document literally covered with statistical data.

Figure 3-6 is the same data converted into graphic form. What is interesting about the graph (Fig. 3-6) is that it was also produced by the computer. It is a visual summary of the data con-

YEAR	SALES*
1964	5
1965	15
1966	20
1967	10

*MILLIONS

3-7 Tabular Data Translated into a Bar Chart, a Line Chart, a Circle Chart, and a Pictograph

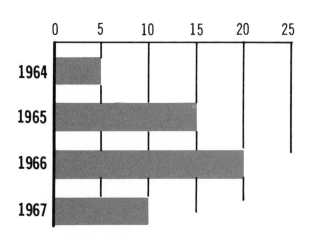

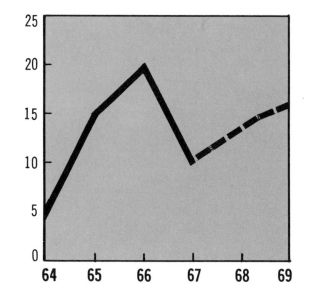

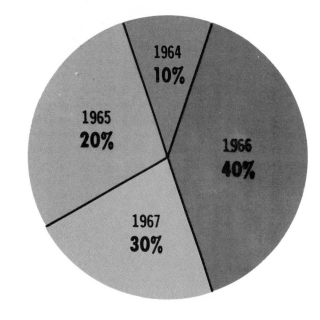

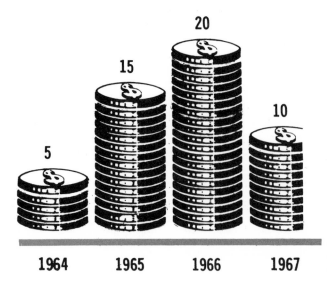

32

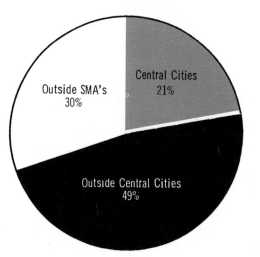

3-8 A Circle Chart (From "A Graphic Guide to Consumer Markets, 1967." Courtesy of National Industrial Conference Board)

3-9 A Graphic Summary of a Study of Advertising Expenditures (Courtesy of Lybrand)

33

tained in the printout (Fig. 3-5). The capabilities of computer plotting devices are rapidly enlarging, and new technology promises to make this technique a very useful summary tool. (See Chapter 12 for a discussion on computer graphics.)

A CHART ADDS VARIETY TO PRESENTATIONS "A chart is a chart is a chart" is not something that Gertrude Stein would have said, nor is it something that anyone should say. All charts need not be monotonously similar.

Within the bounds of effective communication, charts can be conceived with imagination and inventiveness. For instance, the graphic forms used can be varied, color and halftones can be used, photography can be considered as a graphic element, and, where appropriate, pictorial elements can be incorporated. In short, there are countless ways in which variety can be built into the graphics of a presentation, thereby stimulating and maintaining audience interest.

From even the simplest table of figures, numerous graphic interpretations can be generated. Figure 3-7 demonstrates this point by indicating but a few of the many variations possible that interpret a basic table of figures.

Adding variety to charts in turn adds variety to your presentation. The presentation that properly employs visual aids becomes interesting, and easier to understand. When these conditions are met, 80 per cent of the battle to capture your audience is secured. On the other hand, there is no more boring occasion than one spent sitting through a barren presentation that cries with the need for visualization, or a presentation in which the graphics are monotonously similar and poorly executed.

An exciting presentation, supported by good graphics, certainly does not denigrate the stature of the communicator or the importance of his message. Contrary views are mistaken; for surely professionalism is not synonomous with stodginess, nor is conservatism a byword for sterility.

The Pillars of Charting

The communicator, by using the graphic approach, gains certain advantages in the presentation of his material which no other communication vehicle can offer him. These advantages are the pillars on which communications graphics are

built, and constitute the reasons why the visual medium provides an effective means to transmit information.

A CHART IS COMMANDING A visual commands viewer attention, and this is one of the main advantages the communicator gains from putting data into graphic form. Although the mind is arrested more through vision than through the aural or tactile senses, the act of communication can be facilitated even more if the image the mind "sees" is already formed.

Take, for example, Figure 3-8, which is a simple Circle chart depicting net increase in housing inventory by area. This already formed image commands the viewer's attention and he can see, at a glance, that the housing units outside central cities account for almost half of the increase in the study. Without such a picture of comparison the viewer would have had to establish mentally relationships between 49, 30, and 21 per cent, and the communication would have been less direct.

A visual also commands attention by presenting its story in a structured manner: each element contributes an understandable bit of information that is a part of the whole message. Figure 3-9, for example, shows the results of a study that found that in a particular company the reduction of advertising by 50% would reduce sales by 2% but increase net profit by 10%.

There are a number of interesting graphic aspects about this chart that are worth pointing out. First, it announces its premise with an action title: "Reduce Advertising 50%." The concept of advertising is pictorially reinforced by a newspaper clipping. Hence, the viewer immediately identifies the subject matter with the kind of familiar advertising seen in newspapers. The decreased sales volume is represented by an arrow pointing downward, labeled 2%, and captioned "Sales Volume" — a simple device to indicate what has happened to sales. Conversely, the arrow pointing upward is labeled and captioned to show what has happened to the increased net profit contribution. Interestingly enough, the proportion of the upward arrow is not exactly five times the downward arrow (10% : 2%), but it hardly matters; the message is quite clear.

Each element of the chart contributes a bit of information that is part of the story: the action title, the newspaper as a pictorial reinforcement, the arrows indicating increase and decrease. Thus, the message is conveyed rapidly with a minimum amount of explanation.

A CHART IS DYNAMIC A visual is a dynamic force that reaches out and seizes the reader's attention.

No amount of figures or words can convey the drama of a plunging sales curve like a simple line graph (Fig. 3-10).

No amount of explanation or description can have the impact that a pictorial chart has in exposing disparities in related entities. Figure 3-11 is such a chart. It shows the comparative processing capacities of first-, second-, and third-generation electronic data-processing equipment.

No amount of preparation or imagination can match the explosive charge of an effective cartoon (Fig. 3-12).

The graphic form offers these advantages because it is dynamic.

A CHART IS COMPACT A visual has the further advantage of being compact. Surprising amounts of data can be compressed onto a single chart. It has been told that the Navy Department briefed Harry Truman, upon his ascendance to the Presidency, on the entire naval situation in the Pacific with a total of eighteen charts. Whether this story is apocryphal or not, it is nonetheless true that a chart can summarize information more succinctly than any other communication medium.

Summarization, of course, is a process of eliminating details by combining them into totals or averages. Naturally the more data are compacted, the more they are generalized and the broader the overview becomes. For example, to construct a chart showing the results of a thirty-nine year study of consumer prices the minute variances must be omitted, leaving only a general indication of price fluctuation for the period. Figure 3-13 is such a chart.

This representation is an Index chart combined with a Surface chart. Its purpose is to present a broad picture of the price changes of a "market basket" of goods and services bought by families of city wage earners and clerical workers. It is based on prices collected for 300 items in forty-six cities. As such, it is a compact pres-

entation of a great mass of data.

A chart's capability to compact extensive information into a small space is also demonstrated by Figure 3-14. This Word chart summarizes, in a few key phrases, the essence of a complicated discussion on a complex subject.

A CHART IS REVEALING In the process of making decisions, what you don't know will hurt you. Running any sort of operation continually requires selecting one of many alternative courses of action. Somewhere along the line the decisions to take these particular actions must be made, otherwise we would remain inert.

We like to think that the decisions we make are the result of a "diligent analysis of the facts, a prudent consideration of the potential benefits, and a cautious evaluation of the ensuing consequences." But the truth of the matter is that we often deceive ourselves because, after years of reporting these banalities, we actually believe them. The fact of the matter is that we make decisions based on prior experience, intuition, compromise to external and internal sociopolitical pressures, economic realities, and a conscientious appraisal of the information made available to us.

The content of the information made available to us may be good or bad — this is not the concern of this discussion. Let us assume that the information is valid, and let us concern ourselves only with the form in which the information is presented.

Information presented to management is by and large "structured," that is, specific data are requested in predetermined formats. When Mr. Big bellows, "Jones, get me the figures on the XYZ Project!" he means the particular figures accumulated in accordance with set formats. Such formats might include schedules on costs, volumes, expenditures, ratios, past dues, variances, over-commitments, under-commitments, forecasts, budgets, sales, returns, etc., etc. On such schedules, data are amassed, selected and assembled, and subsequently manipulated, converted, and inverted to forge reports that are meant to describe the status of the project.

From these schedules, Mr. Big will glean the information he needs to make new decisions. And provided the information is structured in the proper form, his decisions should be good ones.

35

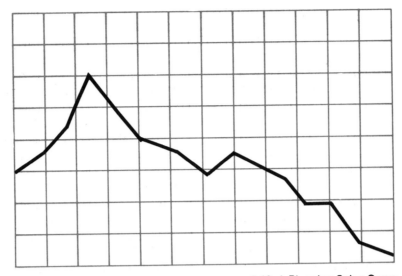

3-10 A Plunging Sales Curve

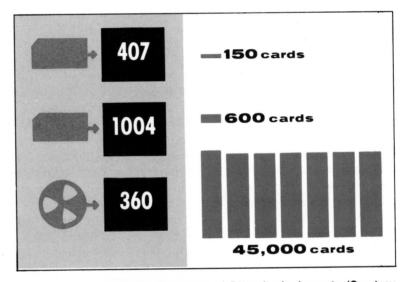

3-11 An Illustration of Disparity in Amounts (Courtesy of Lybrand)

3-12 The Use of a Cartoon

36

3-13 The Use of Charting To Summarize Large Amounts of Data (From "A Graphic Guide to Consumer Markets, 1960." Courtesy of National Industrial Conference Board)

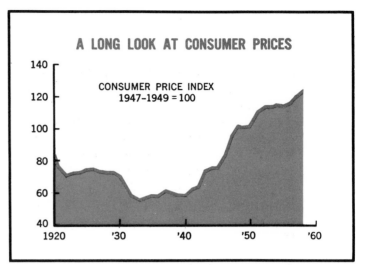

3-14 The Use of Charting To Summarize Large Amounts of Information (Courtesy of *Business Week* © December 10, 1966)

3-15 A Graphic Representation of Findings from a Marketing Study (Courtesy of Lybrand)

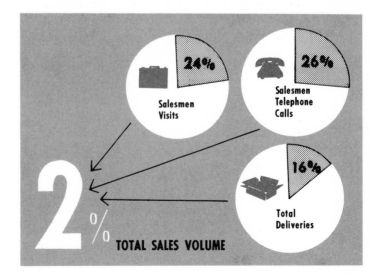

Chances are, however, that even though the information is in the best possible format, many important relationships existing between the figures will not be discovered because the data are in tabular or text form. It is only when statistical material is converted to graphic form that interactions that might be otherwise overlooked are revealed, and the full extent of relationships becomes apparent. Cognizance of these relationships is an important part of the decision-making process.

A CHART IS CONVINCING Because we mainly experience through sight we are more readily prepared to believe something if we see it. By demonstrating visually, instead of merely stating or describing relationships of statistical material, graphics assist the communicator in conveying his message.

Visual amplification is a potent persuader. We can, for example, easily conceive of ten apples being more than one plum, but the idea is not really convincing until we place the items side by side and look at them.

Figure 3-15 demonstrates that visuals can be convincing. It graphically presents the findings from a study of a company's sales effort; this revealed that 2% of the total sales volume required 24% of all salesmen's visits, 26% of their telephone calls, and accounted for 16% of the total deliveries made by the company. Obviously, this is an incredible effort for such a small return. The translation of the data into pictorial form helps bring the facts into perspective by showing the effort expended in proportion to the whole — i.e. the amount of effort that went into the remaining 98% of sales.

A CHART IS VERSATILE Graphics can be used to depict facts, figures, and ideas. This enormous versatility makes graphics an ideal vehicle to inform, report, and educate. For example, suppose management has concluded that cost-reduction investments return about twenty times the amount returned by capital investments. This fact can be reported in a number of ways. One way is shown in Figure 3-16. This chart states that for every dollar invested in a cost-reduction program an approximate return of 400% is possible,

whereas each capital investment dollar can be expected to return about 20%. The chart effectively conveys the fact and dramatically shows the relationship of 20:1, which makes the difference in investment convincing. Of course, the chart could have compared 400 symbols to twenty symbols, but that would have caused unnecessary clutter. The important relationship of 20:1 is held by assigning the value of 10% to each symbol, and thus summarizing the ratio.

Figure 3-17 is a graphic presentation of numbers. The form is a modified Step Surface chart. The figures representing "per cent of total sales" are compared to the "operating cost as a per cent of sales" figures. Although the style of the chart is atypical, in that it is highly stylized, the conversion of these kinds of quantitative data into visual form is a typical use of charting.

The presentation of ideas is a natural for the graphic approach. Ideas are abstract and difficult to deal with. One invariably resorts to "drawing a picture" to get an idea across. Even simple ideas need explanations — witness the muddy-faced kids in their huddle, scratching the soft earth with a stick, explaining to each other how Bobby will carry the football over left tackle on the next play.

To understand an idea the mind must formulate a "picture." When left to our own devices, however, each of us comes up with a different picture. For instance, if several people were asked to visualize an automobile, none would picture the same car, the same setting, or even the same color. The automobile, however, is a familiar concept, and if an exacting description had been specified probably the visualizations would have been similar. But ideas are abstractions, and the introduction of a new idea is the most difficult of all to deal with.

Take, as an example, the concept of "stratification" (as it is used in analytical applications). The word stratification, as defined, does not adequately describe the concept, because the idea has been expanded beyond the narrow dictionary definition. In fact, no other word or phrase within our scope of comprehension can precisely give the meaning of this concept. The concept of stratification is that a few of one thing account for many of another thing, and conversely, many of one thing account for a few of another thing. We can substitute concretions for abstractions and restate the concept as follows: a few items of inventory (say 5 per cent) account for many dollars of sales (say 40 per cent) and conversely 50 per cent of the items in inventory account for 5 per cent of the sales. Or, we can think of stratification in other terms as well. For instance, many merchants own small stores; few merchants own large stores. Between the high and low points are gradations, or stratifications.

The point is that, as an idea, stratification is difficult to communicate, and even more difficult to grasp. Figure 3-18 is a graphic representation of the concept of stratification. Visually, it is shown as two pyramids — one being inverted. Now go back and read the text explaining the concept and observe how the pictorialization aids in the visualization of this idea.

A CHART CAN BE APPEALING A visual aid is appealing provided that it has been well conceived and executed. A chart that is pleasing to look at wins and influences audiences, whereas, in the eyes of most people, data presented in tabular form are formidable. As a case in point, glance through any document filled with statistics, such as the government publication "Survey of Current Business." The voluminous tables, the small print, the endless footnotes are intimidating. On the other hand, well executed charts of the same material appease the viewer's apprehensions and invite him to read on. Certainly, good graphics — those which are well thought out and constructed in a professional manner — cost no more.

Even subject matter which is ordinarily presented in chart form can be made appealing with a little thought and care. For example, in the study of statistics, the various kinds of means, standard deviations and kurtosis are concepts that are explained graphically in every book written on the subject. Usually these illustrations are done as simple line drawings, and, while being frightfully dull, admittedly serve their purpose in communicating the concepts involved. But to facilitate the communication, the additional step of making the illustrations appealing is suggested.

Figure 3-19 is an example of ordinary statistical subject matter handled in a manner that augments its visual appeal. Obviously, the production economics of most statistics books presently precludes the use of color as it is shown in the example. However, color, though helpful, is not an essential element in these charts because tints and tones of black can be easily substituted for it, without a real loss in dimension. Therefore, the presence of color is not the primary reason that these charts are more appealing. What differentiates these charts from ordinary line drawings is that they have body. A dimension of substance is added that makes them pleasing to look at and, hence, more appealing.

The Pitfalls of Charting

As every coin has its other side, so has the use of the visual medium as a communication vehicle. However, the pitfalls encountered when one ventures into the graphic approach cannot fairly be termed disadvantages. If anything, they may be limitations. And most of them need never arise if the communicator's objectives are well defined, well planned, and well executed.

CHARTING IS OPEN TO ABUSES Graphics can be (and are) used to slant or distort facts and figures; this is perhaps the most singular indictment of visual aids. Yet every communication vehicle is susceptible to this charge. Since his very beginnings man has set out to dominate the opinions of those he comes in contact with, and there is no reason to believe that he will not continue to do so.

Perhaps unjustly, this sweeping generalization tends to disparage those whose motives have been acceptable to society. By and large, however, objectivity has seldom influenced our scrupulousness when we desire to convince each other of our own particular points of view. Yet, in all fairness, our failure to abide by the ethical framework of our environment has often been less than deliberate. Naturally, we want people to believe what we tell them. This is a basic human incentive. And naturally, we want people to approve of our actions. Unfortunately, however, many a communicator, while attempting to put his best foot forward, trips over his integriy.

In this regard, the attributes of graphics (i.e. that they are commanding, convincing, dynamic,

39

3-16 A Graphic Representation of Comparing Cost-Reduction Investments and Capital Investments (Courtesy of Lybrand)

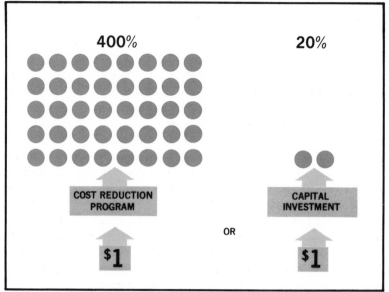

3-17 A Graphic Presentation of Numbers (Courtesy of Lybrand)

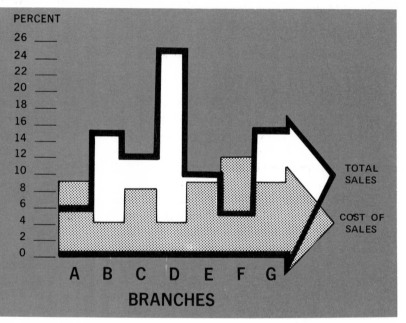

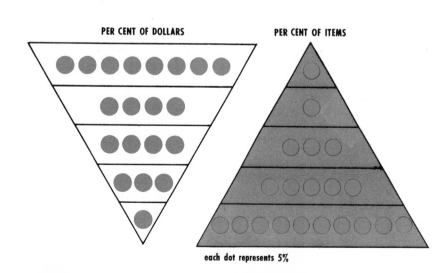

3-18 A Graphic Illustration of Stratification

MEASURES OF CENTRAL TENDENCY

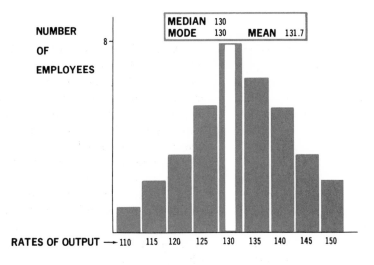

MEDIAN	130	
MODE	130	MEAN 131.7

NUMBER OF EMPLOYEES

8

RATES OF OUTPUT → 110 115 120 125 130 135 140 145 150

PROPORTIONS OF ITEMS INCLUDED WITHIN
$+\sigma +2\sigma$ AND $+3\sigma$ OF THE ARITHMETIC MEAN OF A NORMAL CURVE

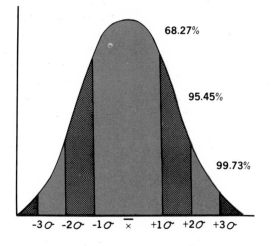

68.27%

95.45%

99.73%

-3σ -2σ -1σ $\bar{x}$ $+1\sigma$ $+2\sigma$ $+3\sigma$

KURTOSIS

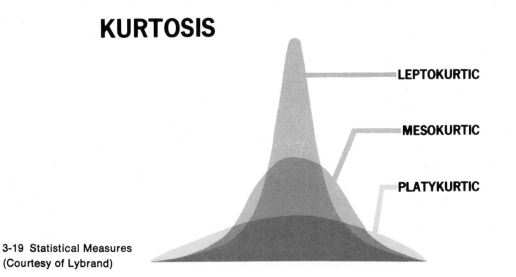

LEPTOKURTIC

MESOKURTIC

PLATYKURTIC

3-19 Statistical Measures
(Courtesy of Lybrand)

41

etc.) present the communicator with a two-edged sword. If indeed they can be employed to persuade, this persuasion can be used in a negative way to distort. There are many ways in which graphics are open to abuses. One way is discussed on page 78.

CHARTS ARE NOT EXPLICIT Data recorded in visual form, for the most part, lack the precision of plain numerical data. Generally, charts are not explicit. For example, Figure 3-20 is a chart comparing the linear measures of a mile, furlong, and kilometer. The scale on this chart makes it impractical to show that there are exactly 5,280 feet in a mile.

Even charts intended for interpolation are not explicit. The values on Line charts, for instance, can be interpolated only with some effort, and, depending on the scale range and interval, with minimal accuracy.

CHARTS ARE NOT QUOTABLE Graphic material does not lend itself to being quoted as does text or tabular material. Except for some broad generalities like up or down, high or low, bigger or smaller, or percentages of a whole, there is little that can be quoted. Of course, the text that appears on a chart can be quoted, but the interrelationships that the eyes transmit to the mind cannot easily be formulated into words.

CHARTS CAN BE SATURATING Invariably, too much of anything will spoil the appetite for more. Proverbially, it's the child who, set free in a candy store, gorges himself to the point of wanting no more (for at least twenty-four hours).

Audiences are also vulnerable to saturation points. Many presentations suffer from superfluous charts. Communicators, in preparing visual material, often fail to be selective when determining the data to be charted. And so, many presentations, burdened with extraneous material, also burden the audience.

Consequently, it is frequently the case that the communicator winds up transmitting everything, but communicating nothing. And this can be a real disadvantage. It is in the selection process that discretion is the better part of charting. It can be said: when in doubt, leave it out.

CHARTING REQUIRES KNOW-HOW The shibboleth that "everybody is a designer" is unfortunately the case—much to the detriment of many graphic presentations. The conception and execution of charts presume a certain amount of know-how, and without this knowledge a graphic program cannot be effectively undertaken. In this sense, know-how must be considered a requisite in the use of graphics.

Conceiving charts is not a simple matter. Many people try, but not all succeed. It requires skill to translate raw data into visual form. Without such skill an effective visual presentation is not possible.

As for execution, operating charts (i.e. crude working instruments) can be executed by almost anyone, but presentation charts require someone who is trained and experienced in graphics. Moreover, the requisite of know-how goes beyond merely producing charts. For instance, the communicator must consider the purpose with respect to the audience, the medium with respect to the facilities, the production with respect to the budget, and a host of other considerations that go into a successful presentation, all of which require know-how.

CHARTS ARE COSTLY The skills, facilities, and material that go into charting can involve significant expenditures. The production of charts takes skill, and some charts take a great deal of skill. Like any other skilled labor, this commodity costs money. It is often a critical mistake to use a spare body to "fill in" on making charts. A good chartist — like a good technical writer, like a good administrator — is part of the communications team, and it is a pity when all the planning and preparation for a presentation go down the drain because of a poorly executed end product. Moreover, it is inconceivable that million-dollar decisions can be made on the basis of evidence presented in poorly conceived and executed charts.

Management must face and bear the costs involved if a graphics program is to work. Facilities, materials, salaries, and professional consulting fees are part and parcel of the cost of communicating. Communicating through graphics is a growing trend—one that is still to reach its apex. The need for good graphics is self-evident. The standards must be set high, but this does not mean that cost should be disregarded. The cost factor of a chart must be reconciled to its purpose and potential benefits.

In order to realize these benefits, however, graphics must be used properly — which means that the communicator must get to know, and be able to use, the devices, mechanics, and forms of charting.

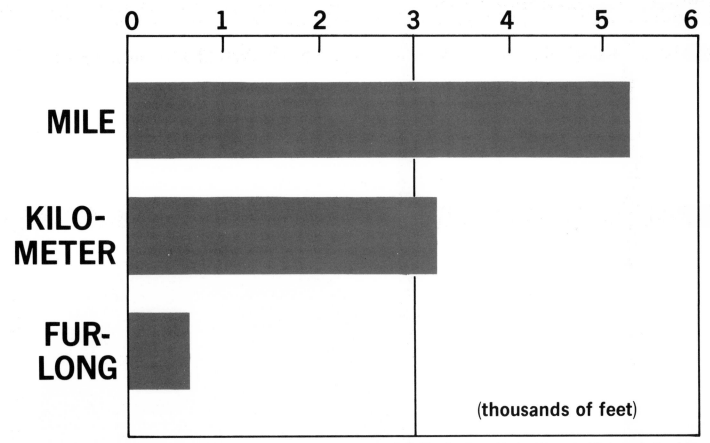

3-20 Charting Some Kinds of Numerical Data Lacks Precision

4

Basic Charting Devices

Essentially charting is a visual method by which one value is compared to another. In order to make a comparison, however, a difference in values must exist. Something must be bigger or smaller, more or less, heavier or lighter, taller or shorter, better or worse . . . than something else.

It is impossible to state the quantification of something without identifying what it is that is being described. For example: ten sea lions; four pounds; three dollars; six months.

It is also virtually impossible to express a comparison without using some implied frame of reference. Witness: sales went up (from last year's performance); John received good marks (with reference to grade standards); production is more this month (than it was last month); inventory is higher (than average levels). Thus, a value stated without a frame of reference is meaningless.

Comparisons need not always be between like entities, such as comparing raw material inventories and finished material inventories, or this year and last year; nor do comparisons need to have a cause-and-effect relationship like sales and profits, or population and housing.

Comparisons can also be made between things that are different in nature. For example, suppose we ask the question: what is the value of the British pound sterling? Well, there are various comparisons which can be made to answer the question, depending on the frame of reference we choose. Each frame of reference involves a different mode of comparison.

For instance, at the present rate of exchange the pound is worth (or compares to) about $2.40 in U.S. currency, about 1,700 Italian Lire, or almost 11 Deutsche Mark, and so forth.

Another frame of reference is time. This form of comparison observes the fluctuation of the pound's value over a period of time — say ten years.

The pound in terms of comparative purchasing power can be related to the cost of a mutton chop, fish and chips, and a generous serving of Yorkshire pudding in London, or Liverpool, or Stratford. The point is that the value of the pound cannot be determined unless it is compared with some specific thing under specific conditions, and these things and conditions can have infinite permutations, with each variation being susceptible to graphic representation as a chart.

The choice of comparisons is almost infinite. But once the choice is made, a method of graphic representation must also be selected. Methods of graphic representation take a number of forms, the most fundamental being geometric devices.

When we were children, and we played the games that children played, we inevitably said: "make believe this is a . . ." — whatever we wanted it to be. While in this state of pretending, our mode of experience transcended reality, and the object actually took on the identity that we assigned to it. And so it is with graphic devices: a line becomes sales, a circle is a dollar, a bar is production, etc. We are able to "pretend" because these basic graphic devices are abstract geometric forms, and as such, they have no specific identity. Abstract forms are used *because* they have no identity, and thus cannot be confused with something that is a nominal part of our body of knowledge.

In sum: the line, the circle, and the rectangle have no meaning per se; they are only symbols, signifying nothing in themselves.* The role of

---

* Pictographs, on the other hand, use symbols that have very specific meanings.

these geometric symbols is to serve solely as vehicles by which a thought is transmitted. They assume identity only insofar as they represent a thought. This identity is transitory, and the symbol never really assumes any permanent meaning in itself.

Actually, the selection of graphic devices has little rationale. While it is true that there are cogent reasons why some devices suit particular needs better than others, it is also true, by and large, that whether a line, or a surface, or a column, or a bar, or a circle is used to represent the data, the communication of thought is still transmitted. And, in most cases, the selection of a graphic device has less effect on the impact of the message than purists would like to think it has. This is not to say that each device does not have particular limitations that should be recognized and considered in its application. Yet, it is realistic to bear in mind that the communicator's selection of device is not the product of a discriminating analysis, but invariably a compromise dictated by preference, and economic and psychological expedience.*

Period and Time Series Charts

Basic charting devices, and their variations, are divided into two classifications: Time Series charts and Period charts. The term *time series* is defined as "a series of data arranged in order of time of occurrence." This is somewhat like saying a walking tour is a tour on which one walks. A more suitable explanation can be given by comparing Time Series charts with Period charts.

The primary difference between the two is that Time Series charts use two scales, quantity and time, while Period charts utilize only the quantity scale. To illustrate: suppose all the products of a manufacturer were to be compared as to sales during the month of June. In this case a quantitative measurement of *many* products is made for a *single* point in time, which is the period of June. The chart would be constructed with one scale (quantity) and would use one period (June). It would be classified as a Period chart.

Now suppose the sales of only Product A were to be plotted over a period of six months. We now have a different condition, namely, how much of Product A (quantity) was sold during the months January through June (time). In this case the quantitative measure of a *single* product is made for *many* points in time. The chart would utilize, in addition to an amount scale, a time scale to accommodate the many points in time. It would, therefore, be classified as a Time Series chart. When these points in time are placed on a scale they form a time series — hence, the name.

Included in the classification of Time Series charts are Column charts, Line charts, and Surface charts, all of which compare the same item at different times and have the identifying characteristics of quantity and time scales. The Period chart category, which compares different items at the same time, includes Bar charts and Circle charts, and uses only the quantity scale.

Conversion of Absolute Numbers into Percentages

A methodology used in almost all the various families of basic devices, and thus requiring preliminary discussion, is the conversion of absolute numbers into percentages. This is a common method used to indicate the relationship that absolute numbers have to their total, when the total is assumed as 100 per cent.

To be more concrete, the following example applies: A=2 days, B=4 days, and C=2 days. The total of A, B, C is 8 days. The numbers 2, 4, and 2 are absolute numbers because they retain the same quantitative meaning no matter what they are used to describe: e.g. two dollars, two tigers, two days.

The figure 8 now represents the total value of A+B+C. As the sum of the parts, the figure 8 also represents the whole — or 100%. Therefore, if B's value is 4, it is ½, or 50%, of 8. Following this logic we can easily convert 2, 4, and 2 into 25%, 50%, and 25% respectively to represent their proportion to the whole. The same ratio would hold true if A, B, and C had values of 200,

* Some people have prejudices with respect to certain graphic forms. For example, they cannot stand Circle charts and will never use them. Charting, like any other art form, is subjective. Economic expedience pertains to time, cost, and skill considerations. It is entirely possible that you can't afford the production of the graphic form that may best fill your requirements. Psychological expedience is typified by the situation in which the "boss" does or doesn't want certain charts, which sets constraints on the type of charts used for presentations to him.

400, and 200 respectively, or if they took on values of 3,300, 6,600, and 3,300 respectively; the magnitude of the numbers has no bearing on the conversion of absolute numbers into percentages.

Mathematically, the technique of calculating percentages is a simple one. The total is always the denominator (the bottom number of a common fraction). The numbers representing components of the total are the numerators (the numbers above the line in a common fraction). To arrive at a percentage divide the denominator into the numerator, and then multiply the answer by 100.

$$\text{E.g. } 4/8 = 8\sqrt{4} = 8\sqrt[.5]{4.0}; \ .5 \times 100 = 50.0 = 50\%.$$

These charts, called 100% charts, have an application in many chart families, and it is well to keep the methodology of conversion in mind, for we shall see it used often in the pages that follow.

Circle Charts

One of the most familiar basic charting devices is the Circle chart (Fig. 4-2). This chart is perhaps better known as a Pie chart, because its wedge-shaped segments look like pieces of pie. The Circle chart is also sometimes referred to as a Sector chart or Segment chart.*

The Circle chart, which falls into the Period chart classification, has great popular appeal probably because it requires no interpolation on the viewer's part, and, therefore, is comparatively easy to understand. Another reason that accounts for its popularity is that its geometric form is a visual "relief" from the rectangles, lines, and grid patterns that all other devices must use.

The construction of a Circle chart requires the conversion of absolute numbers into percentage proportions of the sum value representing the entire circle. Once the sum is converted into per cent values, the 360-degree circle is also divided into 100 parts, with each per cent equaling 3.6 degrees. Thus, the value of a component segment

that is equal to 25 per cent of the sum of component values will occupy a 90-degree segment of the circle (25% x 3.6°) — a quarter pie!

Almost every communicator, at some time or other, has used the Circle chart to explain how the dollar is divided. The virtue of a circle is that it can portray effectively, often dramatically, the relationship the segments have to each other, as well as the relationship each segment has to the whole.

However, in this virtue also lies a defect; because, if the whole, or total, is made up of many components the chances are that few, or no, significant comparisons can be made. At what point the number of components becomes too many is difficult to determine except by applying a visual rule of thumb.

As the number of components required to constitute the sum of the circle increases, the size of each segment gets smaller. And when the segments of the circle are so small that they cannot be visually differentiated from each other, the number of components can be considered too many.

The size of a segment should not be less than 6 or 7 degrees, but too many segments this small will nullify the visual effect of the Circle chart in making comparisons. Larger segments, of course, will visually dominate the circle; this may be a virtue or a defect, depending on the point of your message.

Because a Circle chart has more than one component, it requires some visual means, other than an outline of its segments, to separate and identify one segment from another. Visual means of segment separation can range from the use of simple line patterns (e.g. crosshatching), through shading (i.e. shades of a single color), to the use of different colors, each representing individual segments.

Segment coloring (including shades and line patterns) presents a particular design problem. Circle charts are compact, their geometric shape is a unity, and when color is applied a unique visual mass is created.

Since aspects of color will be discussed in Chapter 7, it suffices to say here that segment coloring has an extraordinary effect on the viewer's "reading" of the Circle chart. Wittingly or unwittingly, the communicator often designs with

---

* The inclusion of the various names for this chart have been made even though a circle by any other name would be just as round. The nomenclature of the basic devices is, unfortunately, loose; and the existence of more than one name to identify the same device often results in confusion. Therefore, wherever possible the identification of each device by its various names will be included in their description.

47

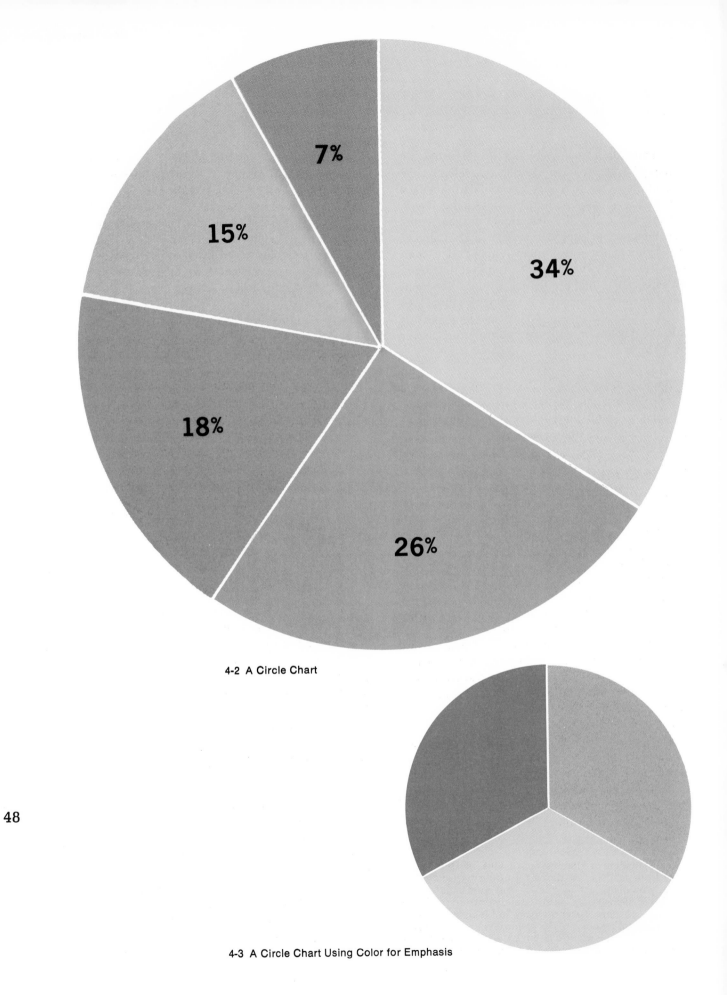

4-2 A Circle Chart

4-3 A Circle Chart Using Color for Emphasis

ITEM AMOUNT

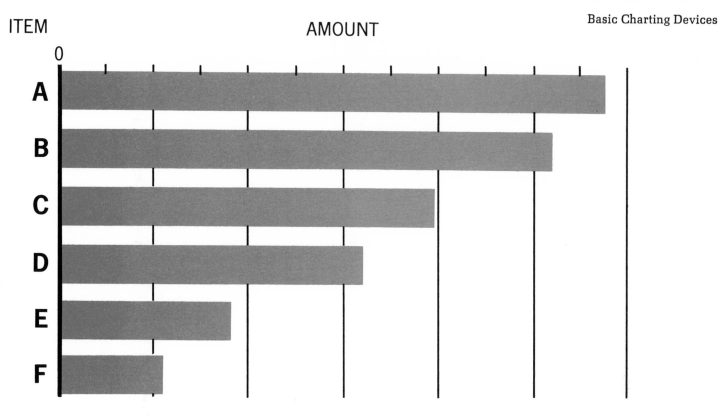

4-4 A Simple Bar Chart

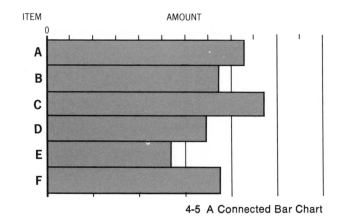

4-5 A Connected Bar Chart

4-6 A Simple Bar Chart Emphasizing One Bar

49

colors that "distort" the viewer's visual perception, resulting in "false" interpretations of the comparisons being made.

A very primitive demonstration of this point can be made using an equal three-segment circle colored green, gray and gray/green (Fig. 4-3). In this example it can be seen how the gray/green and gray segments have difficulty contending with the green segment for the viewer's attention.

Other than the use of color there is very little real designing that goes into a conventional Circle chart. Once the mathematics of conversion and the mechanics of constructing segments are accomplished, the design elements of coloring, positioning, and text are the only steps remaining, and color can work for you or against you.

Bar Charts

The Bar chart family falls into the Period charts classification because it represents a single period of time, and uses only the quantity scale to make comparisons. But against this one scale a great number of items can be measured. No other basic device can compare as many items against a single frame of reference as can the Bar chart.

As a family of charts the Bar has a number of standard variations, all of which have been duly catalogued and recognized by chartmakers everywhere. The number of variations possible is only limited by the inventiveness of the designer. This text, for the sake of practicality, will deal only with the basic variations.

SIMPLE BAR CHART The Simple Bar chart (Fig. 4-4) is one of the most useful and widely used forms of graphic presentation of quantitative data. Its appeal stems both from its ease of construction and from the fact that it is easily understood by "the man in the street" — i.e. by those who are not accustomed to reading charts.

Often the space interval between the bars is omitted, and the chart is called a Connected Bar chart (Fig. 4-5).

In a Simple Bar chart, as well as in all Bar chart variations, the items to be compared are listed on the vertical axis (i.e. up and down), and the quantity, or amount scale, is placed on the horizontal axis (i.e. left to right across the chart). The length of the bar is drawn to correspond to the item's value, or amount, on the horizontal quantity scale. The moment that a second bar is entered a comparison becomes possible. As other bars are added more comparisons are made possible.

The sequence in which the items are listed on the vertical axis is dependent on any one of a number of criteria. By and large, however, the order is adapted to meet the objectives of a study. In other words, the items should be arranged in a sequence beginning with those items that are important to the audience's interest.

In many instances a logical sequence is not discernible, or perhaps even not desirable. In such cases an arbitrary ordering can be used. For example, the items can be listed alphabetically, or geographically, or chronologically. Another method is to arrange the items in relation to the magnitude of their bars, with the largest size bar at the top.

Occasionally, the designer will have a need to show an item that is "different" from the other items on the chart. Examples of "different" items are things like totals or averages. To illustrate this point, suppose the Items A, B, C, D, and E, in the amounts of 3, 7, 5, 11, and 9 respectively, are to be charted. Since no specific order of sequence is intended, the designer arbitrarily chooses to list them in descending magnitude. Thus the items are entered onto the chart as D(11), E(9), B(7), C(5), and A(3). Each bar is constructed in the same width and colored the same color. The space separating each bar is equal.

Now the communicator decides that a bar representing the average of D, E, B, C, and A should also appear on the chart as an additional frame of reference to which each item can be compared. The average bar, having the value of 7 $\left(\frac{11+9+7+5+3}{5} \right)$, is *different* because it is the composite of all the items. This average bar is unique and should be visually set off from the other bars on the chart.

Visual differentiation can be accomplished in a few ways. One way is to change the color of the average bar. Thus, the average bar may be in black and the component five bars in color (Fig. 4-6). Another method is to make the space between the average bar and the first item bar wider, and leave the space between the other item bars equal. Still another method is to make the average bar itself wider than the item bars.

GROUPED BAR CHART   The Simple Bar chart deals with a number of individual items. A member of the Bar chart family called the Grouped Bar chart (Fig. 4-7) goes an additional step and handles categories of individual items.

Suppose, for example, we made a Simple Bar chart indicating the total number of students who flunked algebra in four regional high schools. A Simple Bar chart, with four entries representing the total "flunkees" from each high school plotted against the amount scale, is constructed. But suppose we wanted a representation other than totals — say a representation by sex.

The categorization by sex is part of the entry totals we previously called students. To say it another way, male students who flunked algebra, plus female students who flunked algebra, equal total students who flunked algebra. These two categories of male and female can be represented by individual bars, and the two bars are *grouped* and applied to item entries labeled high schools. The resultant chart is shown as Figure 4-8.

The Grouped Bar chart, sometimes referred to as a Multiple (or Multiple Unit) Bar chart, allows a comparison of items in two, or even three, categories. Bars grouped in excess of three are difficult to read and should be avoided.

The Grouped Bar chart has another very useful purpose. The Bar chart per se is a Period chart, and as such cannot express time beyond the given period assigned to it. But the Grouped Bar chart provides a loophole.

To illustrate: if the entry is composed of two grouped bars, one of these bars can be designated to express this year, and the other bar, last year. Three grouped bars can express, say, budget, actual expenditures, and forecast. In other words, time can become a category or subdivision of an item. So it is possible to construct a Grouped Bar chart showing the marketing expenditures on products A, B, C, and D, with each product item having a group of bars — in this case three. These three grouped bars would indicate budget, actual expenditures, and forecast — all having occurred at different points in time.

In this way (and other ingenious ways the communicator may devise) multiple time periods can be built into a Grouped Bar chart, though it is essentially a Period chart.

BAR AND SYMBOL CHART   A variation of the Grouped Bar chart, hence a member of the Bar chart family, is the Bar and Symbol chart (Fig. 4-9). Actually, the Bar and Symbol chart, like the Grouped Bar chart, is a Simple Bar comparison with a secondary comparison added. The supplementary information provided by the secondary comparison is usually indicated by a crossline, a circle, a diamond, or, for that matter, any other symbol that calls the viewer's attention to the fact that supplementary information is being added to the bar, and that comparisons beyond those of a Simple Bar are being made.

A closer examination of Figure 4-9 will reveal that the symbol on this chart is attempting to take the place of a secondary bar in a Grouped Bar chart. The symbols are used to show, for example, a preceding month, or year, or previous performance.

The symbol is a device intended to catch the eye and say to the viewer, "look at the original bar, and now look at the symbol, and, keeping the original bar in mind, move your eyes up to the symbol and understand that this amount represents a secondary comparison, something different from the original bar."

Admittedly, when written as text, this concept is virtually incomprehensible; but what actually happens here is not complicated because the mind, with the help of the eyes, is accustomed to making this kind of shift.

The Bar and Symbol chart is an easy modification of the Simple Bar chart and a reasonable substitute for the Grouped Bar chart. It can be made quickly and demands a minimum amount of space. As a space saver it is preferable to the Grouped Bar chart. But when space economy is not a problem, and time is available to make a choice, the Grouped Bar chart is a better solution. The Grouped Bar chart provides the advantage that its secondary comparison gives two similar masses (i.e. solid bars) for the eye to compare, and thus eliminates the extra mental step the Bar and Symbol chart requires. In addition, a tertiary comparison on a Bar and Symbol chart is hardly feasible, but is possible on a Grouped Bar chart.

51

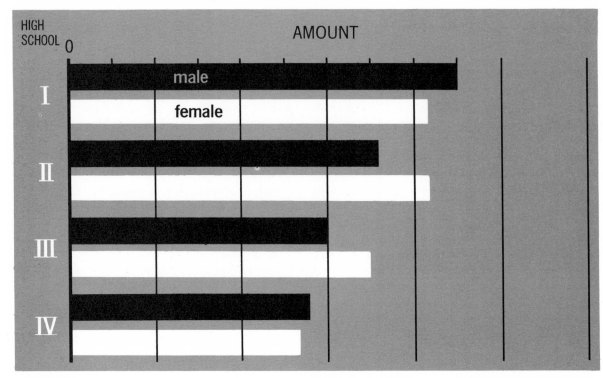

4-7 A Grouped Bar Chart

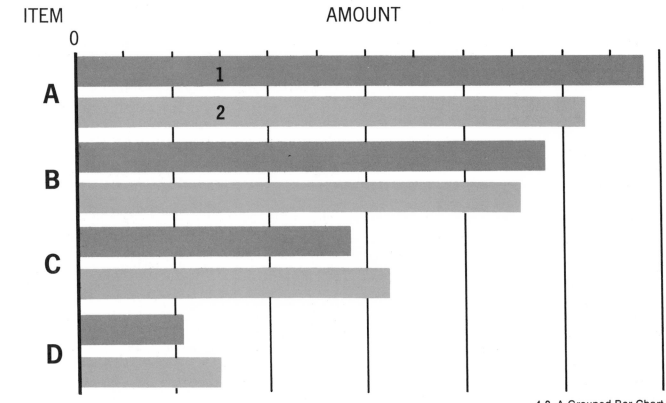

4-8 A Grouped Bar Chart

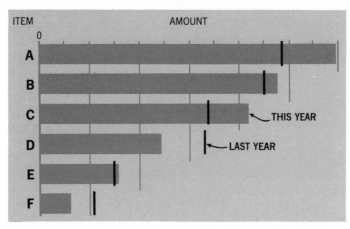

4-9 A Bar and Symbol Chart

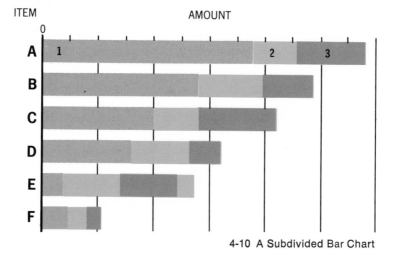

4-10 A Subdivided Bar Chart

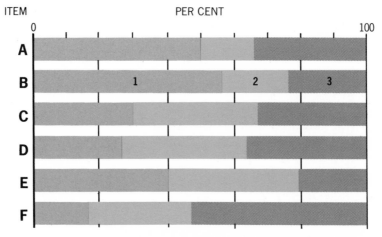

4-11 A Subdivided 100% Bar Chart

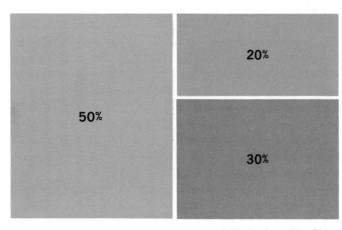

4-12 An Area Bar Chart

53

SUBDIVIDED BAR CHART   Very often data to be charted are made up of bits. For example, an advertising campaign may comprise expenditures for different media: newspapers, magazines, direct mail, radio, television, etc. Each bit is a component of the campaign. The total of component expenditures constitutes the cost of the entire advertising campaign.

In a Subdivided Bar chart (Fig. 4-10) the components of data, as well as data totals, can be charted. The Subdivided Bar chart is also referred to as a Segmented Bar or a Component Bar chart.

The components of a Subdivided Bar chart are added together like a string of beads, and the primary purpose of the chart is to show the relationship of the amount represented by each component to the total of all components. The Subdivided Bar chart, in contrast with the Subdivided 100% Bar, is plotted using absolute amounts.

In addition to its primary purpose, this chart provides the viewer with other comparisons. First, it compares the value of each component with that of other components within the same bar. Second, it provides a comparison of the bar totals. And third, it provides a comparison of *like* components with each other.

The Subdivided Bar chart is a very useful device when two conditions exist: (1) the item totals need to be shown, and (2) the totals are made up of many bits, or components. The Subdivided 100% Bar chart can handle the same conditions plus the condition of disparate magnitudes.

SUBDIVIDED 100% BAR CHART Often the data that are ideally suited to a Subdivided Bar chart treatment contain items whose totals differ so greatly from each other that it is physically impossible to chart them in absolute amounts. Similarly, the components of these totals are also disparate.

For example, suppose certain aspects of the Gross National Products of the United States and Switzerland were to be compared. To compare these totals in absolute numbers on an arithmetic scale would be visually almost meaningless, if not ludicrous. The solution then is not to use absolute numbers but to convert the components into percentages and to construct a Subdivided 100% Bar chart (Fig. 4-11).

The total lengths of all the bars in a Subdivided 100% Bar chart are the same, regardless of the amounts they represent. The scale on the bars is calibrated to 100%; and whether the absolute value (prior to conversion) was 10, 100, 1,000 or 1,000,000, the values expressed as percentages would fill the entire bar.

Understanding the purpose and seeing the advantage of utilizing a Subdivided 100% Bar chart is a little tricky in the beginning, and for this reason the following example simulating a conversion is given.

Item A needs to be compared to Item B. Both items have five *like* components. The total value of A is 2,500, and the total value of B is 300,000. It can be seen at once that a comparison of the two items on the same chart would be, to say the least, difficult. What would be even more difficult is any comparison of the components, because the components of Item A would be barely perceptible against a scale that would accommodate Item B.

To facilitate this demonstration we can translate the data into tabular form:

Item A

Component 1 =	100
" 2 =	300
" 3 =	500
" 4 =	700
" 5 =	900
	2,500

Item B

Component 1 =	20,000
" 2 =	40,000
" 3 =	60,000
" 4 =	80,000
" 5 =	100,000
	300,000

Observe, for instance, that Component 3 in Item A is 1/120th of the same component in B. Bear this relationship in mind, and see what happens when the absolute numbers are converted into percentages:

54

Item A

			Percent of total
Component 1 =	100		4%
" 2 =	300		12
" 3 =	500		20
" 4 =	700		28
" 5 =	900		36
	2,500		100%

Item B

			Percent of total
Component 1 =	20,000		7%
" 2 =	40,000		13
" 3 =	60,000		20
" 4 =	80,000		27
" 5 =	100,000		33
	300,000		100%

Components 3 of A and B are now an equal 20% of their totals, and since the overall lengths of bars A and B will be the same, Components 3 of A and B will occupy the same amount of space in their respective bars.

Thus, the Subdivided 100% Bar chart serves the useful purpose of copying with data in which the magnitude of the numbers varies greatly.*

AREA BAR CHART In a manner similar to the Subdivided 100% Bar chart, the Area Bar chart (Fig. 4-12) can be employed to show the relationship between percentages representing the components of a total. The Area Bar chart adds a second dimension, width, to the Linear Bar chart. To explain: the width of a Linear Bar is stationary, and does not change in relation to the bar's length. That of an Area Bar does change; both its length *and* width represent quantity.

As such the Area Bar chart is a space saver.

---

* The seductive ease of simplifying the relationships of absolute numbers in this manner can also cause trouble, because the magnitudes of difference are easily glossed over in the minds of the viewers. A case in point in real life is that 10% of $100 is *substantially* less than 10% of $1,000,000. Playing with numbers often waters down real values.

It is compact and can accommodate large magnitudes that could not be effectively presented in a Linear Bar. Geometrically, the Area Bar chart's form is a unity, and, as such, is a visual mass more so than is the Linear Bar. The Area Bar, like the Circle chart, is particularly subject to the vagaries of color.

PROGRESSIVE BAR CHART A member of the Bar chart family, and a subtype of the Subdivided Bar chart, is the Progressive Bar chart, sometimes called the Step-by-Step Bar chart (Fig. 4-13). This unusual form of Subdivided Bar shows the components of a bar as a series of steps, one below the other. The top bar represents the total, and each component is progressively shown as a separate item entry.

The Progressive Bar chart is a useful device for a study of details because it calls attention to one step at a time, and emphasizes the number of component steps involved.

The obvious limitation is that on a single chart only one item and its components can normally be shown at one time. It is possible, of course, to show the breakdowns of more than one item on a chart, but this is rarely done.

The total bar and its related components can be in either absolute or percentage numbers.

PAIRED BAR CHART The Paired Bar chart (Fig. 4-14) is used when the items being compared, although akin to each other, create a conflict of scale and require two different *types* or *magnitudes* of measurement.

Most Bar charts have one scale, and when a secondary comparison is added, the designer is required to use the same quantity scale to accommodate it.

In a Paired Bar chart the bars, instead of being grouped one below the other, are placed opposite each other—one set of bars extending to the left on one scale, and the other set to the right on the second scale. This arrangement provides two different scales for measuring the same item, which is identified in a center column between the two separate grids.

An example of different scale types occurs when an item (say, Product A) needs to be measured in 'units produced' and 'cost per unit.' Obviously,

55

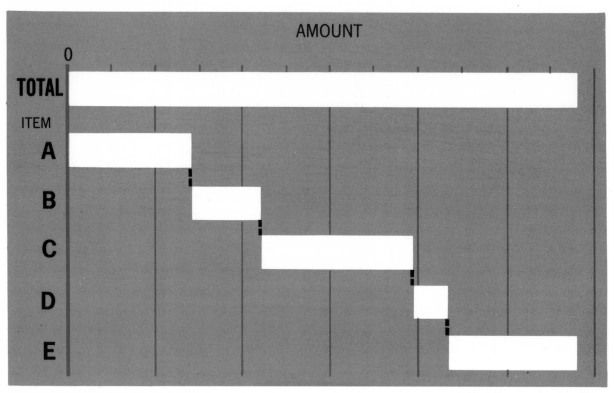

4-13 A Progressive Bar Chart

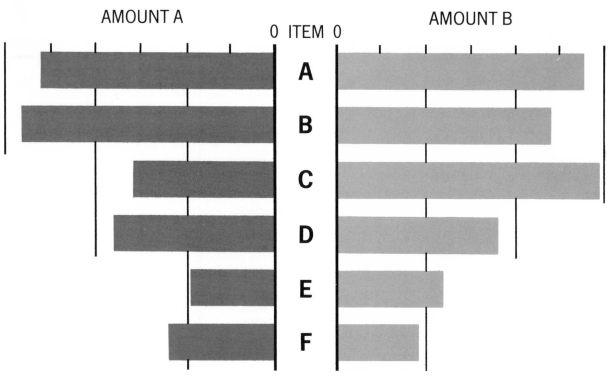

4-14 A Paired Bar Chart

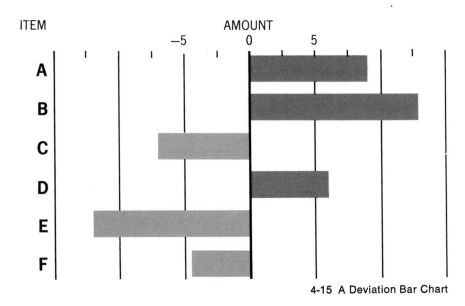

4-15 A Deviation Bar Chart

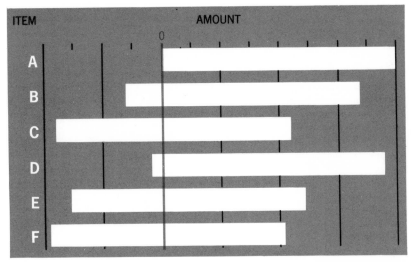

4-16 A Sliding Bar Chart

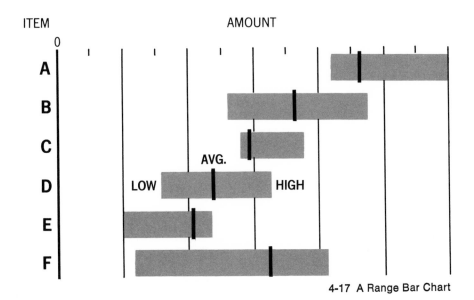

4-17 A Range Bar Chart

57

no one scale can be used to measure both types, since one measurement needs to be made in unit amounts, and the other in dollars.

An example of different scale magnitudes occurs when an item that is in vastly divergent amounts has to be measured. For instance, a staple of life like liquor may be compared in terms of state and national consumption. In this case one scale would be marked in millions and the other in billions of gallons.

DEVIATION BAR CHART A member of the Bar chart family that is effectively used in management-control reporting is the Deviation Bar chart (Fig. 4-15). This chart, sometimes called a Variance or Bilateral chart, is applicable whenever there is a need to show how data deviate from a norm.

For example, suppose the sales quota per salesman for a particular product was 100 units, and four salesmen were each charged with the responsibility for meeting this quota. In this case the 100 units is designated as the norm—an arbitrary assignation, as are all other norms.

The results of the salesmen's efforts were:

Salesman A	95 units
" B	115
" C	80
" D	105

In constructing a Deviation Bar chart to illustrate graphically the results of the salesmen's efforts, a base line is drawn down the center of the chart. This center line represents the 100-unit norm, equaling the quota.

Salesman A's result would be posted as a bar starting at the center-line norm and extending to the left for five units. B's bar would extend to the right for fifteen units, C's bar to the left for twenty units, and D's bar to the right for five units.*

Thus, each salesman's effort is represented by one bar and that bar goes either to the left or right of the center line norm. Notice that the area to the left of the norm is used to indicate the unfavorable differences, while the area to the right indicates favorable results; this is the conventional practice.

In cost-control reporting the Deviation Bar chart is more commonly known as a Variance chart. The norm of a Variance chart is at the point of "zero balance," which is arrived at by subtracting an *estimate* or *standard* from the *actual*.

For example, the estimated cost to produce Item A was $5. The actual cost was $7. The estimate is then subtracted from the actual—$7 minus $5, equaling plus $2. Had the actual been $5, the calculation would have been $5 minus $5, equaling zero. This net of zero is called the "zero balance," and is actually the break-even point. However, since the actual was $7 the result of plus $2 is called 2 *Over* the norm of zero.

The method of calculation is the same when standards are involved. Supposing the standard time for Operation K is 3 hours. A reporting for actual on this operation is made at 2 hours. So again, standard is subtracted from actual and would net out as 2 hours minus 3 hours, equaling minus 1 hour. This minus 1 hour is called *Under* the standard that represents the norm of zero.

Under-zero results appear to the left, and *Over*-zero results to the right of the center line.*

The figures in a Deviation Bar chart can be expressed in either absolute numbers or in percentages.

Actually, what the bars on the chart are showing is the residual value of the zero-balancing. In other words, the entire value of the bar representing the data is not shown, but only the segment of the bar which is left over after the estimate or the standard is subtracted from the actual. If the subtraction results in zero nothing is shown.

---

* This example clearly describes a Deviation Bar chart. However, in anticipation of some misunderstanding, the following comments are intended to clarify the terms used in this chart: (1) The center line in the example happens to be 100 because the sales quota was 100. It could just as well have been 80, or 107 if these had been the sales quota; (2) the center line is technically the base line; and (3) the base line is usually where the deviations equal zero.

---

* A curious observation is that although the debit and credit entries coincidentally follow this logic, and are entered on a "T" account to the left and right respectively, other financial reporting (e.g. assets and liabilities, and profit and loss) reverse their positions.

SLIDING BAR CHART There are times, however, when we may need to show the entire value of the bar in addition to the "net" favorable and unfavorable segments shown in a Deviation Bar chart. To meet this need the Sliding Bar chart (Fig. 4-16) is used. This is a special sort of Subdivided Bar chart in which the length of the bar represents the total of the two main components — one extending to the left (unfavorable) and one extending to the right (favorable) of the base line.

An example of a Sliding Bar chart application would be a quality-control report. Such reports should show the total number of part pieces inspected and the portions of each lot that were accepted and rejected. The base line of a Sliding Bar chart, used for this purpose, would be designated the criterion for acceptance. The number, or percentage, of parts in the particular lot being examined that were rejected would appear to the left of the base line, and those accepted to the right.

In a Sliding Bar chart the bars move, or slide, while the base line, or norm, remains fixed.

Either absolute numbers or 100% bars may be used in this chart.

RANGE BAR CHART The Range Bar chart (Fig. 4-17), as one might expect, shows the range or spread between high and low amounts. This chart is unique in that its bars do not start from a common base, and so they cannot be compared directly with each other from a principal point of reference. Instead, their purpose is to show the differences in size of each range.

The point of a Range Bar chart is that the amount scale remains fixed, and the bars *move* against this frame of reference. As in the Deviation Bar chart, the total value of the bar length is implied, and only the *difference* is charted.

An example of how this chart operates is to suppose that we wanted to estimate the cost of alternative marketing projects. Not knowing the exact cost of each, we can estimate that each one would cost between "this" and "that."

To portray the data graphically a Grouped Bar chart could be used, making one bar represent "this" cost, and a second bar represent "that" cost. The difference between the "this" and "that" bars is, of course, the range. But if we decided to create a single bar to represent only that differ-

ence, or range, we would be rendering the viewer a service. The Range Bar chart does just that: it records, in the form of a bar, the difference between two implied bars that need to be compared.

Column Charts

"Column charts are Bar charts arranged vertically." This often-voiced observation is a valid one from a visual point of view, but from a functional point of view it is only partially accurate, since it does not take into account the essential difference between a Bar chart and Column chart. A Bar chart is classified as a Period chart, whereas a Column chart is classified as a Time Series chart.

Basically, the Column chart has much in common with the Bar chart. Many of the Column chart's subtypes and variations are conceptually, and mechanically, similar to those in the Bar chart family. But here the similarity ends, because the Column is used for comparisons of similar items at different times, while the Bar is generally used to compare different items at the same time.

SIMPLE COLUMN CHART The Simple Column chart (Fig. 4-18) has two axes: one vertical, which is used as the amount scale, and one horizontal, which is used for the time scale. All Column charts have these same axes.

The time scale for a Column chart is usually composed of a number of individual and equal time periods, uniformly arranged in a series, starting at the left and proceeding to the right in chronological order.

What is meant by 'individual and equal time periods' is discussed in some detail on page 86, but broadly, some examples described by this phrase are: January, February, March, April, May; or 1960, 1961, 1962; or Monday, Tuesday, Wednesday, Thursday and Friday.*

A Simple Column chart is constructed with a number of equally spaced vertical bars, each ex-

* Generally speaking, Column charts are not well suited for comparing several different time series simultaneously; nor are they suitable for time series that have unchanging amount values covering extended periods of time, nor for recording data that involve many plottings. Extended time periods and data having numerous plottings are more properly handled by Line and Surface charts.

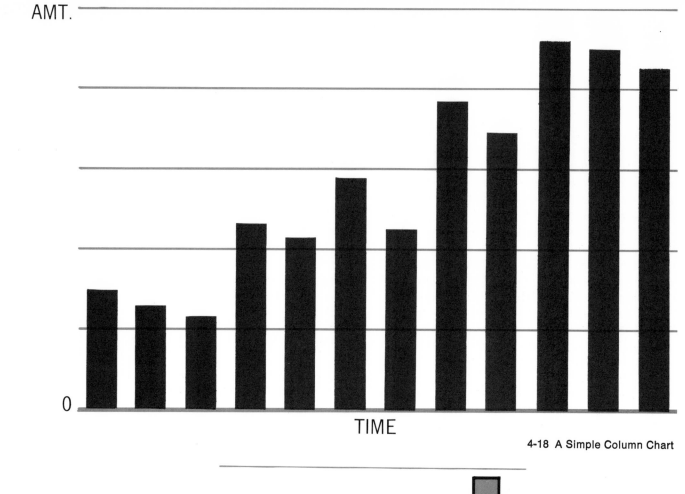

AMT.

0

TIME

4-18 A Simple Column Chart

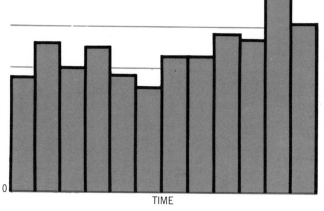

0

TIME

4-19 A Connected Column Chart

100

75

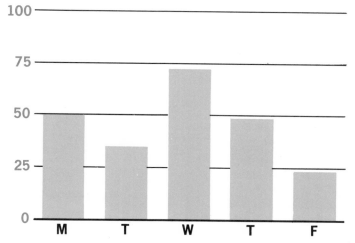

50

25

0

M   T   W   T   F

4-20 A Simple Column Chart

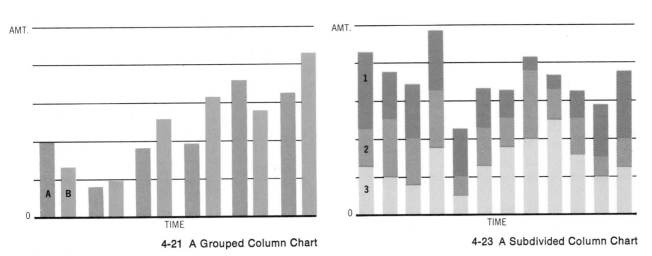

4-21 A Grouped Column Chart

4-23 A Subdivided Column Chart

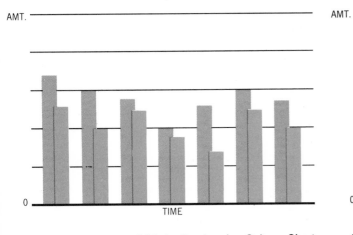

4-22 An Overlapping Column Chart

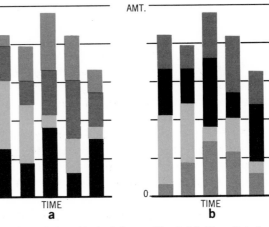

4-24 (a) A Subdivided Column Chart (b) The Subdivided Columns Rearranged

61

tending from the base (or horizontal time line), and terminating at a coordinate point on the vertical amount line. If the space interval between the bars is omitted, and the bars are adjacent to each other, the chart is referred to as a Connected Column chart (Fig. 4-19).

An illustration of how a Simple Column chart is used can be made if we consider measuring the productivity of Clerical Worker Smith. C. W. Smith is assigned the responsibility of processing invoices. The number of invoices she processes per day is dependent on many things (all of which do not concern us here since we wish to chart only the amount of work actually produced).

By checking her daily worksheet we find that on:

Monday	she processed 50 units;
Tuesday	35
Wednesday	72
Thursday	48
Friday	23 (a bad day!)

We can observe by looking at the raw data that her maximum productivity was 72 units. An amount range is then determined to be at least 72 units high to accommodate Wednesday's amount. Technically this range is sufficient, but by setting the top of the scale at 72 we ignore pertinent design considerations.

First, divisable scale increments established on multiples of 2 (i.e. 2/72, 4/72, 6/72) would be awkward to interpolate. Second, if the largest column were 72 units, and the top of the scale were also 72 units, the column would fill the entire grid, so that the chart would appear visually unbalanced.

In view of these considerations, the increment of 5 would be selected, and the amount range extended from zero to 100. This solution meets all requirements. The amount range is then placed outside the grid on the vertical axis.

The time scale, we know, is a series from Monday through Friday. Thus, five increments, labeled accordingly, would be uniformly spaced, and placed along the horizontal axis under the base line.

Vertical bars would now be placed directly over each of the points labeled as days on the time scale, extending from the zero base line,

and stopping where they reach the plotted coordinate point on the amount scale. In the case of Monday, it would be at 50 units. The resultant chart is Figure 4-20.

In this manner a Simple Column chart is very rapidly constructed to indicate the profile of C. W. Smith's productivity.

GROUPED COLUMN CHART The Grouped Column chart (Fig. 4-21) follows the same concept as the Grouped Bar chart. As a Column chart its function is to compare two, but seldom more than two, sets of data for the same point of time in a time series.

For example, sales data for the months of June through December may be reported from Branch Offices A and B. In this case two columns (A and B) are grouped over June and two over the succeeding months, with one column representing Branch A and the other Branch B.

The Grouped Column chart offers the bonus of being a space saver. When space is really at a premium, the columns in each pair could be made to overlap each other and then would be appropriately called an Overlapping Column chart (Fig. 4-22). And, finally, as the ultimate in space-saving devices, the designer may resort to using a symbol to indicate the secondary comparison. This last variation is of course called a Column and Symbol chart, and works the same way as does the Bar and Symbol chart.

SUBDIVIDED COLUMN CHART The Grouped Column chart and its variations nicely handle two sets of data for a single point of time in a time series. But often the problem arises that not only the totals, but also the components of these totals, need to be shown for the same point in time. In such cases a Subdivided Column chart (Fig. 4-23) is used.

For instance, you may want to analyze graphically, for cash-flow purposes, six months of an accounts-payable file. To determine cash flow a charting of totals would be insufficient because it would not show the makeup of the file. However, the components of the file (i.e. what was due in thirty, sixty, or ninety days) would be meaningful information for planning. The Subdivided Column chart lends itself ideally to this type of analysis.

The Subdivided Column chart, also called a

Segmented or Component Column chart, is an interesting one because the order of its components can be sequenced (i.e. arranged) differently; each arrangement presents its contents validly and yet portrays the data in different configuration.

To explain: assume the components of five subdivided columns are represented by this table:

Component	Col I	Col II	Col III	Col IV	Col V
A	4	3	6	2	5
B	6	5	1	3	1
C	3	2	4	5	3
D	1	3	5	4	2

If these data are charted they would look like Figure 4-24a.

Notice how the A components form a pattern, or configuration, as they are viewed across the horizontal axis. Each of the other sets of like components similarly form their own patterns.

In each column the components are *added* to each other to form the column's total. In other words, they are piled one on top of the other. In Column I, for instance, A's 4 is placed on the baseline; B's 6 is added to A's 4; then C's 3 is added to 10 (A+B); then finally, D's 1 is added to 13 (A+B+C) to make the total of 14.

Now suppose the order of arrangement is changed from A+B+C+D to say, D+B+A+C. The configuration of the chart would then look like Figure 4-24b — an altogether different set of configurations, or curves. In this manner the visual appearance of a Subdivided Column chart can be changed. Thus, the communicator, for various reasons, can present his "picture" differently.

Subdivided 100% Column charts in which absolute numbers are converted into percentage ratios are also subject to the rearrangement of components.

DEVIATION COLUMN CHART   The Deviation Column chart (Fig. 4-25) employs the same concept as the Deviation Bar chart to measure data when they deviate from a norm. However, the Deviation Column, instead of showing how a number of different items deviate at a point in time, shows how the same item deviates over a number of different times.

The base line of a Deviation Column chart is drawn horizontally across the center of the chart.

The base line is usually zero but it need not always be — it could be a norm, or average, or some other break-even point that distinguishes what is favorable from unfavorable.

The deviating columns are alternately extended vertically above or below the center line. The area of the grid above the center line indicates favorable results, and below those that are unfavorable. This distinction should be easy to remember if you associate your results with the theological upstairs and downstairs.

FLOATING COLUMN CHART   The Floating Column chart (Fig. 4-26) is the Sliding Bar chart turned sidewards. In this chart the image no longer slides; it floats.

The Floating Column chart differs from the Deviation Column chart because it permits the same bar to be divided so that it appears above *and* below the center line. In doing so the bar is "segmented," with part of its total above and part below.

Unlike the Deviation Column the portion of the bar below the center line need not indicate an unfavorable result. For example, each of the columns may represent the range of temperatures for the day in a week. The center line may represent the freezing point of 32 degrees. Assuming we are in the dead of winter (a chilling thought), the bars could be related to the freezing point, and indicate that portion of the twenty-four-hour day that was above freezing and that portion that was below. The scale can be expressed in either absolute or percentage values.

This example uses days that, of course, have constant totals (twenty-four hours), so that the length of all the bars in the study are equal. Bar lengths, however, are usually uneven when absolute numbers are plotted. In the event uneven bars are not usable, or desirable, the data can be converted into 100% bars and still be handled similarly.

RANGE COLUMN CHART   The Range Column chart (Fig. 4-27) is very much like the Floating Column in that its bars also float — but in the true sense of the word. However, it differs from a Floating Column because its bars cannot extend below the base line, since the base line begins the amount scale. Moreover, the columns need

63

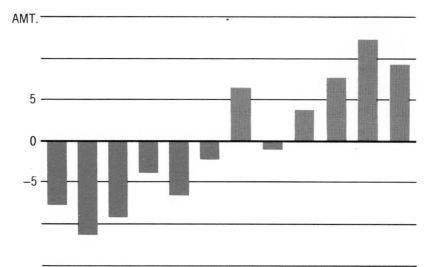

AMT.

5

0

−5

TIME

4-25 A Deviation Column Chart

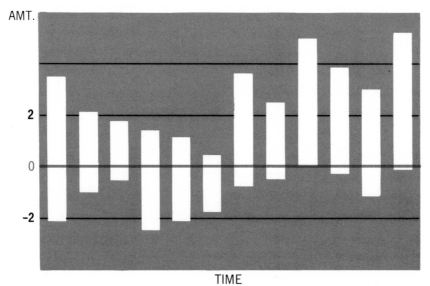

AMT.

2

0

−2

TIME

4-26 A Floating Column Chart

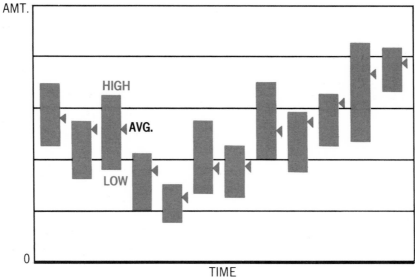

AMT.

HIGH

AVG.

LOW

0

TIME

4-27 A Range Column Chart

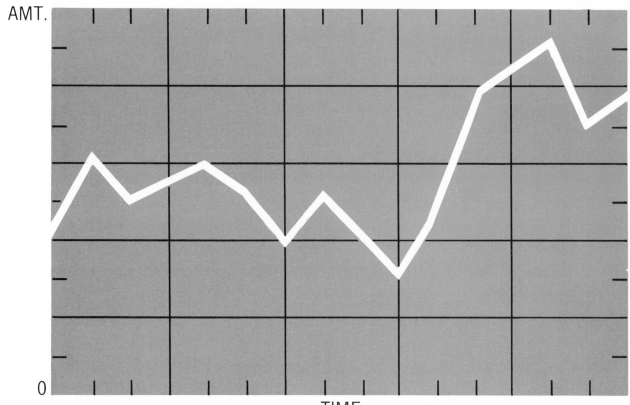

4-28 A Simple Line Chart

4-29 A Simple Surface Chart

not touch the base line, a rare exception in charting.

The Range Column chart, which shows an item's maximal and minimal values within a time series, probably has had more exposure to the public than any other single chart form. It is seen day in and day out on financial pages, in thousands of newspapers throughout the country. In fact, it is often referred to as a Stock Price chart, because it is used extensively to depict the daily highs and lows in stock quotations.

Although made famous by Dow Jones & Co. as a stock-price indicator, the Range Column chart is not limited to this application. It can be used to present the highest and lowest values in any data predominantly characterized by fluctuation. For example: manpower strength, inventory levels, consumer product consumption, productivity of clerical workers, data-processing volumes, and many others.

Supplementary information, such as statistical means, modes, or medians, can be added by using symbols (i.e. crosslines, circles, etc.) to indicate their particular values on the range column.

Line and Surface Charts

The Line and Surface charts are conceptually the same family of charts; the difference lies in the greater visual impact the Surface chart makes. On a Line chart the curve sits out there all alone —naked, so to speak—while the Surface chart, to carry the analogy forward, is clothed by a shading that extends from the base line to the curve.

This is not to say that modesty, or visual considerations, make the Surface preferable to the Line. Rather, it means that they serve the same purpose differently. This difference will be pointed out in the discussion of each member of this chart family.

When a series of plotted points is connected by a line, that line, in statistical jargon, is called a curve, or sometimes a slope.

The Line chart is probably the most widely used form of chart presentation. It is relatively easy to make, extremely flexible, and can be adapted to a wide range of applications. Many disciplines, engineering for example, rarely use any other graphic devices. Line charts are used for the simplest comparisons and for the most complex.

The only other chart family that provides a time series is the Column chart, and it, in comparison to the Line chart, has data-input limitations. That is to say, Column charts cannot generally accommodate presentations that require more than five or six plottings. Line charts can, and do.

The Line chart, borrowed from the mathematician, is capable of presenting a vast amount of data in a compact, not-so-easy-to-interpret form. It is harder to interpret because it carries so many data in its plottings — each of which needs to be interpolated even to approximate its value. But, by and large, Line charts are not meant to be precisely interpolated. Their main purpose is to give a "picture" that describes the relative movement of its data.

SIMPLE LINE AND SURFACE CHARTS The Simple Line chart (Fig. 4-28) is constructed by the extension of a direct line from each plotted point to the next — each plotted point representing a coordinate of time and amount.

Looking at a Simple Line chart one can easily see if the subject has gone up, or down, or stayed about the same. It can be used to depict broad understandings. For example, suppose the rate of crime for 1960 to 1965 were the subject of a Line chart. An ascending curve would indicate the rise in crime from 1960 to 1965. The amount spread between point-1960 and point-1965 indicates how much it has gone up during the entire period of time.

If we were interested in the rate of crime as of the year 1963, it would be quite simple to draw a perpendicular line from the 1963 mark on the time scale upwards until it intersected the curve. At the point of intersection we would then draw another line, horizontal to the base, until it reached the amount scale — and then merely read off the value on the amount scale. Any other "as of" period in the time series would be handled the same way.

The curve on a Simple Line chart can follow almost any pattern from a straight trend line to a fluctuating zigzag line showing drastic amount changes in the data. In the plotting of a line curve, the more points plotted, and the closer these points are to each other, the more likely the curve will appear smoothed.

The Simple Surface chart (Fig. 4-29) is essentially a Simple Line chart, with the space between the curve and the base of the chart filled in by patterns or color, so that it appears as a solid surface. However, there are two characteristics of the Surface chart that differentiate it from the Line chart.

The first difference is that the Surface chart normally shows only amounts. The Line chart, while also showing amounts, can under certain other conditions also show changes in amounts, i.e. rates of changes (see page 81). The other differentiating characteristic of the Surface chart is a visual one: the area under the curve is emphasized because the filled-in surface gives body to its image. This effect is especially useful when the designer wants to dramatize the "substance" in the data being presented.

SINGLE STEP LINE AND SURFACE CHARTS When the data being presented consist of plottings that are widely spaced, or when the plottings reflect data that change abruptly at irregular intervals, a Single Step Line chart is used (Fig. 4-30). In addition, these data are characterized by *constant* amount levels over an entire period of time of a time series — for instance, an average, or a ceiling, or a limit that does not change until the next point in time.

Normally, the connecting line between two plottings is drawn as a direct line (i.e. the shortest distance between two points), but unless successive points are of equal value the connecting line will not be parallel to the base line. The Single Step chart does not follow this principle. Instead it is constructed as a histogram, in that it is formed by a series of 90-degree angles with horizontal lines indicating the levels of constant amounts and vertical lines joining these levels.*

---

* An interesting observation is that the nomenclature of the various charts is for the most part graphic — e.g. Step chart. Attempting to describe a chart like the Single Step is a frustrating experience for both the writer and reader. What with 90-degree angles, horizontal levels, and vertical connecting lines, it is sometimes difficult for the reader to remember what he has read — making the biased assumption that it was clearly written in the first place. With this in mind it is suggested that the Single Step Line chart be remembered as: "the chart that looks like a bunch of steps." The application of similar mnemonic devices is recommended for other charts also.

Naturally, the Single Step Line chart becomes the Single Step Surface chart (Fig. 4-31) by adding the dimension of "body" to the area under the curve, and, for the reasons pointed out in the discussion of the Simple Surface chart, the Single Step Surface chart is different from the Single Step Line chart.

One other observation should be made: the Single Step Surface bears a striking resemblance to the Connected Column chart, except for the vertical lines outlining the columns.

MULTIPLE LINE AND SURFACE CHARTS The Multiple Line chart (Fig. 4-32) expands the Simple Line chart by adding one or more curves to it. Multiple Line charts, however, have a tendency to get sloppy when more than three curves appear on them.*

The curves of a Multiple Line chart may be *related*, such as a total and its components; or they may be *quasi-related*, like profits and sales; or they may be *unrelated*, such as two or more totals representing sales of different products.

When a surface is added the chart is called the Multiple Surface chart (Fig. 4.33), alias the Subdivided Slope-Surface, or Strata chart, or even Layer chart.

The Multiple Surface chart is very effectively used in presentations directed to people who are not generally accustomed to seeing charts as a means of communication. The Annual Report uses them a great deal to make its presentation more impressive and colorful.

In annual reports Multiple Surface charts are often used to explain technical aspects of production or operations, like the layers of earth preceding an oil deposit, or the balance of payments in our economy. In both cases the Multiple Line chart cannot do the job adequately.

The major deterrent in using a Multiple Surface chart is that it can be misinterpreted easily, especially by those not accustomed to reading this kind of chart. Confusion usually stems from the erroneous impression that each stratum of surface begins at the base line — which of course is not the case. The surface strata of a Multiple Surface chart are cumulative, i.e. the second stratum

---

* Charts having multiple curves give rise to additional problems, for instance, double scales (page 84).

67

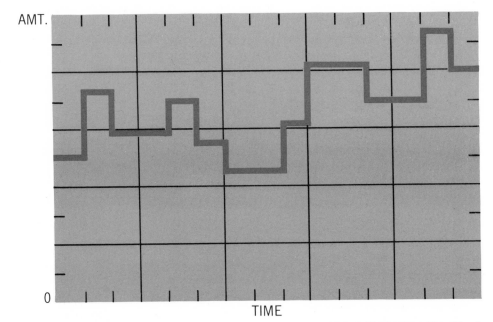

AMT.

0

TIME

4-30 A Single Step Line Chart

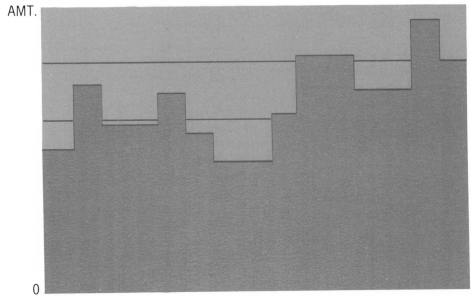

AMT.

0

TIME

4-31 A Single Step Surface Chart

68

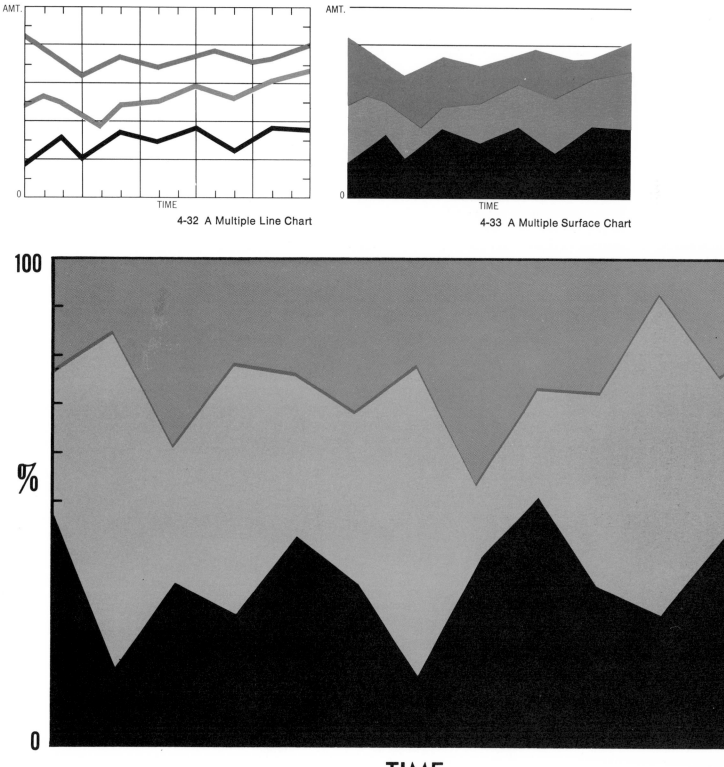

4-32 A Multiple Line Chart

4-33 A Multiple Surface Chart

4-34 A Multiple Surface 100% Chart

is added to the first, the third stratum to the second, and so forth.

The order of the Strata determines the profile of each stratum exactly in the manner discussed in Subdivided Column charts.

The Multiple Surface chart is plotted in absolute numbers, but if the nature of the data requires the conversion of the absolute numbers into percentages of the total, then a 100% Surface chart should be used (Fig. 4-34).

The curves on a 100% Surface chart may be of the Line or Step type. As in all 100% charts the configurations reflect changes in the relative size of the totals' components over the points in the time series.

A caveat must be included in any consideration to use this form of Surface chart. The principal reason for selecting the 100% Surface over the Multiple Surface is that the data's absolute figures are not compatible to a common scale.

However, care should be exercised to determine if the incompatibility is the result of irregular or non-recurring "occurrences," such as strikes, which can cause "freak" points. In other words, determine if the curve is affected by a factor that may never, or at least hardly ever, happen again. If such is the case, caution should lead you to investigate the visual effect this freak point will cause.

A good example of this point is a strike that puts all competitors out of business for a period of time. Naturally, the sole surviving company's sales would skyrocket.

	Normal Years			Abnormal Year
	1962	1963	1964	1965
1st Quarter	300	200	200	300
2nd Quarter	200	300	500	2,000[a]
3rd Quarter	100	200	300	400
4th Quarter	200	200	300	300
	800	900	1,300	3,000

[a](strike period)

Figure 4-35 shows the data plotted in absolute numbers. Now take a look at Figure 4-36 and observe what effect the use of a 100% Surface chart

has on the picture presented. The dramatic portrayal is just the opposite from what really happened. The sales curve is inverted!

Common sense tells us this is not the case, and Figure 4-35, in absolute numbers, portrays the case more accurately.

BAND CHART   A subtype of the Multiple Line and Surface charts is the Band chart (Fig. 4-37). Both curves on a Band chart are plotted from the base line, and their quantities are *not* comulative as is the case in other Surface charts. The function of a Band chart is to take two closely related curves like gross and net, or before and after, compare them to each other, and at the same time lay emphasis on their differences. This emphasis is achieved by using a filled-in surface to represent the space separating the curves.

The significance of this chart is that only the amount of difference between two curves is highlighted. The actual magnitudes that the curves represent are secondary, and as a matter of fact, so is their pattern of change. It is their *relationship,* or the distance between the upper and lower curve, that counts.

Visually the surface band serves to accentuate this spread between the plottings of the two curves, and thus it is an ideal chart for presentations concerned with calling attention to the differences identified by the spread.

INTERSECTING BAND CHART   While the Band chart is predicated on one curve having a greater magnitude than the other throughout the time series, this is not always the case. Very often the two curves intersect at various points in the time series. In other words, sometimes the amplitude of Curve A is greater than that of Curve B, and sometimes it is less.

When such situations occur the use of an Intersecting Band chart (Fig. 4-38) is suitable. This chart, also known as a Deviation Band chart or Overlapping Curve chart, is very useful in analyzing the interaction of two curves. For example, if we designate Curve A as gains and Curve B as losses, we can employ an Intersecting Band chart to portray, with emphasis, when gains have exceeded losses and vice versa.

This emphasis is a necessary part of the presentation, and is accomplished by "color-coding":

be it crosshatching, shading, or applying different colors to the surfaces. Thus, when gains, exceed losses that surface of the band could be colored black, and when losses exceed gains that surface could be colored red. By the use of color in this manner the coincidence of "operating in the black or red" is, of course, intended, thereby adding an extra dimension in communicating.

Combinations of Basic Devices

The graphic devices discussed in this chapter are basic ones. They have been shown in their pristine, generalized forms. Learning the language of graphics necessitates such a simple *ABC* approach.

There is no reason, however, why a designer cannot achieve simplicity and yet conceive a chart that simultaneously employs more than one basic device. In fact, the realities of practice often dictate such needs.

Basic devices can be combined in countless ways, far too many even to attempt to describe them comprehensively. Hybrids or mutations, if you will, are products of the designer's imagination. The communicator's sole criterion in justifying their use is that they communicate more effectively than simpler alternatives he might have chosen. Figures 4-40 and 4-41 present two representative examples possible in creating combinations of basic charting devices.

Naturally, in order to have meaning, basic devices must be set into a chart, which includes its scales, intervals, labels, captions, titles, and such; these can be conveniently termed the *mechanics of charting*.

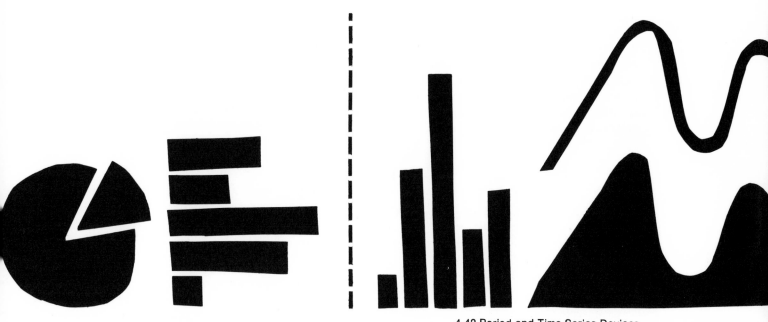

4-42 Period and Time Series Devices

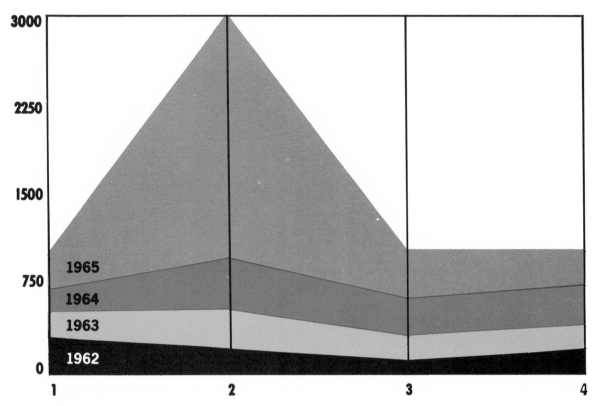

4-35 Sales Data Plotted in Absolute Numbers

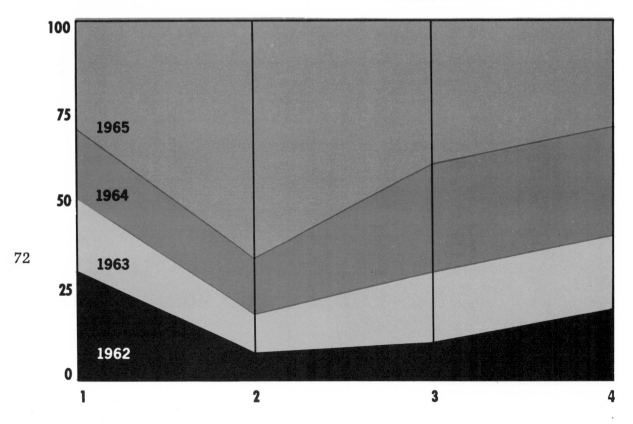

4-36 Sales Data Plotted in Percentages

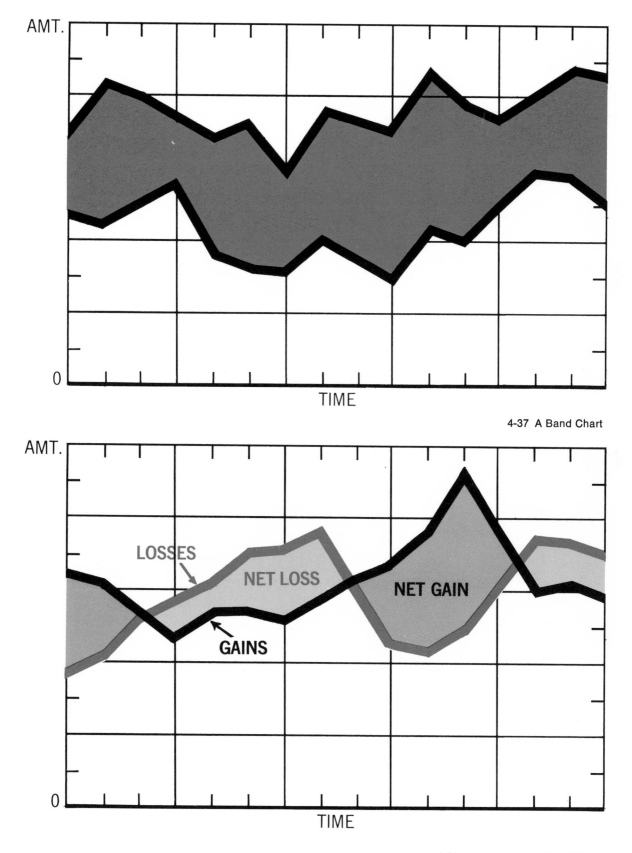

AMT.

0

TIME

4-37 A Band Chart

AMT.

LOSSES

NET LOSS

NET GAIN

GAINS

0

TIME

73

4-38 An Intersecting Band Chart

4-39 A Combination Column and Surface Chart

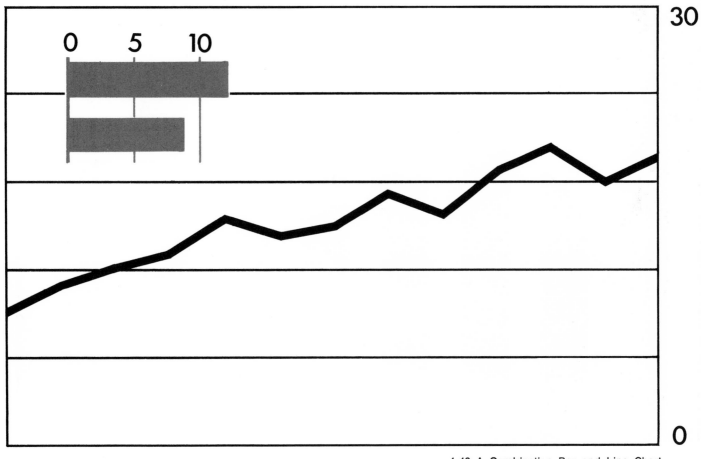

4-40 A Combination Bar and Line Chart

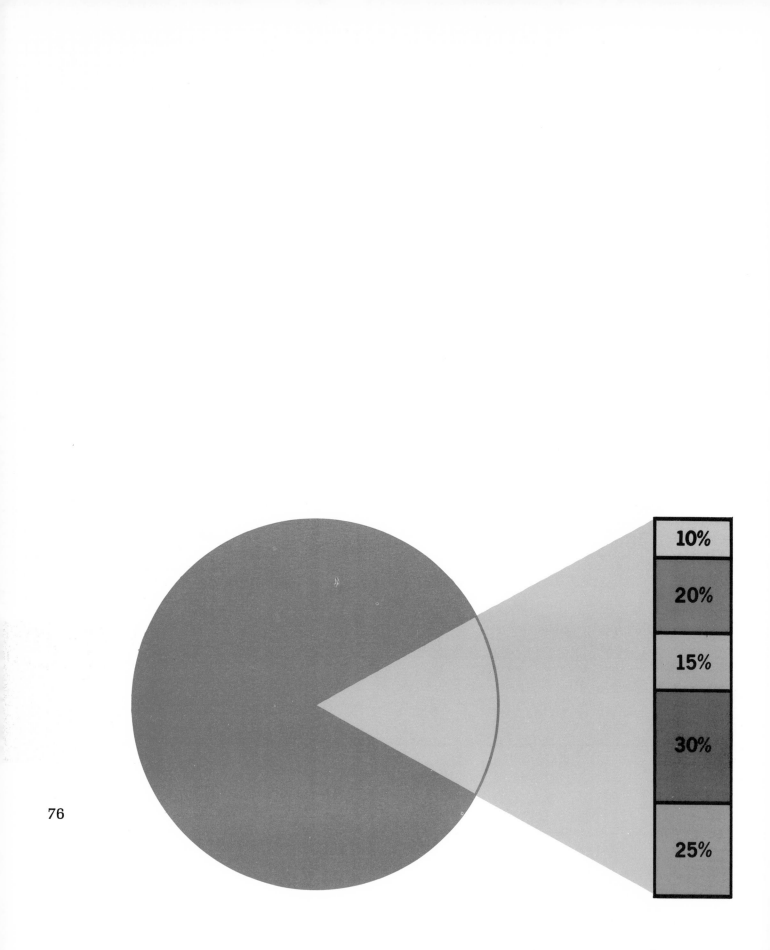

4-41 A Combination Circle and Column Chart

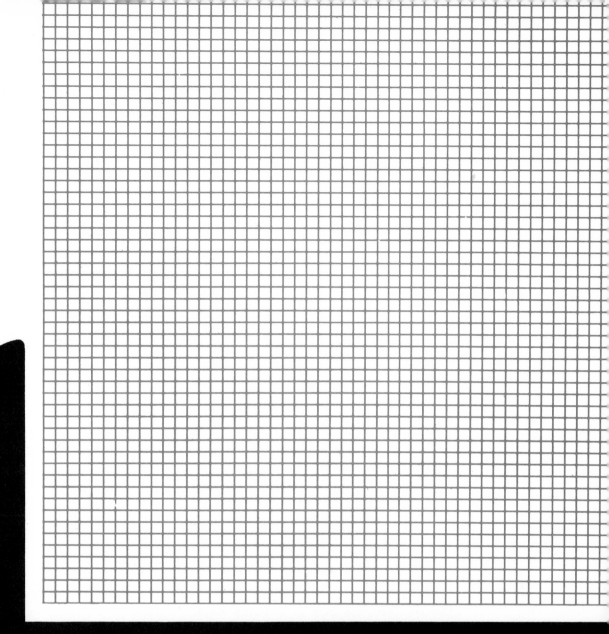

Mechanics of Charting

Mechanics of Charting

The mechanics of charting is probably the least understood and the most misused aspect of graphic presentation. Analogously, mechanics is to charting what syntax is to grammar. In constructing a sentence, it is of little use to pick the precise words if, in the final result, the grammar and punctuation are so garbled that the interchange of thoughts becomes a vain, hopeless experience for the writer and reader. And so it is with graphic communications. If the mechanics is employed poorly—no matter how well the other chart elements are used—the chart's message will be frittered away in confusion and misunderstanding.

From the misuse of mechanics stems the root of distortion. Distortion may be a strong word because it implies active participation by the communicator. In some cases the implication is deserved. People exaggerate with charts and graphs just as glibly as they do with statistics, because charts are merely a visual extension of statistical data. On the other hand, there is nothing intrinsically wrong in wanting the results of our actions to be viewed in their best possible light—which, we happen to believe, lies somewhere near the objective truth.

The proper use of mechanics provides the means of presenting information to its greatest advantage. More basically, mechanics provides the vehicle for successfully communicating results. To examine the validity of this statement, observe in Figure 5-2 how the same bit of statistical data is affected by the selection of amount and time scales.

Using the original scale as a constant frame of reference, observe the presentation of a simple curve and trend (dotted) line in the other charts and see what happens when either the amount, or time, or both scales are varied.

In this demonstration, a picture is literally worth a thousand words. With each presentation so obviously different, how is the viewer to know which to accept? Actually, it is impossible to determine which of these graphic representations positively reflects the objective truth. We may feel some are "fairer" presentations than others, but even so, it can be validly argued that each one accurately portrays the same data.

This kind of sophistry is possible because the graphic technique is essentially an abstraction or interpretation of objective reality. The communicator must therefore take care to avoid the potential for distortion in his interpretation. In this light the important thing to remember is that the context in which the representation is used is the only frame of reference that establishes the integrity of the communicator. For instance, if a company is increasing its sales, but losing profits rapidly, it would be nothing short of deception to elongate the time scale purposely to lessen the sharp decline of the profits curve, while shortening the time scale on the sales curve to make its incline rise sharply.*

Obviously, this is not the right way to handle such data. And ironically, there is no "right" way. There is only a preferred way, established by two criteria (which are not mutually exclusive). The

---

* Caveat Lector! (Reader Beware!) There is no doubt that some of the burden of proof rests with the reader's ability to be discerning. This does not, however, mitigate the communicator's unethical or deceptive intent. Meanwhile, understanding mechanics and its implementation makes one a better reader as well as a better maker of charts.

first criterion is the communicator's subjective view. The chart should meet his aesthetic sense, and transmit the message ethically and advantageously to his purpose. The second criterion is to work within, and adhere to, guidelines drawn from standards compiled by professional organizations such as ASME.*

These criteria are always held in a delicate balance. Certainly, the first one deserves the greater attention. That is not to say the other can be forsaken, for it holds the key to a common language of charting.

The various signs and symbols used in chart-making are a type of shorthand. As with other uses of abstract symbols, such as in mathematics, music, or chemistry, the ability of the receiver to follow the transmitter's thought is largely dependent on the "language" they have built between them. Therefore, the more standardized symbols of the language become, the more effective they are.

The various aspects of mechanics set forth in this chapter are intended as guidelines for the preparation of graphic presentations. These guidelines represent generally accepted standards. While these standards serve as a frame of reference which should be followed, they should not necessarily be followed so rigidly that elasticity of innovation is precluded.

Amount Scales

All charts classified as Period or Time Series charts have amount scales. The amount scale on a Period chart runs from the left to right along the horizontal axis of the grid, beginning at the left with the smallest value. Amount scales on Period charts are usually placed at the top of the grid.

On a Time Series chart the amount scale begins with the smallest value at the base of the chart and extends upwards on the vertical axis, terminating with the largest value. Amount scales

---

* American Society of Mechanical Engineers. Much of the material in this chapter has been built around the principles and standards set forth in ASME's publication *American Standard Time-Series Charts* *(ASA Y15.2-1960)*. The field of charting is indebted to this organization for its efforts in establishing uniformity and generously making its work available to the public.

on Time Series charts can be placed at the left and/or right of the grid. These rules are elementary and there should be no reason to deviate from them.

AMOUNT RANGE SELECTION The selection of an amount range is a key step which should be approached with care.

There are four simple guidelines in this selection process; by using the following hypothetical table we can explore their application:

January	10 units
February	5
March	23
April	19
May	29
June	20

The amount range should be greater than the largest value in the data. The largest value in the table is 29 (in May). Thus, the amount range should be large enough to accommodate a magnitude of at least 29.

The amount range should be conveniently divisible. Technically, the amount range for the data in the table could be from zero to any value more than 29. Yet a figure like 33, which satisfies the requirement, is difficult to divide into uniform scale intervals.

If the chart is to be interpolated it is better to use multiples that are easily divisible. Ordinarily, these are even numbers; uneven numbers are awkward to work with. For instance, half of seven is three and one-half, whereas half of eight is four.

If the chart has to do with money, however, the choice is fairly simple since the amount values can be based on the decimal system.

The amount range should make provisions for an acceptable graphic image. The range selected will directly affect the configuration or the image representing the data. Care should be taken in selecting a range that ensures that the visual image is not crowded into the extreme top or bottom of the chart.

Figure 5-3 demonstrates this point. There can be no question that Figure 5-3c makes the most sense graphically, and graphic sense should always be a prime objective.

79

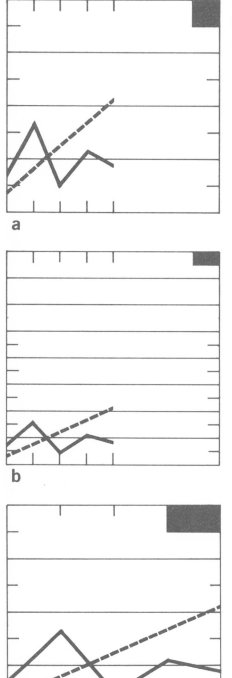

a

5-2 Effects of Altering Time and Amount Scales (a) Original Scale (b) Contracting Amount Scale (c) Contracting Time Scale (d) Expanding Amount Scale (e) Expanding Time Scales (f) Contracting Amount and Expanding Time Scales (g) Contracting Time and Expanding Amount Scales

b

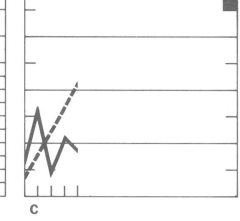

c

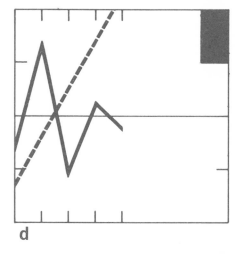

d

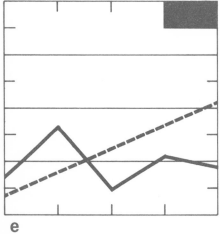

e

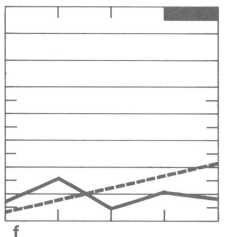

f

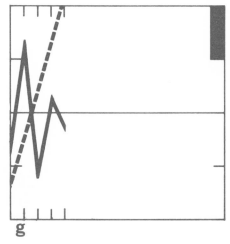

g

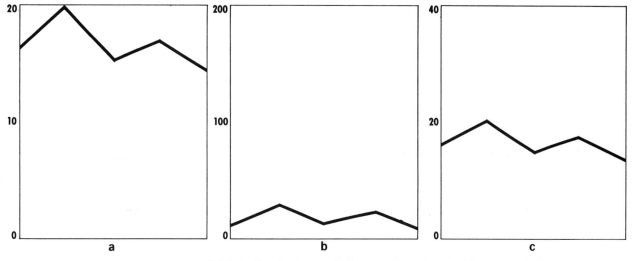

5-3 Selecting Proper Scale Range (a) Too Small (b) Too Large (c) Preferable Range

The amount range should be uniform for a set of charts. Charts are often made in "sets." For example, three separate charts showing last year's levels of inventory, this year's levels of inventory, and next year's forecasted levels of inventory are considered a "set" because they all deal with the same inventory. The amount ranges on all three charts should be uniform to allow valid comparisons to be made.

STATISTICAL "FREAK" VALUE Occasionally, because real life has tendencies to provide the exception to the rule, data contain a freak value, as in May of the following table:

January	10
February	5
March	23
April	19
May	58
June	20

The same data we dealt with previously now have a highpoint of 58 instead of 29. How is this handled?

One method is to increase the amount range (Fig. 5-4). This treatment results in a flattening of the curve and sacrifices profile definition for the sake of accommodating an oddball value.

The common practice is to treat a unique variation — a one-time peak — as an *exception* and run it off the chart, identifying its value as shown in Figure 5-5.

RATE-OF-CHANGE COMPARISON Amount scales should start at zero. There should be only one exception to this rule. This exception occurs when there is a need for showing rates of change rather than levels of amounts. Both the rate of change and the amount level are drawn from the same data; what differs is the point of emphasis.

For example, take as basic data these production figures:

Time	Amount
January	100
February	110
March	95
April	115
May	105
June	100

There are two ways to analyze this data for comparison purposes. First, in terms of amount levels, the scale begins at zero and includes every piece in order to show the levels of production (Fig. 5-6).

But often, our concern is not so much the amount of units produced as the rate of change. And this is, of course, the second way to analyze the data.

A rate-of-change analysis involves an examination of the *movement* of production levels. For example, as compared to January, the February level increased by 10 units; in March it fell 5 units; in April it rose 15 units; and so on until it reached the same level in June as it had in

81

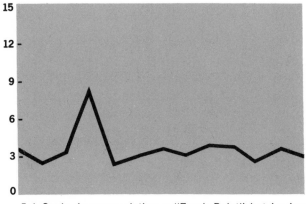

5-4 Scale Accommodating a "Freak Point" but Losing Line Definition

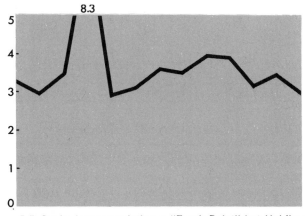

5-5 Scale Accommodating a "Freak Point" but Holding Line Definition

January. In this case the change and rate of change are significant, and therefore emphasized (Fig. 5-7).

In this last comparison, the principal reference point of zero is not needed, and the scale begins at an amount common to all items in the study. For this production example, such an amount is 90.

The rate-of-change comparison is also suitable to situations in which the magnitude of the data is so great, and changes in this magnitude so relatively small, that any fluctuation of levels would not be perceptible if the amount scale were to begin at zero, and cover the entire range.

Take, as an illustration, an assignment to depict the levels of population in the United States, adjusted monthly by births and deaths. Obviously, a population of almost 200 million would create a scale against which a 1 or 2 per cent net change would be an insignificant visual ripple in a configuration of this magnitude.

To meet the problem we would depict the changes in population (i.e. the rate of population change) rather than the total population at any given time.

A dangerous generalization (nevertheless one worth indulging in) is that when the question posed asks, "how much," in one form or another, the amount scale must begin with zero, and the

82

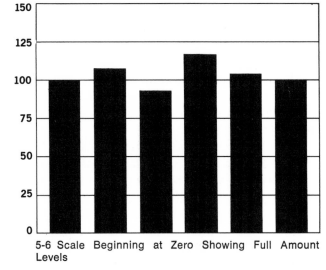

5-6 Scale Beginning at Zero Showing Full Amount Levels

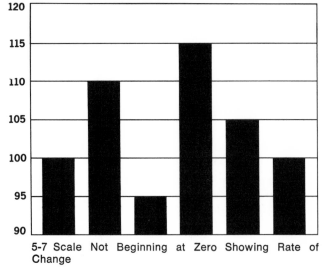

5-7 Scale Not Beginning at Zero Showing Rate of Change

range must show the entire magnitude. But when the question posed asks about "the difference" in amounts, only that portion of range focusing on the changes needs to be shown, and the zero can be omitted.

BREAKS IN AMOUNT SCALE   There are situations in which an amount scale cannot remain intact and still graphically serve the communicator's purpose. Scales involving large magnitudes and studies concerning comparisons of growth account for most of these situations.

When a scale cannot accommodate an entire amount, it must be *broken*. Any disruption of a scale's numeric continuity represents a break in the scale. Except for rate-of-change comparisons, the amount scale should not be broken. This is especially true for Column, Surface, and Bar charts.

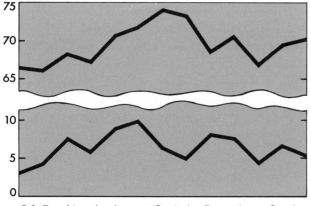

5-8 Breaking the Amount Scale by Removing a Section

A break in the amount scale is usually accomplished by removing a section of the scale (Fig. 5-8). The removal is often used to bring amount levels into greater proximity, for closer comparisons. While this is a valuable analytical technique, the designer must be aware that by using this technique he creates the impression of a greater degree of variation in the data than actually exists.

Another method of breaking a scale is omitting "zero"—the chart's principal point of reference. As a rule, when the chart is comparing levels of amount the zero must be used as a base. But when the chart is comparing the rate of change in amounts the zero can be omitted.

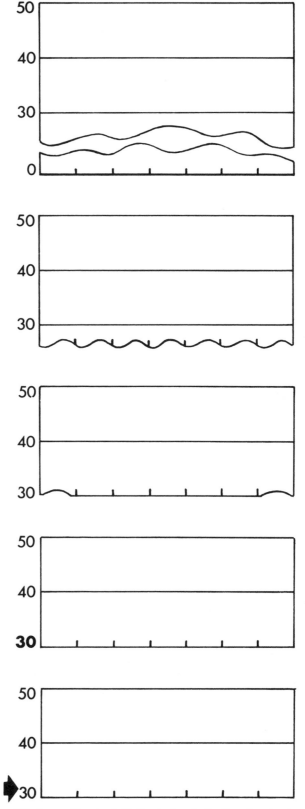

5-9 Some Standard Methods for Indicating Breaks in Amount Scales

83

Regardless of the method used to break the amount scale, the important point is that the reader must be apprised of a break. It is not uncommon to find charts omitting zero without explanation; the omission of this pertinent information often does the reader a great disservice.

Figure 5-9 shows various standard methods of indicating the omission of part of the amount scale. Any one of these methods can do the job, but experience will undoubtedly lead you to discover that different methods fit different circumstances. You may even wish to innovate your own method to fit a particular problem. In any case, the omission must be properly identified.

MULTIPLE AMOUNT SCALES   When the information required on a single chart demands amount ranges that are incompatible, the solution may very well be the use of two separate amount scales. Charts employing more than one scale are called Multiple Amount, or Double Scales, and are not uncommon (Fig. 5-10).

Normally, the need for multiple scales stems from one of two conditions: (1) the presence of a large disparity in the items being compared or (2) an incongruity in their descriptions. As an example of disparate magnitudes, consider comparison of the speed of a rocket to the speed of a jet. An example of a description incongruity is a comparison of tons shipped to export dollars.

In the construction of a chart with multiple scales, the spacing and positioning of amount intervals on both scales are important. The interval spacing on both must be the same, even though the interval values may differ, and the position of the intervals on both scales must coincide.

The value of "zero" need not appear on the chart. However, when amount levels are being compared both scales must use zero as a theoretical starting point (Fig. 5-11). Rate-of-change charts can ignore zero as a starting point, actually and theoretically. However, since rate-of-change comparisons are intended to portray relative growth, the increment values of the two scales should be arranged so that somewhere on the chart the two curves meet at a common juncture that serves as the principal point of reference (Fig. 5-12).

84

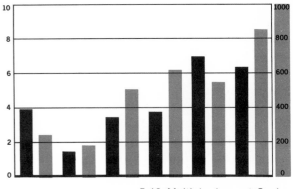

5-10 Multiple Amount Scales

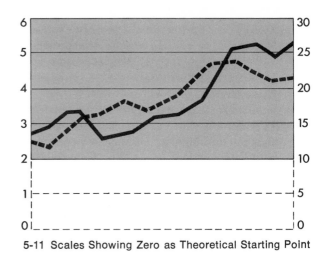

5-11 Scales Showing Zero as Theoretical Starting Point

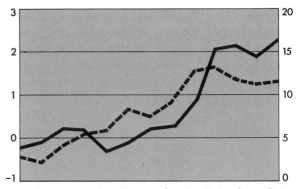

5-12 Scales Ignoring Zero as Starting Point Show Relative Amounts of Change

There is one important caveat concerning the use of two scales. Which curve belongs to which scale is often difficult to determine, especially when printed in a single color. Consequently they should be carefully labeled and their use restricted to audiences that are accustomed to them. When sufficient audience knowledgeability is lacking, care should be taken to accompany the chart with an explanation of the purpose and use of the two scales.

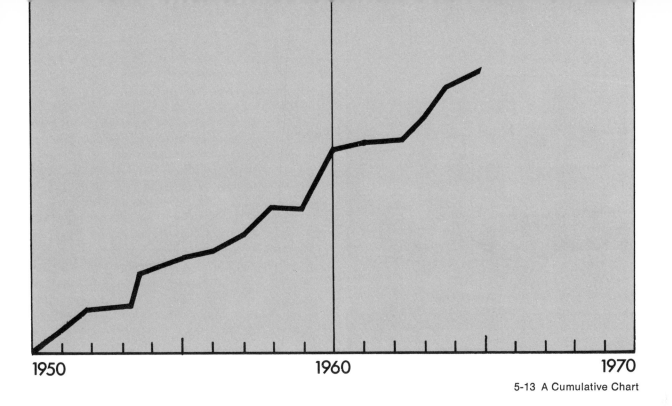

1950   1960   1970

5-13 A Cumulative Chart

Time Scales

Time Series charts have, in addition to an amount scale, a time scale that is usually placed along the base line of a grid. This scale can, however, be placed at the top of the grid if the designer has a "legitimate" reason for doing so. Just what constitutes legitimacy is difficult to say. Like all such questions in graphics concerning a "right way" or a "wrong way" there are no pat answers to justify use of innovation. There are only guidelines arrived at by testing certain criteria. For example:

Does the innovation impede communication or cause confusion?

Would the generally accepted standard method serve just as well?

Does the innovation look right visually?

These guidelines are meant for "soul searching," and not to inhibit or discourage being "different." Being different for difference's sake is a thin rationale for burdening the graphic language with useless material.

TIME RANGE SELECTION The selection of a range for the time scale is comparatively easier than choosing an amount range because the span of time is prescribed by the data—it is definite and inelastic. For example, charting employee absenteeism records for a six-month period automatically dictates that the time range must be six months — certainly no less, and usually no more. However, under certain conditions, as for example in a Cumulative chart (Fig. 5-13), the time range can be extended beyond the bounds of the current data to provide for data yet to come. In Cumulative charts the last amount of the data is added to the *accumulated total* of prior amounts on a continuing basis. Accordingly, the chart is constructed to allow space for anticipated posting sometime in the future.

Once the time range is determined, intervals must be selected. Interval selection is a bit more involved because the increments of time are reducible to smaller increments, i.e. years can be reduced to months, and months to weeks, and weeks to days.

The choice of intervals should be guided by two practical considerations. The first concerns the desired extent of *completeness* to be conveyed, and the second involves the constraint of available *space*. The absenteeism-record example can be used to illustrate the implementation of these considerations. Since the absenteeism occurs daily, the most complete record possible would be one showing daily occurrences. Accordingly, the smallest unit of measure would be one day.

If the consideration of completeness were to dictate the selection of interval, a chart with about 180 plottings would be required to show the day-by-day rate of six months' absenteeism. Such a chart would appear crowded because the designer was forced to condense the space between intervals to accommodate the plottings.

85

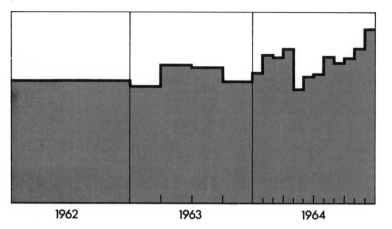

5-14 Provisions Left for Increment Spacing

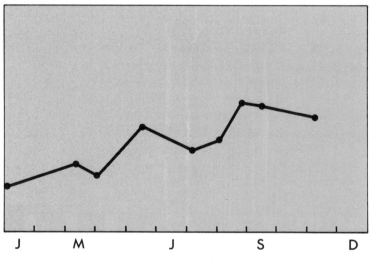

5-15 Space Left for Uniform Plottings

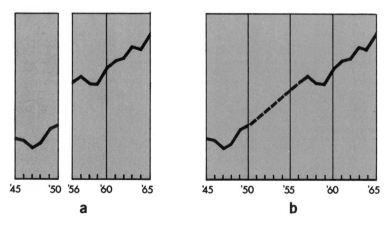

5-16 (a) Omissions of Time Shown Improperly (b) Omissions of Time Shown Properly

If the consideration of space were to dictate the selection of interval, the completeness of daily plottings would somehow have to be compromised. The extent of compromise must be determined by the communicator to meet the objectives of his study.

For instance, is the objective to show absenteeism in detail (e.g. attendance on Fridays is poor)? Or, is the objective broader, merely to show that the movement of the data goes up, or down, or stays pretty much the same (e.g. the excessive absenteeism in the month of April must have resulted from spring fever)?

Certainly, the broader the interval chosen, the more general the graphic picture becomes. Choosing an interval of a month would, of course, provide a picture with only six plottings. This may be too broad. If the record were accumulated on a weekly basis it would produce twenty-six plottings. This may still be too many plottings. Perhaps a bimonthly increment would be the better solution.

In essence, the interval is often best selected by trial and error — i.e. rough the chart; look at it; shake your head; throw it aside; re-evaluate your considerations, and start anew.*

Intervals using *like* time increments should be equally spaced on the time scale. This rule is simple enough to follow when only one kind of increment is used. To illustrate: suppose the increment chosen were "months"; then for a six-month series the time scale would be divided into six equal intervals. But suppose more than one kind of increment needs to be shown — say, "years," "quarters," and "months." The activity of months and quarters cannot be compared to the activity of an entire year — one is an apple, one is a pear, and the other is an orange, so to speak. In this case, the space interval for each year should be equal to four times the space allotted for each quarter and twelve times the space for each month (Fig. 5-14). In this manner the smallest time value becomes the common

* The problem of completeness does not always require an "either-or" solution. A complete and detailed presentation can be made without compromise if more than one chart is used to depict the absenteeism records. Detailed charts may show a single week by days, and summary charts may show months or groups of months.

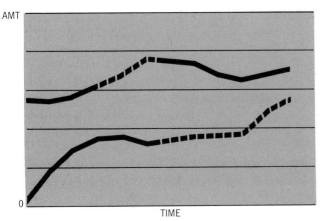

5-17 Two Methods To Show Omissions of Time

unit denominator and is used as the basis for proportionately allocating space to larger time units.

As shown in Figure 5-15, space must be allotted uniformly even though there are no plottings to represent particular points in the time series under study. Time is continuous — it marches on — and must be accounted for on the time scale despite the fact that no quantitative happening has occurred.

BREAKS IN TIME SCALE It is unequivocally wrong to indicate breaks in time by removing an interior section of the time scale (Fig. 5-16a). This is one of the very few hard and fast charting rules. The removal of part of the time scale violates the continuity-of-time principle. You can no more omit a period of activity that has occurred in a time series than you can omit a period of human history (although some periods can wishfully be forgotten).

Activity that is recorded on an amount scale is variable — it can go up, down, not move, or even quantitatively not occur. Yet no matter how the levels of amount change, time is always the constant frame of reference, if comparisons are to be made.

When actual amount data are missing from a period of time, this is treated in the same manner as amount data that are forecast or estimated — i.e. by a dotted-line extension to a solid line (Fig. 5-16b). It should be noted, however, that when a dotted line is not an extension of a solid line, but stands alone as a means of labeling to differentiate one curve from another, the dotted line does *not* represent non-actual data, and should not be confused with this concept.

The concept of a dotted line (as an extension of a solid line) is becoming part of the graphic language. Its frequent and consistent use will enable readers eventually to recognize that it indicates the presence of non-actual data. Whether the dotted line extends a solid line or joins two solid lines together does not make a difference (Fig. 5-17). Conceptually, these two methods mean the same, just as to a musician the notation of Middle C is always the same note, no matter on which clef it appears.*

REPEATED TIME SERIES It is not unusual to find data that are cycled over similar time increments in a series. To explain: suppose the data covered monthly salary costs for a three-year period. The data for each of the years are different, yet the time increment of a year is common, and is repeated three times.

Of course, it would be possible to construct a chart with thirty-six monthly intervals. Such a chart would serve to show the continuous

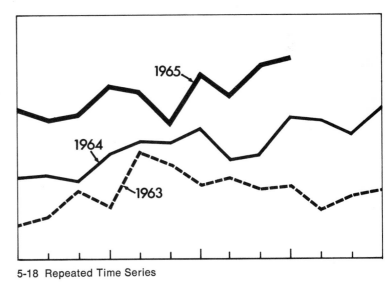

5-18 Repeated Time Series

---

* Unfortunately, most chart viewers do not have the benefit of reading books (like this one) that tell them that a solid line extended or joined by a dotted-line means non-actual data representation. However, good practice dictates that when the dotted line method is used, it is appropriately labeled, so that the method will eventually be recognized as common practice and be universally understood.

monthly fluctuations of salary costs, and would be very large or very crowded.

It is also possible to show the same fluctuations by constructing a smaller, or less cluttered, chart with twelve uniform monthly intervals to present the same span of time. This chart, called a Repeated Time Series (Fig. 5-18), is actually a Multiple Line chart that stacks three separate curves, each of which represents one year. This interpretation adds the advantage of allowing a comparison of comparable points in time; for example, the levels of salary for the month of March in each of the three years.

The Repeated Time Series technique is very effective for comparative analyses of comparable series of time periods, and is used extensively in management reporting.

PARALLEL TIME SEQUENCES   While the Repeated Time Series can be used for evaluating continuous data, Parallel Time Sequences (Fig. 5-19) are used when data are not continuous, but represent different historical periods in which parallel or similar events occurred.

Although we can readily concede that no two historical periods are exactly the same, we should likewise concede that some periods do have basic characteristic similarities. Examples of periods of time having characteristic similarities include periods of war, recession, boom economy, and tight-money markets.

Suppose, for example, we wanted to compare initial consumer response of Product B to Product A, which was introduced into the same test market five years ago. Both products can be

5-19 Parallel Time Sequences

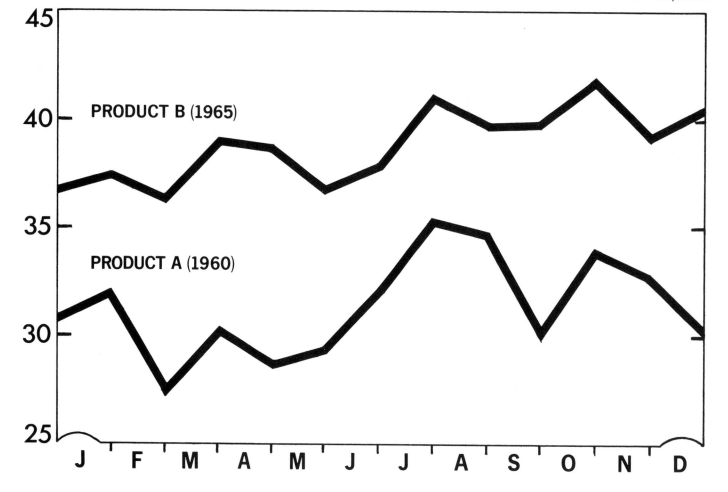

PRODUCT B (1965)

PRODUCT A (1960)

considered similar in being (a) directed to the same consumer group; (b) priced approximately the same; (c) packaged somewhat the same, and merchandised in an identical manner.

Of course, to consider the circumstances surrounding these products absolutely identical is unrealistic because time continually alters our environment, economy, and attitudes so that things can never be the same. Nevertheless, for some comparative purposes, approximations of this kind serve an informative and useful end.

A Parallel Time Sequence that employs the concept that different periods of time can be analogous presents non-continuous data in the same manner in which the Repeated Time Period chart presents continuous data.

The Parallel Time Sequence is at once a useful and tricky device. Its value to the communicator lies in his ability to match parallel sequences of time. His definition of where the corresponding periods begin and end shapes the relationships to be established and compared.

That there is a growing use for the type of representation provided by the Parallel Time Sequence concept is unmistakable. Take the marketing function as one example. The practice of forecasting has been built on the projection of historical data for similar (and continuous) periods of time. For instance, the activity forecasted for next January was projected on the basis of what happened last January. The selection of a calendar-year cycle was arbitrary, and January was compared to January without consideration of any other factors.

Following World War II, forecasters began employing "moving averages" techniques and matching corresponding seasonal patterns of activity behavior. Although this refinement compensated for many of the "oversights" made by the cruder period selecting methods, it still relied primarily on the "matching-of-the-months" technique.

But with the advent of the computer the selection of Parallel Time Sequences has been facilitated. Also, new scientific management approaches have replaced conventional techniques by introducing concepts that are not predicated on the fiscal year, or calendar year, or seasonal cycles but rather on more precise parallel periods. By utilizing the prodigiousness of the computer, the management scientist is able to translate eco-nomic, social, political, and business factors and forces — the raw material from which the predicated behavior of future activity is extrapolated — into probability hypotheses. The output of these programs is in both non-continuous and continuous periods of time, and the techniques of Parallel Time Sequence and Repeated Time Series can be effectively applied in charting the data for analysis of the output.

Ratio Scales

Ratio scales are used on Semilogarithmic charts and are increasingly becoming accepted in the presentation of studies and analyses to "ordinary" people. The Semilogarithmic chart, which has its vertical axis ruled logarithmically, and its horizontal axis arithmetically, has long been regarded with suspicion as being too "technical." Indeed, if a ratio scale is read as a linear scale it can be confusing, and in some cases misleading. Yet, although it may appear as a highly technical and complex bit of mechanics, the Semilogarithmic chart is not an especially difficult chart to use. Neither proficiency in mathematics nor an understanding of logarithms is necessary. Anyone who can make a chart using arithmetic scales can make a chart using ratio scales, provided he has a basic understanding of the difference between the two representations.

So, although Semilogarithmic charts using ratio scales seem quite formidable, they actually are not. First of all, ratio scales are used to show relative rates of change; that is to say, they show proportional or percentage relationships. Accordingly, magnitudes of values are compared by their ratios and not by their differences (as is the case with arithmetic scales). In an arithmetic chart, the same *numerical* difference is always represented by the same interval distance on the amount scale, whereas on the ratio scale the same *percentage* difference is always represented by the same interval distance on the amount scale.

Figure 5-20 illustrates this point. Notice that the interval between 1 and 2 on the arithmetic scale is the same as between 5 and 6, but on the ratio scale it is not. In fact, all the increment intervals on the arithmetic scale are the same distance apart. When a series is increased by constant increments it is termed an "arithmetic progression." The ratio scale is different in that it uses a

89

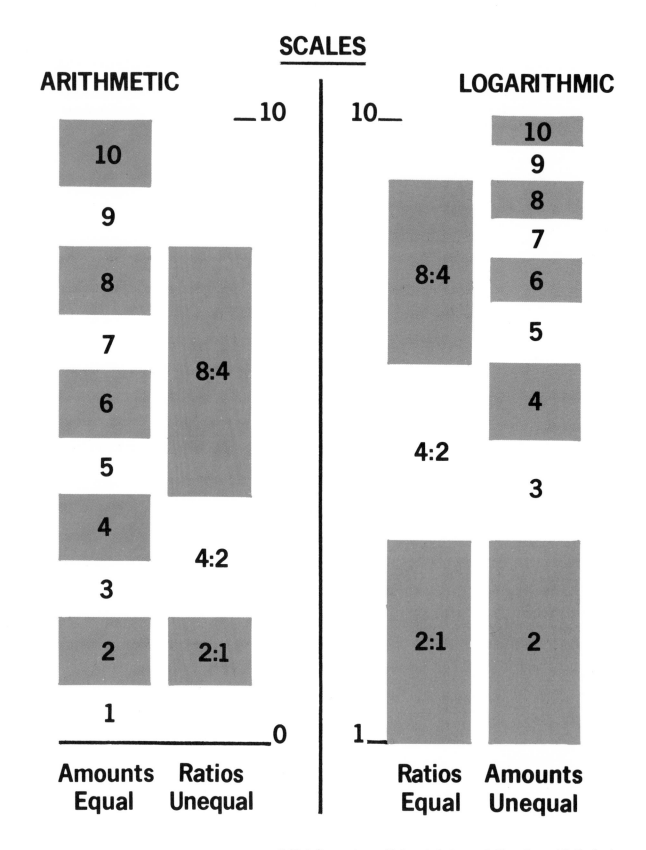

5-20 A Comparison of Intervals between Arithmetic and Ratio Scales

"geometric progression," which is a little harder to define. A geometric progression is increased by the application of a constant multiplier. For example, take the multiplier "2" and observe that the interval of *1 to 2* on the ratio scale is the same as *2 to 4* (2 x 2). Also, the distance between 4 and *8* (2 x 4) is the same as between 2 and 4. Likewise, the intervals between 8 and 16, 16 and 32, 32 and 64, etc. will also be the same distance apart because the increase is always double, or 100 per cent of the prior amount. If the multiplier is "3," the interval distance between values bearing a ratio to the multiplier "3" would also be the same (e.g. 3:9, 9:27, 27:81, etc.).

The application of these concepts to a constant increase or decrease on an arithmetic scale, in opposition to a ratio scale, is demonstrated by the example in Figure 5-21. On the arithmetic scale, the increase of 50 is always represented by the same interval distance. For example, an increase from 50 to 100 is represented by the same vertical distance as an increase from 500 to 550, or 5000 to 5050. Similarly, a decrease from 200 to 150, or from 600 to 550, or 10,050 to 10,000 will always be represented by the same distance on the arithmetic scale. The magnitudes of the base numbers have no bearing — 50 units are 50 units. However, on the ratio scale the magnitude of the base number makes a great deal of difference because ratio scales deal in percentages. Observe: an increase of 50 units when going from 50 to 100 is a percentage increase of 100%. But from 500 to 550, it is only 10% (10% of 500 is 50), and from 5,000 to 5,050 it is a mere 1%. The same is true for decreases considered in percentages. A decrease from 200 to 150 is 25% (50 is ¼ or 25% of 200); from 600 to 550 it is 8.3%; and from 10,050 to 10,000 it is 0.5 (½) of one per cent.

Thus, the arithmetic scale emphasizes absolute

an increase of 50 units...	percentage of increase...
50 to 100	= 100%
500 to 550	= 10%
5,000 to 5,050	= 1%

a decrease of 50 units...	percentage of decrease...
200 to 150	= 25 %
600 to 550	= 8.3%
10,050 to 10,000	= 0.5%

5-21 A Comparison of Absolute and Percentage Increases and Decreases of a Constant Increment

91

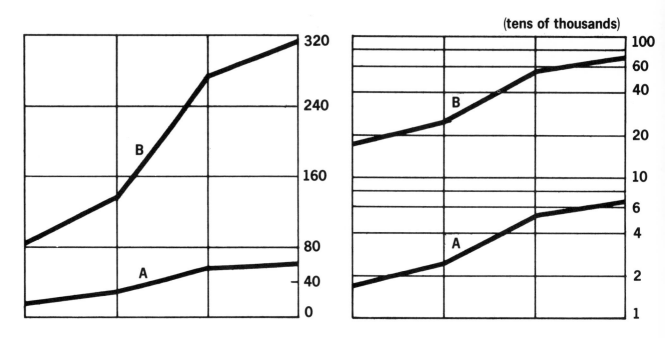

(tens of thousands)

5-22 A Comparison of Identical Data Shown on Arithmetic and Ratio Scales

changes while the ratio scale emphasizes rates of change. Plotting absolute numbers on a Semilogarithmic chart creates a totally different "interpretation" of the data than it does on an arithmetic chart.

For instance, supposing the performance of this year's growth for two sales offices were to be analyzed. Last year Office A had sales of $50,000, while Office B did $250,000 worth of sales. This year's accumulative quarterly results were:

	Office A Cumulative		Office B Cumulative	
1st Quarter	$17,500	35%	$ 87,500	35%
2nd Quarter	27,500	55	137,500	55
3rd Quarter	55,000	110	275,000	110
4th Quarter	62,500	125	312,500	125

A cursory examination of the sales figures (without percentages) only reveals that both offices increased sales, B by some $62,500. It could be said that Office B's increase is five times that of A's, which, in fact, it is. But as a measure of growth this observation is not true. By looking at the percentages of growth during the year, we see that both offices grew uniformly *with respect to their bases*. Figure 5-22 represents these data in graphic form. The absolute numbers plotted on the arithmetic scale give the impres-

sion that B's performance was much better than A's. However, when the absolute numbers are plotted on the ratio scale (which translates them into percentage ratios), the true measure of growth becomes apparent, and the chart indicates a uniform rate of growth for both offices.

Either chart validly depicts the performance of the offices; what differs is the point of view. It is up to the communicator to select the scale to fit the message he is attempting to convey. Moreover, he must inform the reader what the charting is depicting, and how it is to be interpreted so as to avoid misinterpretations and distorted meanings.

For practical purposes, a Semilogarithmic chart gives a "picture" of the relationship between two curves. Measuring (i.e. reading off) exact percentage changes takes some practice, and, more often than not, readers cannot be expected to interpolate a ratio scale as they would an arithmetic scale. Most statistic textbooks devote a good deal of space to the intricacies of constructing and interpreting Semilogarithmic charts. While a little knowledge may be a dangerous thing, it is nevertheless germane to this brief review to offer some generalizations on the interpretation of ratio curves. Figure 5-23 illustrates the various types of configurations that appear on a Semilogarithmic chart. Notice that seven general patterns appear;

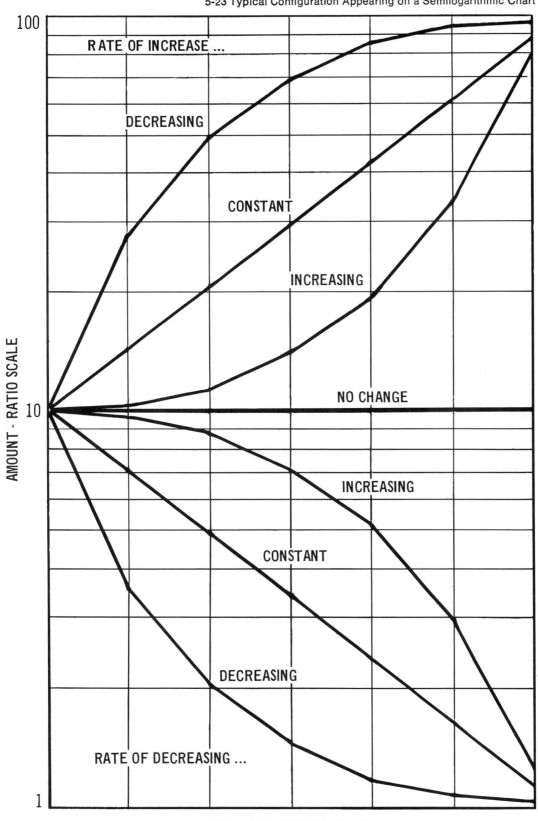

5-23 Typical Configuration Appearing on a Semilogarithmic Chart

each one manifests the characteristic of the data being plotted as follows:

When the ascending configuration is convex (as in the top curve) the magnitudes of the data are increasing at a decreasing rate. In other words, as the total magnitude increases the increments grow smaller (e.g. 1, 11, 20, 28, 35 . . .)

When the configuration ascends in a diagonal manner, the magnitudes are increasing by a constant rate (percentage).

When the configuration descends in a concave

fashion, the magnitudes of the data are increasing at an increasing rate — for example, production rates that double and treble with the learning curve.

When the curve is horizontal with no movement, up or down, the magnitudes of the data are uniform.

When the configuration of the curve descends convexly, the magnitudes are decreasing at an increasing rate.

When the configuration descends diagonally in

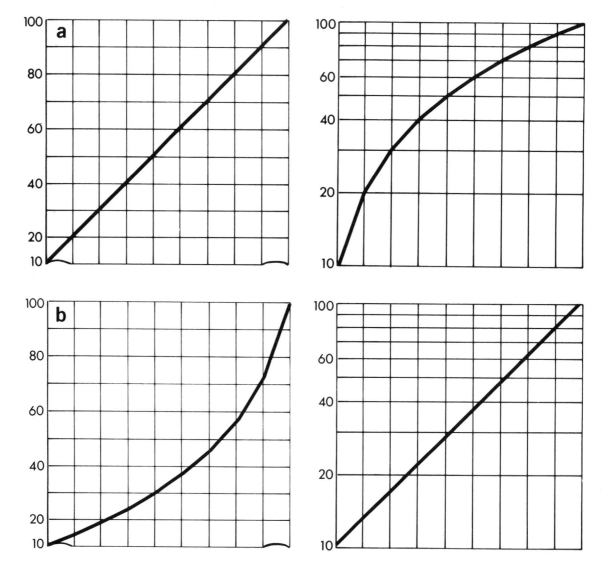

5-24 (a) A Constant Increase of Absolute Numbers Shown on Arithmetic and Ratio Scales (b) A Constant Increase of Percentage Shown on the Same Scales

94

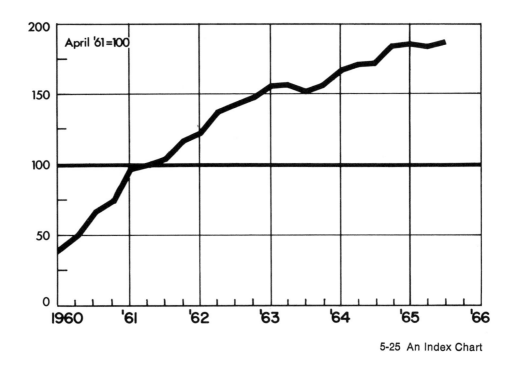

5-25 An Index Chart

an almost straight line, the magnitudes are decreasing at a constant rate. For example, suppose the constant rate of decrease were 30% and we started with a magnitude of 100. The first plotting would be 100, the second 70 (100 minus 30%), the third 49 (70 minus 30% of 70), and so on.

When the configuration of the magnitudes is concave, and is descending, the data are decreasing at a decreasing rate.

These guidelines can be used generally to "read" a Semilogarithmic chart. What must be borne in mind is that the same data on an arithmetic chart would not look the same. For example, Figure 5-24 shows a base of 10 units increased by a constant 10-unit amount on both an arithmetic scale and a ratio scale. The chart also shows a base of 10 units increased by a constant rate of 30% on both types of scales. Observe that what is an arc on the ratio scale is a straight line on the arithmetic scale and vice versa.

Many readers are completely unfamiliar with ratio charts. Some dislike these charts because they cannot manage them. For these or other reasons the communicator may want to avoid using them. In such cases he has other recourses. An alternative to the Semilogarithmic chart is the Multiple Amount chart (page 84), which uses double scales. A two-scale chart can perform virtually the same function as a ratio chart because it depicts, and emphasizes, the relationship between two or more configurations.

Another alternative is to convert the data into percentages and plot the percentage ratios instead of the absolute numbers; a method employing this technique is the Index chart.

INDEX CHART   The Index chart (Fig. 5-25) is a device familiar to most of us. Perhaps it is not readily recognized, but when your friendly newscaster tells you that the cost of living has risen 3.4%, he is, of course, referring to an Index chart kept by the Federal government.

To construct an Index chart, an arbitrary figure is represented as 100%. For example, the government agencies may decide that the cost of living in 1960 is now to be considered a "base." This base becomes 100 (per cent). If today the costs exceed that base by 3% the entry on the chart is 103, or if they go below the base by 3% (it should only happen), the entry is 97. In this manner, any data can be converted to percentages of a base figure that has been established as 100%.

The Index chart is a handy device that presents little difficulty in understanding. It is simple to calculate and easy to construct. It does not, of course, record actual amounts. Only the deviations from an arbitrary norm are shown. Other than this qualification it is a practical solution to the communicator who wishes to avoid using the Semilogarithmic chart with ratio scales.

95

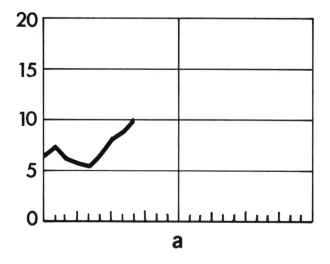

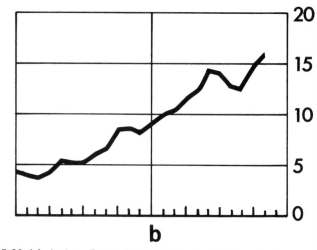

5-26 (a) Action Occurring on the Left Side of the Chart (b) Action Occurring on the Right Side of the Chart

Labels

Labels provide identification of some chart elements, thereby explaining to the viewer much of the information necessary for an understanding of the comparisons being made. One cannot be too fussy about good labeling. Labeling produces positive and negative effects that are not always consciously attributed to it. For example, when a chart is poorly labeled, the viewer does not bother to say, "Gee, that chart is poorly labeled."

He knows, however, that he is working a little harder to grasp the information. He may be annoyed because he cannot distinguish elements easily. And, he may end up forsaking the entire message because he cannot be bothered with unraveling the confusion. In short, a viewer will accept or reject a chart for reasons he is required neither to understand nor care about. The burden of communicating lies with the communicator.

AMOUNT SCALE LOCATION An aspect of labeling is the location of scales. The location of the amount scale is easy to determine, because there is a rationale for placing it either at the left or right of the grid.*

96

---

* In order to assist the reader, it is possible to put the amount scale on both the left and right of the grid, but it must be remembered that Multiple Scales utilize both sides and thus confusion may initially arise until the viewer realizes that the scales are identical.

Normally, since we read from left to right, the amount scale is placed on the left. Moreover, engineering drawings, as well as other scientific charts and graphs, uniformly label their scales on the left. However, for charting purposes we need not be so rigorous.

Design circumstances, for instance, may suggest that the scale location be at the right of the grid; this is a bona fide reason for putting it there. Except for design considerations, the location of the scales can follow this simple rule of thumb: *locate scales as close as possible to where the action is on the chart.*

If the action is occurring on the left side of the chart as in Figure 5-26a, then place the scale on the left. If, as Figure 5-26b shows, the emphasis of the data is occurring at the right side, then put the scale at the right. This rule is especially pertinent when the reader is expected to interpolate the data on the chart.

Scale designations (i.e. numerals) on amount scales should be placed as close to the grid as possible. Provided there are not too many rulings, at least every major horizontal and vertical grid line should be identified with a label. Interval indicators, like tick marks used in lieu of rulings, are generally not labeled.

The positions of numerals on the amount scale should be juxtaposed to their respective grid rulings in a manner that leaves no doubt as to what the numerals identify. The bottom and top numerals are exceptions. The bottom numeral should

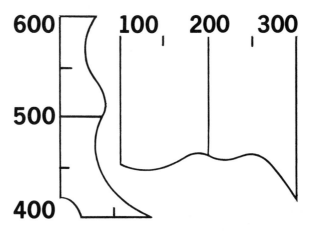

5-27 Position of Numerals on Amount and Time Scales

sit on the base line, and the top numeral should butt its top against the top ruling (Fig. 5-27).*

The number of digits in the amount label should be limited to four. Numbers of greater magnitude can be handled in other ways by captions (see page 101).

The digits located at the left of the chart should be flush to the right, and conversely, digits located at the right should be flush to the left.

As to the type face and point size of the numerals it would be presumptuous to make concrete suggestions because of the infinite variations that are possible. It is wrong, moreover, to design by formula, since each graphic problem has its individual design solution. However, the following generalization may serve some purpose: labels describing scales are secondary information needed to set the scene so that the chart's message can be highlighted; accordingly, labels should be relegated to the background so as not to compete for viewer attention with the chart's main emphasis.

TIME SCALE LOCATION   The time scale offers less leeway in its location. Except for design considerations there is very little reason to place it other than at the bottom of the grid. Moreover, placement at the grid's bottom visually augments the base line — a very good reason for putting it there.

Here again, although design is not shackled to convention, one should nonetheless carefully consider what is visually sound, and familiar to viewers.

Labels on time scales are generally not difficult to cope with. Their designations and divisions are familiar to most people, and so are their abbreviations. Accordingly, it is even possible to omit some labels without causing confusion. For example, if a time scale representing a year had twelve divisions, and every other division is labeled — Jan, Mar, May, Jul, Sep, Nov — it is clear that the omissions were Feb, April, Jun, Aug, Oct, Dec. Abbreviations, like M, T, W, T, F for the

days in a work week, or '59, '60, '61 as the years 1959, 1960, and 1961, are familiar symbols and present no barrier to understanding.

Time-scale labels should straddle the vertical grid rulings they identify, except those labels beginning and ending the series, which should be positioned flush left and right respectively (Fig. 5-27).

In cases where explanatory, qualifying, or supplementary information concerning time-scale labels is needed, it can be handled by a footnote symbol (Fig. 5-28).

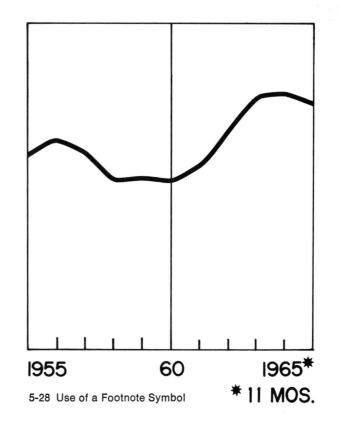

5-28 Use of a Footnote Symbol

* 11 MOS.

---

* Comments on where and how graphic elements should be placed are not meant to "art-direct" the design of a chart. These suggestions merely represent what are considered the standard methods as recommended by the American Society of Mechanical Engineers.

97

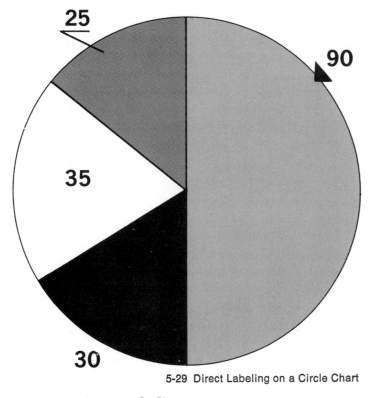

5-29 Direct Labeling on a Circle Chart

Direct Labeling

Direct labeling is a technique that can be effectively used in practically all kinds of charts to identify amount, time, and subject matter.

CIRCLE CHART   Circle charts use direct labeling exclusively. Each segment of the circle is identified as *what* and *how much* it represents. The label can appear on the segment itself or adjacent to the segment (Fig. 5-29).

BAR CHART   The Bar chart often uses direct labeling as a support to facilitate interpolation. For example, in addition to the amount scale the value of each bar is added as a label either on the bar itself or immediately following the bar's end. Sometimes the label identification of the bar is also handled this way.

A word of caution, however, is offered. The placement of a label outside the bar tends to extend visually the length of the bar, and may disrupt the profile of the bars, causing some visual difficulties in making comparisons (Fig. 5-30).

Sometimes the subject description of the bar is of a nature that is inconvenient for placement outside the grid. Or, the chart may be designed so that no area outside the grid is allotted. In each of these instances, the bar can be labeled directly, as shown in Figure 5-31.

The apparent drawback of the direct labeling used in this manner is that the visual line created by the lettering or type is sometimes visually mistaken for the actual bar. In other words, the viewer is apt to substitute the label for the bar and compare the length of letters rather than the length of bar. This point is not farfetched if you stop to consider that the viewer is primarily drawn to the words because words mean something to him.*

The abstract shape of the bar is basically meaningless, and can be comprehended only after an intellectual effort. In such situations, the letters and abstraction fight each other for attention, and the viewer is asked to serve as referee! Cynicism notwithstanding, the directness and simplicity of communicating a simple comparison may be lost, and its interpretation becomes a mental challenge when no challenge is necessary. (Moreover, the viewer may not meet the challenge.)

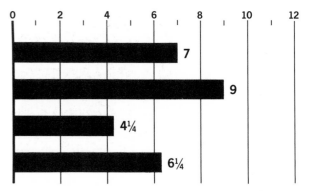

5-30 Direct Labeling as an Extension of the Bar Chart

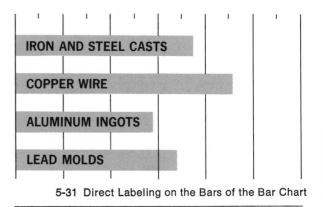

5-31 Direct Labeling on the Bars of the Bar Chart

* A famous Rapid Reading School advocates that students practice speed drills in books printed in foreign languages, so as not to be hampered by familiar words while developing scanning techniques.

Also, one large New York printer prepares the text for layout mock-ups in Latin to discourage the viewer from reading, so that he may concentrate only on the graphic appearance of the dummy.

COLUMN CHART The Column chart can also be directly labeled. Generally, column values are placed at the top of the columns to assist the viewer's interpolation. As in Bar charts the use of this technique is intended to facilitate "reading." However, direct labeling used to indicate amount values in this manner often leads to the misinterpretation of column length, and has the same drawback as described above for the Bar chart.

Direct labeling of subject matter on Column charts can be done on the columns themselves, or by visually associating labels to columns by means of arrows, lines, and other connnective devices (Fig. 5-32). When labeling directly onto columns, care should be taken not to bisect the column completely (Fig. 5-33a), which produces a visual and unnecessary break. Figure 5-33b shows how to meet the objectives of labeling and visual continuity.

SURFACE CHART Surface charts offer little choice to the designer for direct labeling. The label should be placed within the surface or as close to the surface as possible, with a connective device that clearly identifies the stratum it is describing. Because Surface charts must use colors or shadings to differentiate their strata, labeling, applied directly, should be done in a manner that makes it easily visible within the surface area. Two ways to accomplish this are to set the label in bold type and to spare-out the area immediately surrounding the label so that it sits on a field of white (Fig. 5-34).

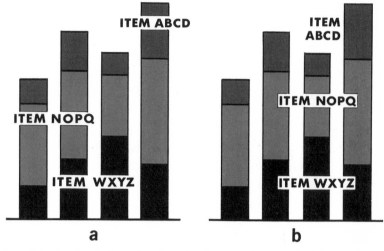

5-33 (a) Direct Labeling Bisecting the Columns Improperly (b) Bisecting the Columns Properly

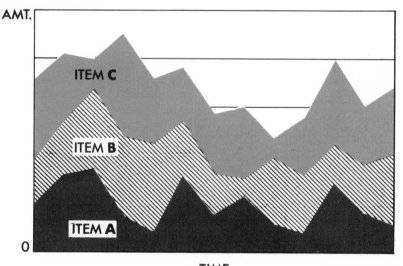

5-34 Direct Labeling of a Surface Chart

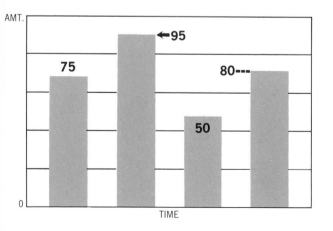

5-32 Direct Labeling on a Column Chart

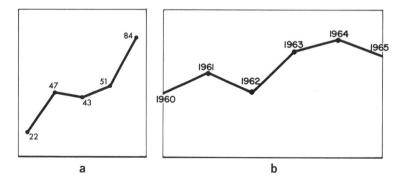

5-35 (a) Direct Labeling of an Amount Scale on a Line Chart (b) Direct Labeling of a Time Scale on a Line Chart

LINE CHART The Line chart offers many possibilities for direct labeling. For example, the amount scale can be omitted and the plotted points directly labeled, as shown in Figure 5-35a. In the same manner, the time scale can be omitted, as shown in Figure 5-35b. In both cases the number of plotted points should be limited, since too many readings will clutter the chart and defeat its purpose.

Techniques used to identify curves with labels should be kept simple. Some guidelines for clarity and simplicity follow:

Obvious labeling should be avoided.

Connecting arrows or lines should be employed sparingly.

There should be no doubt as to which curve the label is identifying.

The visual impact of the label should be secondary to that of the curve it is describing or identifying.

Random placement of labels should be avoided. The placement of labels should be *where the action is!*

Figure 5-36 makes these points illustratively. Notice that the labels are obscure. In addition, their placement leaves the identification of the curves uncertain. And more important, the positioning of the labels ignores the dramatic right side of the grid — where the action is. Figure 5-37 corrects these deficiencies.

Keys

A common form of labeling is the key, or legend. The key is a convenient technique sometimes used in lieu of direct labeling to describe or identify chart elements. Generally, keys are used when direct labeling would result in unwanted clutter.

Probably one of the most familiar uses of a key is found on an ordinary road map, identifying main and secondary roads, sizes of cities, scale of miles, etc. The concept is the same for all kinds of charts. Each pattern, color, and symbol in a key is assigned a meaning. As a group they become an established "code." Subsequently, each chart element is entered onto the chart using the code, so that when the viewer needs to identify an element, he consults the key and translates the information according to the code.

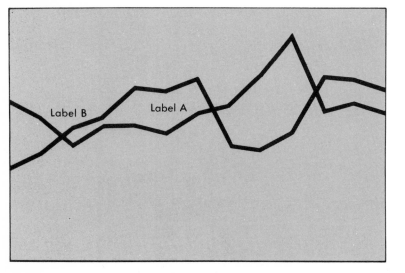

5-36 Improper Direct Labeling on a Line Chart

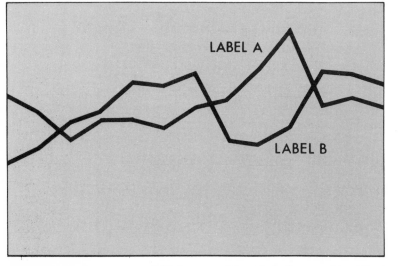

5-37 Proper Direct Labeling on a Line Chart

The key has different forms and locations. For example, it can be an inset and located within the grid (Fig. 5-38). This is the conventional treatment. It can also take the form of a subtitle (Fig. 5-39). Or, it can be omitted from the chart altogether and have the viewer rely on a pre-established code to identify chart elements. An example of pre-established keys is the color-coding used in electrical wiring to identify various wires and their connections. This color-coding of wires is standard throughout the electrical industry and therefore is pre-established. An example of a pre-established symbol is an airplane silhouette that indicates the presence of an airport on a map.

Keys are rarely used on soft copy because they require the viewer's eyes to flit from the code to the element in order to make identifying connections. This procedure usually takes an instant, yet this instant may be too long and cause confusion. In an oral presentation the key can be given by the speaker. For example, he can say, "The figures in red indicate losses."

Captions

Captions are words and symbols that explain units of measure. For instance, dollars, pounds, and per cent are captions. Functionally, captions modify labels by identifying what it is that the label is describing. For example, a label will say "50" and the caption will say "dollars."

Captions should be kept short and precise so that they relieve visual congestion by minimizing the amount of text required to explain the chart's contents. For example, the quantity "one thousand dollars" can be written as $1 thousand. It can be shortened to $1,000. And it can be abbreviated as $1M. This flexibility is valuable because the less text used to communicate, the less cluttered the chart will be and the less time required for its preparation.

Captions are versatile. They can be used in a number of ways, and they can be located in a number of places on the chart. Following are some of their salient features:

Captions can be abbreviated. As we have seen, captions can reduce cumbersome text to a few meaningful characters that make possible a quick exchange between minds.

Every audience is unique in that its capability

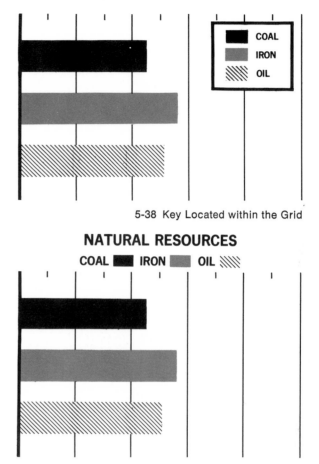

5-38 Key Located within the Grid

NATURAL RESOURCES

COAL ■ IRON ■ OIL ▨

5-39 Key Used as a Subtitle

for understanding the chart depends on its familiarity with the subject matter being presented. For example, a chart on the thermonuclear reaction process is comprehensible to a small audience of scientists. Very few of us are able to penetrate the mystique of the scientists' world and understand their language. However, the "languages" of most other fields are not as esoteric. More commonly, the terms and nomenclature of most professions are easily within the grasp of the layman. But this is not always true of the abbreviations connected with these languages.

For example, examine the following simple abbreviations: sq. in.; bbl; bd. ft., and cwt. These are abbreviations for square inch, barrels, board foot, and hundredweight — some, or all, of which you have had occasion to deal with as a unit of measure. Even the abbreviations of familiar terms are often not recognizable. The use of caption abbreviations should consider the audience which

101

the chart is addressed to. For instance, if the term "board foot" were used in a presentation to lumbermen, the abbreviation "bd. ft." would be easily understood. However, when the term is to be used in an annual report, which reaches a broad spectrum of stockholders, it would be prudent to spell it out completely, or at least partially, like "board ft."*

Therefore, while the shorthand of abbreviations is a time- and space-saver, it often confuses an audience that is not conversant with its meanings. Accordingly, a judicious compromise between full disclosure and coded jargon should be made to keep the caption as short as possible and still understandable.

Captions can be abbreviated using symbols. Captions are extensively used as symbols. Many symbols are *conventional,* such as $ (dollars) and % (per cent). Many are exclusive, such as σ (standard deviation) or ° (degrees). And many are *special-purpose* symbols like L^5, which to a limited circle of readers is mutually agreed upon to mean "lots of 500."

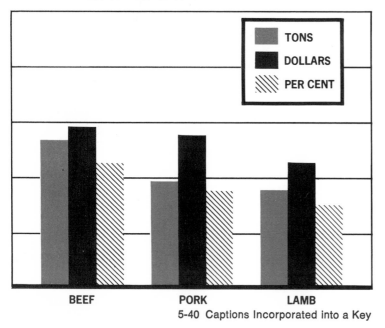

5-40 Captions Incorporated into a Key

When common symbols are used, no explanation is necessary. However, unique symbols — ones that are exclusive or special-purpose — require varying degrees of explanation, depending on the nature of the audience viewing them.

Captions can be incorporated into a key. Captions, like labels, are often built into keys and can be abbreviated or symbolized to form a code for identifying elements on a chart. Figure 5-40 shows the application of captions in a key.

Captions can be in the form of titles or subtitles. The caption can also be built directly into a title — for instance: "Millions of Tons of Bubble Gum Chewed Daily Since January 1." A caption can also be a subtitle, such as "Annual Consumption of Popcorn (in Millions of Tons)."

Captions can be used to reduce the number of digits in a label. The labels on an amount scale may read, for instance, 100, 200, 300, 400, and 500. These three-digit numbers can be reduced to the single digits 1, 2, 3, 4, and 5 by using a subcaption reading "in hundreds," or by using the device "(00)." These subcaptions should be located somewhere on the chart, preferably under the main caption identifying the unit of measure — for example "Pounds (in hundreds)" or "Pounds (00)." The use of captions to alter or modify labels should be carefully done, and the captions should be located in a manner that makes it perfectly clear just what the communicator is trying to convey.

While the caption can be located in the title or a key, it is usually placed in relation to the chart's grid. For example, Figure 5-41 shows the caption conventionally placed outside the grid. Figure 5-42 shows the use of captions within the grid.

Captions are important and should be used whenever there is doubt as to whether the viewer will fully understand and identify the elements on a chart. The designer should never hesitate using them, but he should use them sparingly. The reader must be informed, but there is no reason to give him visual indigestion! The more put onto a chart, the more concentration required of the reader. Conversely, if too much information is omitted from the chart both the communicator and the reader are in trouble. That golden mean is what constitutes the art of charting.

---

* Spelling out the term "board foot" is, of course, only one of many solutions to this type of communication problem. Another solution would be to asterisk the abbreviation, and in a footnote explain that "bd. ft." is the standard abbreviation for "board foot," indicating that the abbreviation will appear as such throughout the text.

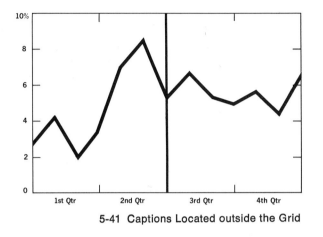

5-41 Captions Located outside the Grid

5-42 Captions Located inside the Grid

Titles and Subtitles

The first thing on a chart that a viewer reads (not sees, but reads) is the chart's title. Ideally, a title is a succinct group of words that should immediately clue one as to what the chart is about. Many titles do anything but that. Good titles are difficult to write. They are difficult because they require experience and skill to condense the subject, scope, and action of a chart into a few words that tell the story. Any student of journalism can attest that this is not an easy task.

The writing of titles stresses content, and, in doing so, offers some literary concessions. For instance, punctuation can be virtually ignored, and rules of capitalization can be waived. Also, while a title should express a complete thought, it does not have to be a structurally correct sentence. For example, "Average Monthly Consumption of Vodka in Russia" is structurally poor as a sentence, but conceptually complete.

While brevity is a criterion of title writing, it is not the primary one. The primary criterion is sense. Moreover, the title must say something. A title like "Sales Program Accomplishments" is a say-nothing title. Stop to think of it — 'what accomplishments?'; 'which program?'; 'when?'; 'how much?' The point is that such titles are much too general and should be avoided.

Diametrically opposite the say-nothing title is the say-everything title, which, for obvious reasons, should also be avoided. An example is a title like "The Number of Brick Homes Built Since the Great Depression That Have No Electricity in the Southeastern United States Exclud-

ing Metropolitan Areas." (The chart may have to be placed on the following page since the title leaves no room for it on the same page!)

Fortunately, the dilemma of title-writing has some remedies. First of all, titles can be omitted. If they add nothing to the chart, there is no reason to retain them. Secondly, in many instances the conventional style of title, which descriptively names the chart's subject, can be replaced with an action title. To illustrate: a conventional title like "Regional Distribution of Personal Income" can be activated by the addition of the verb "shift." As an action title it would read: "Regional Distribution of Personal Income Shifts." Now the viewer has a clue as to what is happening.

Action titles are borrowed from the journalist. Sometimes they are referred to as "headline titles," and that is precisely what they are. A newspaper headline principally contains a subject, verb, an adverb, and a direct object — and so should a chart title.

For example, a newspaper headline might announce an increase in the local schoolboard budget somewhat like this: "City School Budget Rises Next Fiscal Year." (They may also add as a subtitle "Taxpayers Complain.") Reading this headline, we immediately know: where, what, how, and when, even before we read the text.

Similarly, for the communicator's purpose, "Sales Program Accomplishments" can be given an injection of vitamins to read: "Sales Program Increases Profit Ten Per Cent" — or whatever else it did.

Action titles give the reader the immediate

103

clues to understand more easily the balance of the explanation. Moreover, they amplify what the chart is conveying. And, more important, they can precondition the reader to be favorably disposed to the communicator's point of view, pictorially expressed in the chart. This kind of repetition creates a double impression, which psychologists say is important to memory retention.

The mechanics of titles is not so dramatic. The position of the title is the designer's prerogative. Examples of some standard placements are shown in Figure 5-43. Keep in mind that, no matter where the title is placed, it must command primary attention. The title must stand out in the crowd of other elements on the chart.

Titles can be supplemented by subtitles. Functionally a subtitle carries some of the main title's burden. For example, the main title might read: "New York City Traffic Increases," and the subtitle might add, "Per Cent Changes in Public and Private Vehicles, 1960-1965." (New Yorkers might further add: what else is new?)

Subtitles also function as captions and keys to provide pertinent background information for the viewer.

Both titles and subtitles must be logical when read at a glance, especially if they are long enough to require two lines. Accordingly, when more than one line is needed the title should be separated at a logical point.

For instance, suppose the title was, "Selling Performance Beats Sales Quotas in First-Quarter Record" — a perfectly good title, but perhaps a bit long for one line. Design logic might dictate that the title should be broken into two even sections:

SELLING PERFORMANCE BEATS SALES
QUOTAS IN FIRST-QUARTER RECORD

But a closer look at this arrangement reveals that it does not quite make sense. How can selling performance beat sales? Obviously, the break is in the wrong place. "Sales Quotas" is one thought and the words constituting that thought belong together. Therefore, the symmetry of this design has to be sacrificed (a melodramatic overstatement) for the sake of good sense. Thus, the title should be segmented:

SELLING PERFORMANCE BEATS SALES QUOTAS
IN FIRST-QUARTER RECORD

Acronyms

The length of titles can sometimes be shortened by using acronyms and abbreviations. Acronyms are words formed from the initial letters or successive syllables of an entire title. SAC (Strategic Air Command), NASA (National Aeronautical and Space Administration), and Amex (American Express Company) are acronyms.

Abbreviations also follow the principle of initial letter formation. FBI (Federal Bureau of Investigation), IBM (International Business Machines), and MIT (Massachusetts Institute of Technology) are examples of abbreviations. The problem in using acronyms and abbreviations is that, once they go beyond the knowledgeability of the viewer, their usefulness turns into a liability.*

Unfortunately, the scope of the problem is im-

TITLE CENTERED

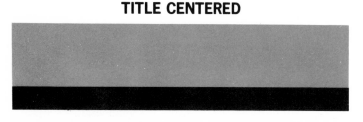

TITLE FLUSH LEFT

TITLE IN GRID

5-43 Standard Placement of Titles

---

* The government and military are notorious for their use of this technique. "Notorious" is used with irony because the proper identification of the countless agencies would be an impossible burden if every one of them had to spell out its long and complex name.

mense. For instance, the *Encyclopedia of Associations* lists over 12,000 organizations, of which more than 3,000 are national in scope. Each and every one of them has either an acronym or an abbreviation, and many of these are the same for more than one organization. For example, the American Medical Association, the American Management Association, and the American Marketing Association all answer to AMA!

Also, familiarity breeds abbreviations. There is hardly an alumnus who does not think of his old alma mater as "Ol' USC" (University of Southwest Calabunk). Businessmen daily mix indigestion with the IRS or SEC. And finally, the corporate policy and procedures manuals are virulent breeders of abbreviations and acronyms. Within its walls the company's true moniker is forever lost in oblivion—it exists only as CWC, or GAF, or IP, or ITT.

These strange words and letters often address themselves to little cliques or in-groups. To the outer world this unfamiliar language may have little meaning and much confusion. Thus, acronyms and abbreviations should be used judiciously and always with the audience considered. When necessary they should be explained with footnotes, or in the text of the presentation.

Relationships

Legend has it that the great masters of painting first diligently learned fundamentals, then practiced the rules, and *then* began to innovate. And so it is in all fields of endeavor. Every discipline has its basics whence spring all the new ideas, new techniques, and new avenues that provide us with the countless tangents to convention.

In the field of charting, the techniques of Relationships can be catagorized as being "different," yet close enough to the principles of graphics to be considered sound, and of practical use. These techniques (Perspective, Third Dimension, and Proportional Representation) apply to charting another dimension beyond the flat plane of height and width. Although implied, this dimension optically appears "real," and visually adds a dynamic quality to an image.

Relationships are the fun and games of charting. They are interesting to work with because they excite the imagination and test ingenuity.

But they also have drawbacks—perhaps more than most other charting techniques. It is not unusual for a designer to get caught up in the artistic snares of these techniques and lose sight of his communication objectives.

PERSPECTIVE Perspective is perhaps the most realistic of the relationship techniques. Perspective was "invented" by the marvelous Renaissance man of the fifteenth century. Prior to this time perspective was little regarded and less understood. Its advent, however, succeeded in forever changing the visual world of pictorial representation.

Perspective adds to a picture a dimension that corresponds to our sense of reality. Without it, a picture may appear flat and unreal.

The application of perspective to charting is tricky. In our natural environment we see in three dimensions. It is not especially difficult for us to compare height and width of objects that are equidistant from us, but we have the darnedest time trying to relate the sizes of things at varying distances. What is close to our line of vision is big and what is far away is small—even though both may be the same size.

Thus, in charting, if we simulate perspective we may emulate reality, but we also inherit our limitations to judge size differentials at a distance. This point is made convincing by observing Figure 5-44a, showing an ordinary curve in two dimensions. Apply perspective to it and it becomes Figure 5-44b.* Each projection of the image is valid, yet presents a seemingly different comparison to the viewer.

Figure 5-45b, showing a Column chart in perspective, provides a more specific example. The angle of viewing succeeds in leading the viewer to believe that the chart's first column is substantially larger than the other columns, and the last column in particular. Actually, the difference in column height is rather miniscule, as shown in Figure 5-45a.

Perspective is a favorite technique for Circle-

105

---

* The examples shown are in pseudoperspective, i.e. they have been modified to appear as being in perspective. True perspective would cause such distortion that the representation would be unusable for charting purposes.

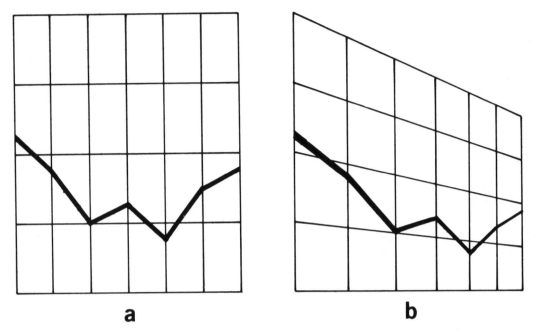

5-44 (a) Line Curve Shown in Two Dimensions (b) Line Curve Shown in Perspective

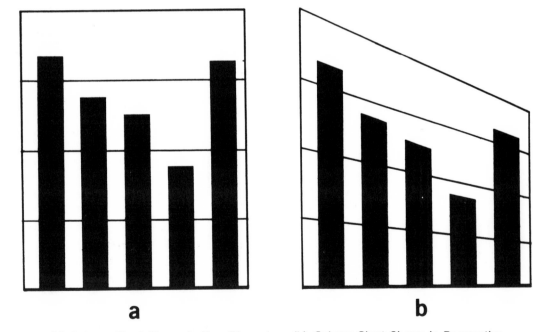

106

5-45 (a) Column Chart Shown in Two Dimensions (b) Column Chart Shown in Perspective

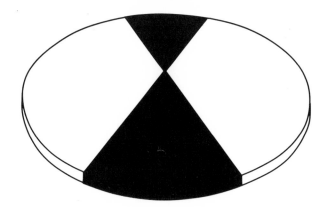

5-46 Circle Chart Shown in Perspective

chart presentations, especially when the designer is explaining how "the dollar is spent." The application of perspective to a Circle chart is an excellent illustration of the potential distortion inherent in the technique. For example, it is hard to believe that the two segments in Figure 5-46 are equal, but they are! So, when your mayor reports to you that the segment in the foreground is the amount of money he is spending on you, and the rear segment is the amount of his take, you can assume that your suspicions have been right all along.

Perspective is frequently used by designers of annual reports — and with some justification. After all, their job is to create an exciting and attractive piece of work that will inflate the pride of stockholders. (Many stockholders may prefer to inflate their pocketbooks and have the expenditure in the form of dividends.) Nevertheless, perspective can enhance the artistic aspects of a report.

The designer using perspective must bear in mind that its application should be restricted to matters that are not critical to an analysis of the report. Important information, which cannot afford even implied distortion, should use other graphic forms. And never try to use any graphic form in lieu of financial statistics in an annual report. In particular, the income statement and balance sheet should remain in cold hard numbers.

The rendering of a drawing in perspective requires skill. The mechanics of determining perspective is much too complex to be given definitive treatment in this book. More than adequate explanations can be found in any good encyclopedia or book on the mechanics of art. However, at the risk of oversimplification, Figure 5-47 attempts to illustrate the concept of constructing a chart in perspective. It must be remembered, however, that only pseudo-perspective can be used in charting.

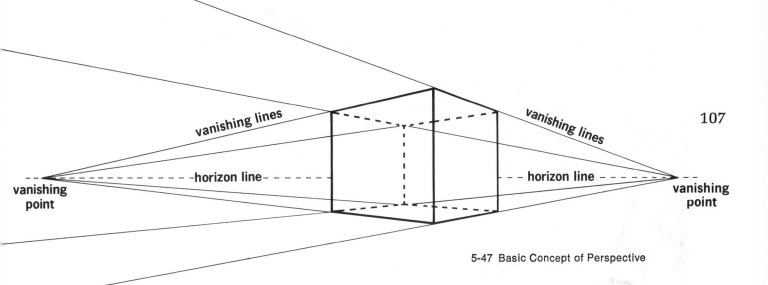

107

5-47 Basic Concept of Perspective

THIRD DIMENSION When the projection of perspective is made to indicate only the depth of an object, that extension of depth is referred to as the "third dimension." The extension of depth is usually accomplished by a shading that lends body to the graphic form, and serves to give the object additional visual interest.

The third dimension is a familiar technique, especially to the doodler. Functionally, it usually serves little or no purpose. Its use is primarily decorative, providing a visual relief from the monotony of two-dimensional charts.

There are some pitfalls in employing a third dimension that should be brought to the communicator's attention. For example, Figure 5-48a uses the technique of looking downward at a set of columns. A cursory glance at this chart finds it quite acceptable. But observe what happens when you try to determine the value of the columns. Question: how is the viewer to determine whether the horizontal grid line is related to the top of the bar in the foreground, or to its projected third dimension?

Now look at Figure 5-48b, which views the columns from the bottom upwards. Question: does the base begin at the end of the projection, or at the beginning of the bar proper? Again, the viewer has no sure way of knowing how to interpret the value of the columns.

The representation in Figure 5-48c appears to avoid both these questions. However, this does not mean this method is the only third-dimensional representation that can be used. The following suggestions are offered to facilitate the interpretation of the various representations of the third dimension:

Label the value of the columns and avoid guess work on the part of the reader.

Make the primary column (i.e. the column in the foreground) visually more powerful than its depth perspective. This emphasis can be achieved by using strong colors or shades on the primary column and weaker colors or shades on the depth dimension.

Make the width of the primary bar greater than its projection. The depth dimension should appear as a shadow of the subject column.

Do not change perspective in mid-presentation. Once the perspective of the third-dimensional projection is selected, keep it uniform throughout any accompanying charts being presented with it.

Where possible make the third dimension serve a function. For example, in Figure 5-49 you can see how cleverly the designer has incorporated what amounts to a variation of a Connected Bar chart into a visual three-dimensional effect.

PROPORTIONAL REPRESENTATION Proportional representation, though used frequently, is perhaps the weakest of the Relationship techniques. Its weakness lies in the difficulty the designer encounters in proportionately increasing or decreasing a representation, and the difficulty the viewer has in interpreting the relative size of the proportion.

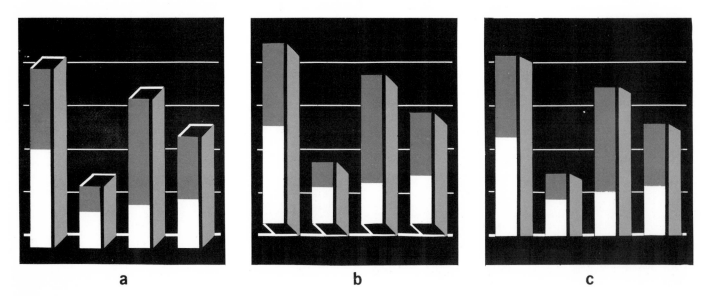

a b c

5-48 Three-Dimensional Chart (a) Seen from Above (b) Seen from Below (c) Seen Straight On

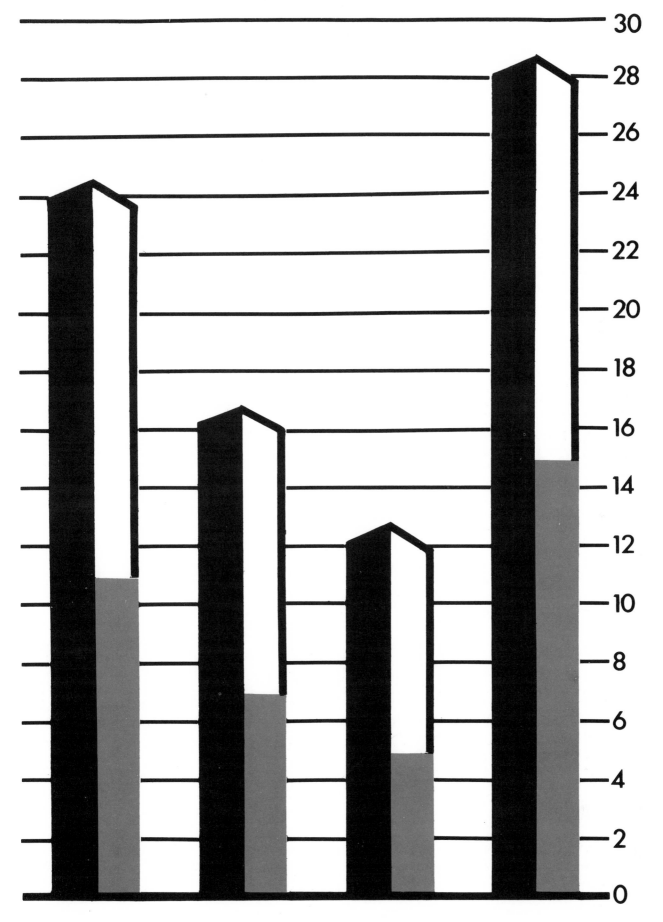

5-49 Utilizing the Third Dimension To Construct a Connected Bar Chart

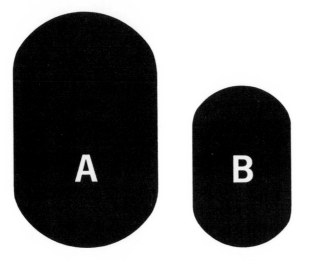

5-50 "A" is Twice as Big as "B"

For example, look at Figure 5-50. We can readily see that A's image is larger than B's; but we do not know how much larger. If we read the text we learn that A is twice the size of B. But actually, is the image of A twice as big? By what method of measurement is it twice as big? For instance, is A double the height of B? Or, is it double the width? Perhaps both the height and width are doubled? Could A be either twice the area, or twice the volume? Or, really, does it matter at all how A is measured, as long as it *looks* twice as big? To answer this question let us examine how the various methods of measurement affect an image. And to make such an examination let us try to pictorialize a proportional representation of this statement: "Railroad commuter travel has doubled since last year."

In Figure 5-51, Image I represents last year's amount of travel, and is the *constant*. To double this constant an image must be constructed to proportionately represent an amount that is twice as big. Accordingly,

Image II is double Image I in height only. But this will not do, for it is readily apparent that the visual relationship created by this measurement is ludicrous. Incidentally, Image II is not strictly proportional because only the dimension of height has been doubled.

Image III, which doubles both height and width, is even more ridiculous when compared to Image I because it offends our sense of reality.

Although it is mathematically accurate it *appears* to be about four or five times larger than the original image.

Image IV takes a different approach. It doubles the area of Image I. This representation is visually more within the realm of credibility, but still seems considerably more than twice the size of the original image.

Image V approaches a reasonable representation of an image that is twice as big as the original image. This image is measured in volume, i.e. it is twice the volume of Image I. But unless you are a mathematician, or have such skills available, it would be even more difficult to calculate volumes than areas. And, assuming that you did mathematically accomplish the task of translating the original image accurately and faithfully to twice its volume or area, would the viewer be the wiser? Would he know the difference? Should he care?

Image VI has no mathematical logic behind it. It merely attempts to represent Image I doubled *visually*. This image probably comes the closest to satisfying visually the viewer's sense of proportional relationship in real life.

Thus, to satisfy visual impressions a proportional representation does not require mathematical accuracy. As a matter of fact, not even the "experts" can tell for sure whether a proportional representation is geometrically valid.

The point is that the representation must convey to the reader the impression that one image is proportionately bigger than another. And this must be done "realistically." To say how much bigger requires labels or text. Therefore, if you succeed in making the comparison *look* visually believable, you have accomplished a proportional representation.

The techniques of Relationships have a very definite place in graphic presentations. While some conservatives continue to disparage their value and contribution to the field, more and more practitioners are adopting these techniques because they add spice to the garden variety of charting forms, which at times can become prosaic and monotonous.

If the techniques of Relationships are used properly they can provide the communicator with variety and flexibility in his presentations. And these are certainly among his most valuable assets, if only because the communicator should be flexible enough to vary his vehicle as his audience varies, and as his purpose varies. Just as reporting to operating personnel is different from reporting to management, and both are different from reporting to stockholders, so the communicator too should be able to meet differing situations.

Mechanics, although tedious, is obviously an important part of charting. The temptation to relegate this job to comparatively "less skilled" individuals should be resisted—*how* something is said requires the same skill as determining *what* to say, and *what to use* in saying it.

Equally tempting is to disregard the mechanics of charting when pictorial forms are used. Although freer in scope, most pictorial chart forms are subject to the various principles of mechanics.

5-51 Proportional Representation (Illustration by Ib Ohlsson)

112

5-52 Evolution of a Slide

114

Pictorial Charts

The hallelujah land of charting is pictorial representations. Pictorial charts, which visually tell a story through pictures, rather than through abstract devices, have great audience appeal. For the communicator, pictorialization as a chart form offers a wider latitude of expression, and fewer restrictions, than geometric forms. And among designers it has many adherents simply because it more closely simulates the field of art than does any other chart form.

The value of pictorial charts for presenting quantitative data, however, depends chiefly on how the charts are used, and to whom they are presented. For instance, to a trained person viewing his technical subject they may add little, or nothing, to what might be conveyed by a well designed conventional graphic form. But to a layman, who has only a slight understanding of the subject, or perhaps even a dislike for conventional charting, pictorial techniques may be most effective.

While the use of pictures is optional in the presentation of quantitative data, it is indispensable in communicating abstract ideas. Accordingly, the transmission of concepts is greatly facilitated when they are presented in picture form. For example, in an electronic data-processing system a "bit" of information can be stored in a punch card, magnetic tape, or disc. Each of these modes works in a different way, and to try to explain the differences would take a great many words, all of which would probably lose many listeners. The idea can be conveyed simply, however, with a picture. Figure 6-2, a simple pictorialization of how the bit of information is stored in each mode, illustrates the point.

Easily understood, the picture is, in fact, a universal language. Pictures are often used to bridge communication barriers between foreign tongues. Figure 6-3, for example, was taken from an annual report written in Japanese. Although we have no knowledge as to whether it represents sales, or profits, or purchases, there is no doubt that it concerns television sets, automobiles, and sporting goods.

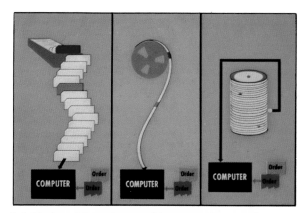

6-2 Modes of Data Storage (Courtesy of Lybrand)

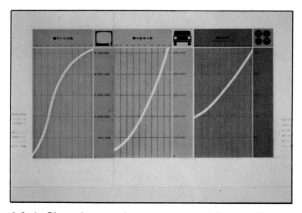

6-3 A Chart from a Japanese Annual Report (Design by Levy and Kimura)

115

RURAL AND URBAN POPULATION

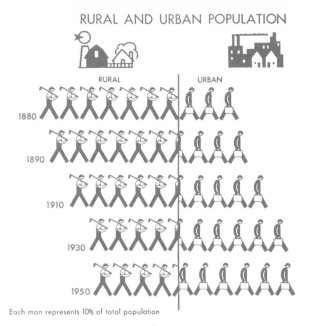

Each man represents 10% of total population

6-4 A Pictorial Sliding Bar Chart

LAND USE IN THE UNITED STATES

EACH SYMBOL REPRESENTS 200 MILLION ACRES

6-5 A Pictorial Subdivided Bar Chart

Pictographs

Some disagreement exists concerning the definition of a *pictograph*. Each source that has used the word has seen fit to apply its own meaning. Hence, confusion has arisen because one man's pictograph is another man's *pictogram* and a third man's *ideograph*. At the risk of further semantic hair-splitting, pictographs can be defined as "pictorial symbols used as numerical counting units in substitution for an amount scale on a conventional chart." Used in this way the symbol is an integral part of the chart.

For example, Figure 6-4 is a Sliding Bar chart depicting the shift of rural population to urban communities. Symbols of men are substituted for the normal bar, and each man-unit represents 10 per cent of the population. The fact that the symbols identify a farmer, as opposed to a city dweller, further amplifies the message.

Figure 6-5 is an example of a Subdivided Bar chart that uses pictorial representations to show the use of land in the United States. In this chart, the concept of time is portrayed by using the buffalo, horse, and tractor. Each counting unit, representing 200 million acres, can be easily identified by its picture (even without a word label).

Figure 6-6 is a Simple Bar chart that uses a horse's head (connoting horsepower) as a counting unit. In this case, the counting unit remains constant; the sources of power available on farms in 1930 are the variables.

Finally, Figure 6-7 is a percentage chart in which the counting unit is a pig. Conceptually, it

POWER AVAILABLE ON FARMS IN 1930

ELECTRICITY

ENGINES ON COMBINES

STEAM AND GAS ENGINES

WORK ANIMALS

TRACTORS

TRUCKS

Each symbol represents 2,200,000 H P

6-6 A Pictorial Simple Bar Chart

is an amusing variation on the familiar "this little piggy" theme — here the lucky one cried all the way home.

These charts are pictographs because they use symbols to act as counting units. The symbols are substitutions for a basic device and are incorporated into a conventional form. The counting units, assigned numerical values, are used in lieu of an amount scale.

116

REE-FOURTHS OF PIGS GO TO MARKET BY TRUCK

UBLIC DEBT

PER PERSON

$59 $300 $1,970 $1,735

3   1922   1945   1951

Pictogram

Pictograms

Pictograms, like pictographs, also use pictorial art. However, the pictures in a pictogram are merely part of the graphic narrative, whereas in a pictograph they are an integral part of the chart. The picture element in a pictogram supports a conventional chart form in the presentation of quantitative data. Actually, pictogram pictures serve to set the scene by providing a recognizable backdrop against which the message is transmitted.

For example, Figure 6-8 shows a group of pictograms drawn from a report (Profile of California) issued by the Bank of America. Notice that each of the charts uses pictorialization to identify its subject matter. The graphic portrayal of the statistical data, however, appears as a basic charting device ingeniously integrated into the composition.

6-7 A Pictorial Percentage Chart (From "Automobile Facts, September 1938." Courtesy of the Automobile Manufacturers Association)

Figure 6-9 is another example of the manner in which pictures are used as a support element. Obviously, the symbols have no function other than conveying the impression of varying magnitudes.

Figure 6-10 is actually a hybrid. The coins, although serving as pictorial columns, are not really counting units, and so the chart must be classified as a pictogram. The chart's main interest, by the way, is its humor, which is carried through by having the figure struggle to carry the burden of the increased public debt. The humor ingeniously adds emphasis and amplifies the message.

In general, the artistic latitude of the graphic narrative, using pictograms, is greater than in any other method of graphic device because it has fewer rules and restrictions. In practice, it has only those imposed by one's imagination and plain common sense.

6-9 A Word Chart Using Pictograms (Courtesy of *Business Week* © October 9, 1965)

Country	Number of people per car in 1964
U.S.	2.8
Canada	3.9
France	6.6
Britain	7.1
W. Germany	7.6
Belgium	8.8
Italy	13.1
Netherlands	13.6
S. Africa	15.7
Venezuela	28.4
Argentina	30.8
Mexico	60.3
Japan	76.9
Brazil	86.8

The worldwide scramble for a passenger car:

In the U.S., nearly three people per car—but in Brazil about 87 people per car

118

6-8 A Series of Pictograms (From "California Profile— A study of the Market Served by the Bank of America." Designed by Tom Kamifuji. Courtesy of Bank of America)

6-11 A Conventional Reference Map of South America

6-12 A Road Map

6-13 A Map Used To Emphasize Programs as Nationwide (Courtesy of Lybrand)

6-14 A Map Showing Standard Time Zones

Maps

Maps are probably the oldest kind of formal charting known to man. Created to show certain features of land and sea, the map contains almost all the elements used in the graphic language: scales, symbols, shapes, colors, labels, captions, keys, titles, figures, text, and lines. Moreover, the concept of a map is founded on spatial relationships: far and near; one to another; big and small; high and low. Overall, the map is perhaps the most complete communicative device we know.

However, because we are so accustomed to using maps, we seldom think of them as visual aids. To most people, a "map" is a concept, quite divorced from the forms of charts normally used in presentations.

The conventional reference map (Fig. 6-11) and the ubiquitous roadmap (Fig. 6-12) are common examples of how maps are used. But the communicator must go beyond the familiar usage of maps and think of them as powerful tools for conveying ideas of space, and for establishing geographical frames of reference.

Figure 6-13, for example, speaks of "central training programs," but it is the map that indicates that the programs are on a national scale.

Figure 6-14 employs a map as a geographical frame of reference to indicate the standard time zones in the United States.

There are endless applications for maps as graphic elements, either as an integral part of the chart or as a frame of reference against which relative placements can be made.

119

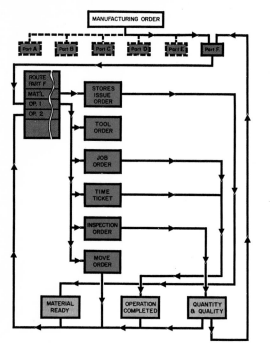

6-15 A Flow Chart Describing the Processing of a Manufacturing Order

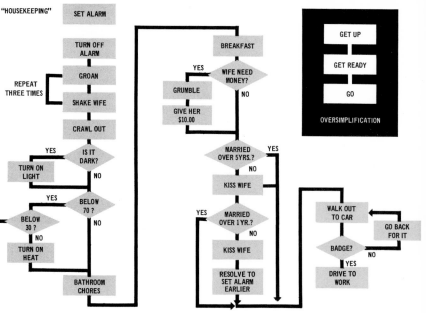

6-17 An Atypical Example of Programming

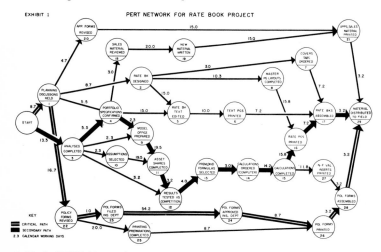

6-16 A PERT Network

Flow Charts

Flow charts are a kind of map. They are especially helpful in explaining the step-by-step logic of a system. Without Flow charts, systems and procedure writers would be utterly lost. Words alone could not explain the multirelationships existing between operations in a system.

Figure 6-15 is an example of how a Flow chart integrates shapes, symbols, lines, and colors to tell a story. This chart describes the flow of a particular manufacturing order that is part of a system. When many Flow charts, like this one, are linked with others (describing other subsystems) the entire operation of a company can be revealed in visual form.

Some flow-charting techniques incorporate time.

One excellent example of such techniques is the PERT chart (Fig. 6-16). Although PERT (Program Evaluation and Review Technique) is a relatively new technique, it has gained considerable acceptance. For the most part, this recognition is due to its successful application to diversified projects. For example, a metals manufacturer schedules an around-the-clock mining operation with this new approach, and saves money by cutting time from maintenance and repairs. This technique is also used in the planning of moves, constructions, and installations, among others.

The novelty of PERT lies in the graphic and conceptual integration of all components of a project into a network. In PERT, a detailed breakdown is made of all elements or activities in a project, with associated completion times and costs. Their interrelationship is then graphically portrayed in a Flow chart, and an analysis of all network sequences establishes the sequence of activities in which no delay can occur without delaying the total project. This sequence of activities is known as the "critical path," and its determination identifies for management those activities that require priority attention in case of delay. In the event of a delay, manpower and other resources can be rescheduled (usually from peripheral events) to minimize the effect of the delay on the entire project.*

---

* A detailed explanation of this technique can be found in the IBM publication "PERT General Information Manual E20-8067."

120

Carolus Magnus

121

6-21 The Family Tree of Charlemagne. (Illustration by William Metzig)

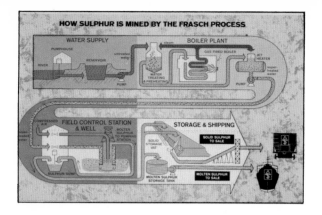

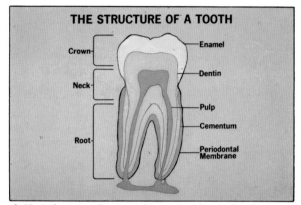

6-19 A Cutaway Process Chart of a Human Tooth

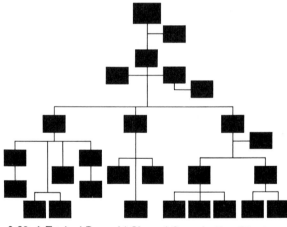

6-20 A Typical Pyramid-Shaped Organization Chart

Modern data-processing systems also make extensive use of flow charting. Before any program is made operative, a Flow chart is constructed and the logic of the routing is carefully checked out. Although the Flow chart in Figure 6-17 is not a typical program, it is an interesting one.

Process Charts

The Process chart is a form of Flow chart that uses pictorial art, instead of lines and symbols, to simplify the explanation of complex processes. Figure 6-18 is an example of a Process chart that

depicts the various steps involved in mining sulphur by the Frasch process.

This particular technique of process charting is commonly used to advantage in annual reports directed to lay audiences. The purpose of the chart is merely to provide the reader with a broad understanding. Therefore, the steps shown are usually grossly generalized, and the pictorialization is highly stylized.

Process charts used for teaching purposes, however, demand greater fidelity to the actual workings of an object. For example, the cutaway technique shown in Figure 6-19 permits the viewer to see the structure of a tooth. While, for clarity's sake, the number of parts has been reduced to a minimum, and stripped of unnecessary detail, the parts shown are positioned in their exact functional relationship and in their proportionate sizes.

Thus, the composition or operations of even the most complicated structure or mechanism can be made comparatively easy to understand through the techniques of process charting.

Organization Charts

Organization charts are diagramatic representations that depict the structures of organizations by delineating levels of authority, delegation of duties, lines of responsibility and channels of command. In doing so they expose the relation of one function to all other functions. No other form of graphic representation so forcefully demonstrates the power of a visual to reveal multiple relationships.

In many companies, where the organizational structure is a complex and delicate issue, the Organization chart is an anathema. As a matter of fact, some companies refuse to commit theirs to paper; and others, which have made organization charts, will not publish them. This is not especially surprising since an individual's status with his peers, subordinates, and superiors in his most valued professional possession.

Obviously, a hierarchy must exist in every organization, but it is not until the structure is crystalized in visual form (for everyone to see) that trouble arises. Individuals vie for the vertical levels at which their little boxes appear. The lateral distances of boxes from the chief executive are scrutinized for hidden meanings. The

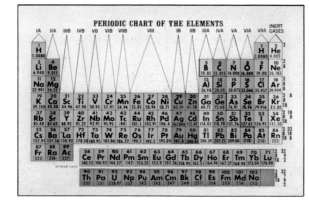

6-24 A Periodic Chart of the Elements

6-25 A Word Chart Designed Around the Text (Courtesy of Lybrand)

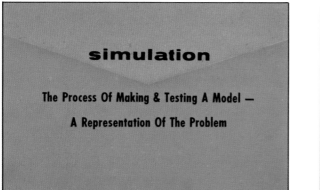

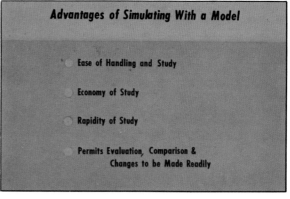

6-27, 6-28 Word Charts Designed Through the Text (Courtesy of Lybrand)

solid and dotted connecting lines are subjected to vague interpretations. And the sizes of the boxes, and the typography thereon, are invested with promiscuous speculations. In short, the Organization chart is one of the most sensitive projects to undertake.

The mechanical aspect of making an Organization chart is a simple exercise in draftsmanship. Although a number of variations in form are possible, the standard (and most common) is the pyramid shape, shown in Figure 6-20. The placement of functions on the pyramid conforms with the order of hierarchy within the organization. Thus, the organization's chief executive officer is positioned at the apex, and the functions of descending importance are placed on subsequent horizontal levels. Each function is represented by a box containing a descriptive caption and usually the name of the individual filling it. Connecting these boxes are lines. Normally, a solid line indicates functional and administrative control over subordinate boxes, and a dotted line usually means less than absolute control.

Organization charts, by and large, are executed as simple black line schematics. Color is seldom used because organizational changes are so frequent that expensive color printing would be an extravagance. However, when available, color can be used for purposes of differentiation.

There are other forms of the Organization chart that are used to portray relationships of one entity to other entities, within a given structure. The *family tree* (Fig. 6-21) is an example of another type of Organization chart. The study of family relationships, and the pattern they follow back through the years, can be facilitated for the student if the ancestry is visually plotted in chart form.

Another form of the Organization chart is the *historical chart,* where time is used as a frame of reference to place the events that occurred in their proper chronology (Fig. 6-22).

The concept of the Organization chart can also be used for the classification of things. Take, for example, the chart in Figure 6-23 which depicts a *tree of learning,* with all its divisions and subdivisions.

And, finally, the *Periodic Chart of the Elements* (Fig. 6-24) is a member of this family of charts. Here again, the emphasis is on the relation of one part to all the other parts of the whole.

The concept of the organization is a flexible one

123

that has many applications in determining the relationship of one group to every other group within a total structure.

Word Charts

Invariably, in every presentation, there are thoughts or ideas that cannot be visualized by any graphic form, and therefore must be expressed in words. These become Word charts. The Word chart is one of the most difficult types of visual aids to handle because, by nature, it is graphically sterile and monotonous. Accordingly, Word charts require a considerable amount of thought to make them interesting and effective.

Many communicators, however, fail to approach Word charts as bona fide visual aids. Some, for example, may go to great lengths to avoid having words appear without some sort of pictorial embellishment, no matter how irrelevant the embellishment may be. More often than not, they concoct the most improbable images to portray or support a thought or idea. And usually this artificial approach amounts to a game of charades, in which all but the most astute and imaginative viewers can only guess at the significance of the pictorial images.

At the other extreme, there are communicators who approach Word charts as the alpha and omega of visual communication. Consequently, they load charts with superfluous text, so that these charts resemble pages from the *Encyclopaedia Britannica*.

Obviously, both extremes are poor ways of handling the problem. Basically, there are two ways to approach the making of a Word chart: one is by designing *around the text,* and the other by designing *through the text.*

DESIGNING WORD CHARTS AROUND THE TEXT The design of a Word chart around the text is accomplished by making the graphic element extraneous (but not superfluous) to the main body of the message. Conceptually, the graphic element is treated in a manner similar to the pictorial element in a pictogram. As an example, see Figure 6-25. The main body of the message is the text: "Training is Part of Forward Planning." If this text appeared without graphic support it would be informative but rather uninteresting. However, when the message is amplified pictorially, the chart takes on an added dimension, and the Word chart is no longer merely a sterile phrase void of visual interest.

Often communicators encounter situations in which a great many words are required to explain an involved message. In order to avoid cluttering a single chart, a solution would be to segregate the text into logical units of thought, and to employ a series of Word charts that are visually tied to each other. In these situations the techniques of designing around the text can be effectively used to establish the visual continuity needed to sustain the message.

The series shown in Figure 6-26 is an application of this point. In this case the header slide (upper left) was presented first to serve as a summary and an introduction to the slides to follow. The communication problem in the subsequent slides was to describe, in more detail, the services appearing on the header slide. Moreover, each slide had to stand alone, and yet be visually related to the other slides in the series.

The solution was to split the screen, and on the right side put words and phrases from which the speaker, in giving the presentation, took his

| Stone Age | Early Middle Ages | Late Middle Ages | Renaissance | Baroque | Louis XV - XVI |

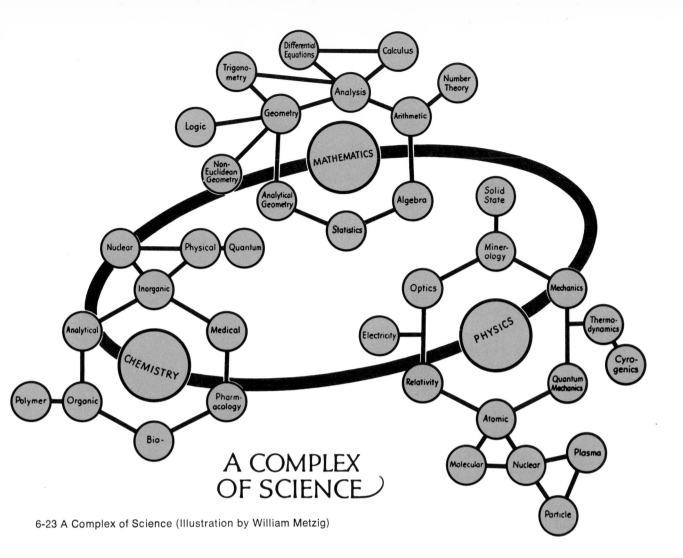

A COMPLEX
OF SCIENCE

6-23 A Complex of Science (Illustration by William Metzig)

cues. The left side of the screen was used for a visual symbolization of the slide's topic. Notice that the graphic part of each chart is extraneous — it acts only as a visual support to the main body of text. The format of the series (i.e., split screen with graphic at the left and text at the right) served to establish a visual continuity to the presentation. In each case, the designing was done around the text.

DESIGNING WORD CHARTS THROUGH THE TEXT The graphic element in designing through the text is *built into* the overall visual aspect of the chart. In other words, it has no particular identification — it is pure design. In Figure 6-27, for example, the text is the predominant matter on the chart. The background design does little more than make the naked words visually palatable. The same holds true for Figure 6-28.

6-22 An Historical Chart of Costuming (Illustration by Ib Ohlsson)

Directoire   Third Empire   Early Automobile Age   Post World War II   Present Times   Future?

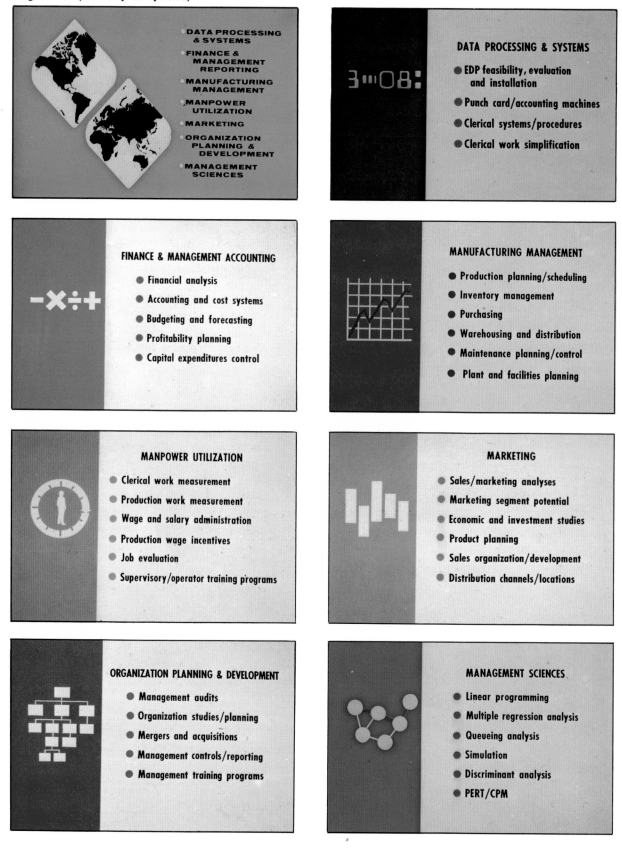

6-29–6-32 Word Charts Designed for Impact (Courtesy of Lybrand)

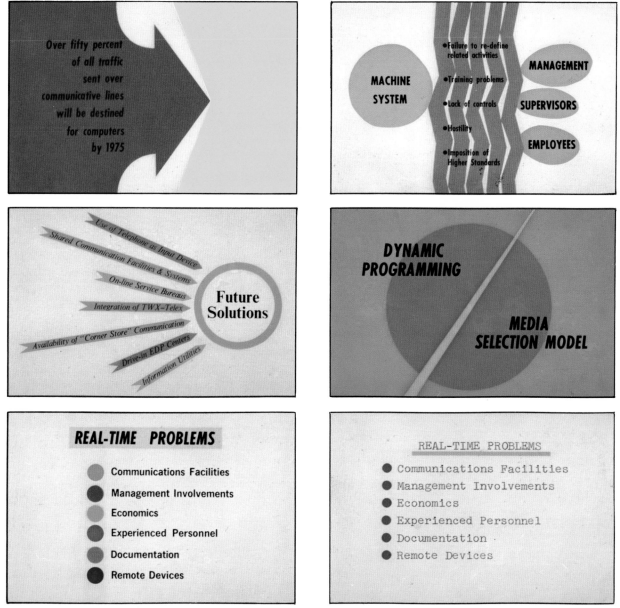

6-33 A Simple Word Chart (Courtesy of Lybrand)   6-34 A Very Simple Word Chart

127

But in Figure 6-29 the design is more forceful, and gives a feeling of movement that emphasizes the text. Designing through the text can be handled dramatically by creating a sense of motion in the graphic element. Figures 6-30, 6-31, and 6-32 are further examples of the kinds of things that can be done by deploying the graphic element as an animate force.

However, all Word charts need not become so visually involved. Figure 6-33 demonstrates that even a minimum amount of design visually relieves the harshness of plain words sitting nakedly on a chart. Figure 6-34 is merely a typewritten version.

Word charts, as visual forms, offer the communicator unlimited opportunities to apply his thinking creatively, and thereby enhance his presentations.

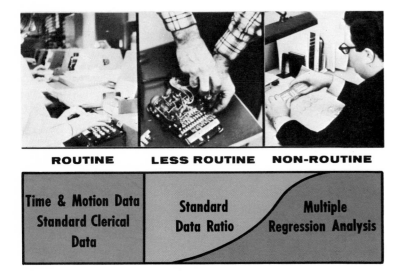

ROUTINE   LESS ROUTINE   NON-ROUTINE

Time & Motion Data Standard Clerical Data	Standard Data Ratio	Multiple Regression Analysis

6-35 A Chart Using a Photograph as a Graphic Element (Courtesy of Lybrand)

6-36 A Photograph That is a Chart (Courtesy of Mosler Safe Company, 1963 Annual Report)

Photographs

The photograph is one of the most versatile graphic elements available to the chartist. When properly used it can lend to a visual a dimension of reality that is impossible to achieve with illustrations. Photographs and illustrations are two different techniques, and the application of photographs to charts requires a distinctly different approach.

The technique of illustration is accepted by the viewer as a conceptual representation of reality. And since an illustration merely suggests a real-life situation, it has a broad span of interpretation. As a result, the viewer bears a relationship to the illustration wherein the object depicted is symbolic of all such objects, past, present and future.

But a photograph is different. It is rooted in reality. To the viewer it has a narrower span of interpretation because it depicts a specific object bounded by space and time. Therefore, the photograph as a mirror image of real life requires different criteria of perception — accuracy, for one, and detail, for another. Consequently, the photo-

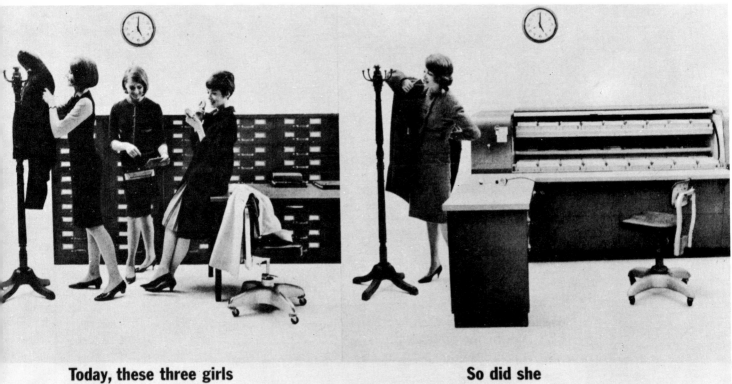

Today, these three girls filed 12,500 checks   **So did she**

6-42 *Medici Coat of Arms* (Design by William Metzig)

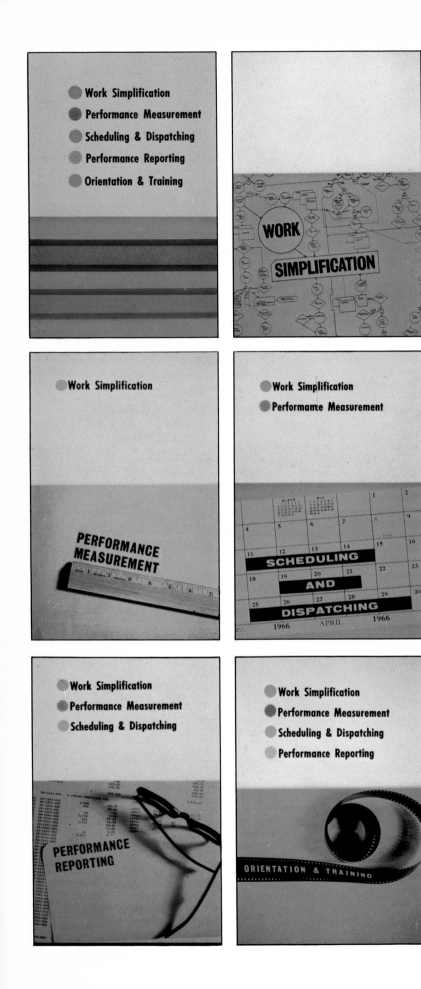

graph must meet certain tests to be effectively utilized as a graphic element. It must serve a bona fide function. It must be germane to the chart's subject matter. Additionally, it must have a self-contained composition capable of standing apart from the other graphic elements on the chart. Finally, it must be visually compatible with the other graphic elements on the chart.

With the chart shown in Figure 6-35 the criteria a photograph must meet as a graphic element can be evaluated. For example, the photographs are used to demonstrate pictorially the concepts of "routine, less routine, and non-routine" types of work. Thus, the criterion of function is satisfied.

The photographs, when placed in the context of the chart's subject, serve to support the ideas being expressed because they are germane. Observe, also, that each of the photographs can be lifted out of context and stand alone as a piece of photography—meeting the test of self-contained composition. Finally, there is no visual conflict between the photographs, nor is there a conflict with the other graphic elements on the chart. Thus, in this case the application of photography successfully meets the tests imposed by the criteria for effective utilization of the photograph as a graphic element.

In constructing a chart the photograph can be used as a primary or secondary graphic element. When used as a primary element the photograph itself *is* the chart (Fig. 6-36). As a primary element it can also be a photograph of real objects. When used as a secondary element the photograph becomes part of the chart, supporting the main thrust of the message. Figure 6-37 is an example of photographs used in Word charts designed around the text. In this series the points being made are carried progressively forward and amplified, using the photograph as a secondary graphic element.

There has been little exploration of photography as a primary and secondary graphic element in soft-copy applications. And there is room for a great deal of experimentation in this area. Hard copy, in the form of printed matter, has made use of photography. Most publications have accomplished great strides in effectively using photography as a form of visual communication, both as primary and secondary graphic elements.

6-38 Symbols Used by Medieval Alchemists

Symbols and Symbolism

Our most precious legacy from antiquity is a written language. Without it the vast body of knowledge discovered and developed throughout the centuries would not be known to us. Nor would we now have the ability to record our thoughts, possessions, and visions, so that future generations might profit by them.

Most early civilizations developed their written language in similar manners. For example, the cuneiform of the Babylonians and Assyrians, the hieroglyphics of the Egyptians, and the characters of the Chinese language began by using symbols having conventional fixed forms and meanings. These symbols, which are in effect picture writing, were drawings representing objects. Thus, to convey the idea of a tree, these peoples drew a picture of it. Gradually, over the centuries, from the simple picture used to ex-

press a single idea (ideography), there evolved more complex multiple signs to express words (logography), and eventually phonetic combinations (syllabic) that sounded like words in order to express abstract ideas. Today, the alphabets we know evolved from these earlier forms of picture writing.

Yet pictorial representation has lost none of its appeal, nor its value as a basic means of communication. Symbology continues to be a form of shorthand language, whereby a single mark, picture, or sign can convey or identify meanings that would require considerable explanation in words.

The symbols we use are either obvious representations of familiar objects or abstract symbols signifying some familiar concept. For example, a pictorialization of a flame is an obvious repre-

131

6-39 A Pictorial Symbol

sentation of fire, while the Rx on a doctor's prescription has become a symbol generally representing the concept of pharmacology.

In effect symbolism is a contract between users and viewers, whereby an abstract picture or sign is agreed to have a specific meaning. The process of understanding by common consent is the same premise upon which the entire vocabulary of language is built.

Any classification of symbols cannot possibly be rigorous, because the meanings of symbols continually alter and shift. Even symbols having historical significance change as different ages and cultures adapt them for their own purposes. A classic example of this is the sign of the swastika.

At the dawn of time, early man lived in awe of the sun. Because the image of the sun lent itself easily to an ideograph, much of his picture writings were of sunbursts. The swastika was a visual corruption of these sunbursts, and was used to decorate his possessions. To primitive man, the swastika was a symbol of "life" in all of its ramifications.

The advent of Christianity brought another meaning to the swastika. Like so many other pagan concepts, the Christians borrowed the symbol and interpreted pagan "life" to signify "life resurrected." Hence, the swastika became a cross, formed by four capital gammas (the third letter of the Greek alphabet, which looks like our "L"), and symbolized Christ as the cornerstone of the Church.

Modern times saw a new and notorious mean-

6-40 A Conventional Symbol

ing attached to the swastika. Because it was adopted as the emblem of Nazi Germany it now symbolizes all the evil we have come to associate with the era of Nazism.

A classification of symbols is also difficult to make because, through usage and acceptance, the limited symbols of yesterday may become common symbols tomorrow. An example of such an evolution is the pawnbroker symbol. Universally recognized, this three-ball symbol actually had its origins in the Medici family coat of arms. The Medicis, who were Florentine bankers, were famous as money-lenders to the world as it was known in the fifteenth century, when literacy was rare. The Medici crest, Figure 6-42, had six balls; somehow only three of them have passed down to us as a symbol of money-lending.

Finally, rigorous classification is hampered be-

6-41 A Symbol with Historical Significance

cause many symbols serve multiple purposes. Thus a symbol may be commonly accepted to mean one thing in one context, and something altogether different, but equally accepted, in another context. A simple example is the sign "X," which marks the spot, indicates multiplication in a mathematical context, signifies the cross in a religious context, and represents an unknown factor in a theoretical sense.

Overall, symbology is a dynamic force of communication, but must be carefully applied to minimize misinterpretations by the reader. Since all symbols are in a large sense abstractions, they must meet certain requirements to be understood.

One of these requirements is that they be defined, *traditionally* or *especially*. An example of a traditionally defined symbol is the Star of David. An example of an especially defined symbol is a circle assigned a particular meaning for a particular presentation.

Another requirement is that the meaning of a symbol be understood by the community using it. The community may be as large as a culture or as small as an individual audience viewing a particular presentation.

Last, but not least, symbols must be consistent in their meaning. Thus, traditional symbols, which have become part of the vocabulary, should have the same meaning every time they are used in similar contexts. On the other hand, special symbols have transitory meanings, which need to remain consistent only within the context of a particular presentation.

Despite the many difficulties, the various symbols we know can be broadly classified as:

Pictorial Symbols — which are illustrated representations of familiar things.

Conventional Symbols — which, by common consent and extensive usage, have come to have certain meanings. The dollar sign and musical clefs are examples of such symbols.

Limited Symbols — which have been created to identify specific entities, but have restricted applications. Trademarks are good examples.

Special-Purpose Symbols — which are adopted to take on special transitory meanings that exist only within, and for the life of, a presentation. The geometric forms of basic charting devices are examples of such symbols.

PICTORIAL SYMBOLS   The most common form of symbolism is the pictorialization of an object or idea. Pictographs and pictograms are predicated on such symbols.

Usually, these symbols have a direct meaning. For example, in Figure 6-43 the calendar months are divided into seasons, and the seasons are represented by picture symbols that have strong associations with the idea being conveyed. Pictorial symbolism harks back to picture-writing and is one of the most basic forms of communication.

The use of pictorial symbols as a communication vehicle, however, is contingent on the viewers' ability to associate pictures with ideas. Although most of them are fairly obvious, there still remains the possibility that they can be misconstrued.

As far back as 1923 this possibility was a very real one to visual communicators. In Vienna, at that time, a pioneer in the field of pictorialization, Dr. Otto Neurath, attempted to create a visual language by instituting a system to standardize the meaning of pictorial symbols. He called this system ISOTYPE, which is a coined word meaning *International System of Typographic Picture Education*. Isotypes are the basic symbols proposed as an international picture language. Dr. Neurath established a considerable reputation, and throughout his lifetime he devoted his time and energies to the development of his system and to promulgating isotypes as a universal picture language.

In the United States, Dr. Rudolph Modley, who was an associate of Dr. Neurath, has done much to continue and further the use of pictorial unit charts. Today many of the standardized pictorial symbols used in charting stem from the pioneering work of these men.

There is nothing especially difficult in creating a pictorial symbol, and there are a number of styles and techniques that can be used. But basic to any approach are these guidelines:

Symbols should adhere to the principle of good art. They should be well executed, and be able to stand alone as a piece of graphic art, however humble.

Symbols should be made as simple and clear as possible. They should be easily distinguishable as the object being portrayed. Even when the

133

6-44 Variations in Pictorial Symbols

symbol is highly stylized it should unmistakably represent the object.

Symbols should be self-explanatory and instantly bring to mind a common concept. For example, a symbol of an automobile should look like an automobile. A farmer should look like a farmer — not just a man, or worker, but a farmer.

Symbols should be flexible. They should be capable of being reduced or enlarged without a loss of identity.

Symbols should be adaptable to different techniques. For example, they should work in color, or black and white; in silhouette; as a line drawing; or in any other medium.

Symbols should be simple when functioning as counting units. They should be capable of being segmented without completely losing their identity. Also, symbols should be able to withstand being repeated without becoming visually disturbing or boring.

Symbols should never change their sizes when functioning as counting units. Proportional masses should be avoided (see page 108). When a change in quantity occurs, more or fewer symbols, not larger or smaller symbols, should be used.

CONVENTIONAL SYMBOLS. Conventional symbols abound. In business, science, and the arts the use of common signs and symbols is a principal means of communication. Music, for instance, is almost completely a symbolic language; so are mathematics and chemistry.

Conventional symbols differ from pictorial symbols in that they are abstract signs whose forms have little resemblance to the idea they represent. Nevertheless, these symbols, whose origins are buried somewhere in the past, have become widely familiar through years of usage. A dollar sign is an example. A less obvious example is an arrow used to indicate direction.

Conventional symbols present few or no problems in communication. They are widely understood and have become part of our sign language. The communicator should, however, take precautions to assure himself of the symbol's familiarity within the community he is concerned with.

For example, common the world over are the symbols used to represent male and female in the biological science. Also common to our culture are the colors black for death, blue for boys, and pink for girls. Figure 6-45 has incorporated these conventional symbols to convey their common meanings.

Some newer symbolic "languages" are less well known at this time, but nevertheless should be classed as conventional. An excellent example

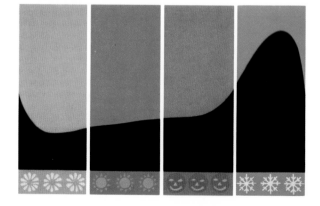

6-43 A Chart Using Pictorial Symbols

134

6-45 A Chart Using Conventional Symbols

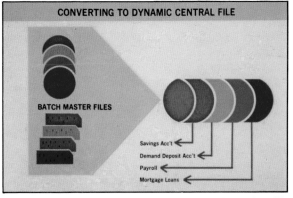

6-47 The Use of Abstract Symbols in Depicting Electronic Data-Processing Systems

of the development of such a visual language can be found in the field of programming for automation technology.

It has been estimated that within a decade we will have more computer programmers writing machine instructions than doctors writing prescriptions for patients; the language of such a potentially large community cannot be ignored.

Figure 6-46 shows part of a template with some of the symbols used by programmers. Considerable standardization is still required to make the precise meanings of symbols consistent among users, but through the efforts of agencies like the American Standards Association, and the wide and continual use of these abstract shapes, a language is now developing with which countless individuals will be able to communicate.

Figure 6-47 is an example of some of these symbols used in a chart that depicts a system. The circular shape is symbolic of a magnetic tape reel. The rectangular symbol (with a corner cut) is a punch card. And the cylindrical shape is a symbol for a random-access file.

LIMITED SYMBOLS Many symbols are limited by virtue of their unique purpose — heraldry, for example, whose meanings are by and large forgotten. Guild symbols also had meanings, many of which are no longer remembered. Some, however, are still with us, and by now have become conventional. The barber's pole, with its red and white stripes, is a symbol that has survived from the early days when barbers not only cut hair and trimmed beards, but were also the local surgeons who practiced blood-letting, tooth-pulling, and other kinds of impromptu surgery.

The twentieth century fully developed the corporate trademark, which is a limited symbol,

since it is created to identify a company and has no function beyond this. Nevertheless, as in the case of the barber pole, some of these modern trademarks are slowly becoming conventional because they fill a void in our vocabulary, or because they are so strongly associated with the idea they represent. The trademark "IBM" is a case in point of a symbol that has entered into our vocabulary to represent, in general, the concept of electronic data-processing equipment.

SPECIAL-PURPOSE SYMBOLS Any shape, sign, letter, color, or numeral can become symbolic of anything the communicator wants it to, provided its relationship is defined and its meaning assigned. Thus, any symbol can serve a special purpose to fill an immediate and temporary need to label something so that its identification can be facilitated.

The best examples of special-purpose symbols are basic charting devices (Chapter 4). These geometric forms assume transitory identities for the purpose of a particular communication.

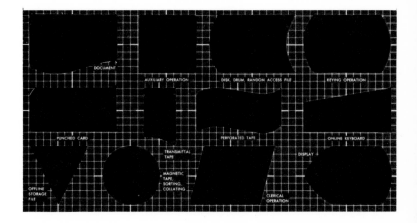

6-46 Part of a Symbol Template Used for Programming

Actually, special-purpose symbols are codes or keys that, by mutual consent, identify things conveniently. Suppose, for example, we were making a presentation in which we had to discuss the locations of plants, warehouses, and sales offices of a particular company.

Figure 6-48 indicates the number of ways in which we could differentiate these entities on a map. One way would be to use words: "Plant," "Warehouse," and "Office." Another way would be to use pictorial representations of the entities as symbols. These are, however, conventional ways. The special purpose symbol would be to choose certain abstract shapes to represent them: like a circle (plant), a triangle (warehouse), and a square (sales office). If color is available, we may choose to make all the entities circles and color-code them — one color for the plant, another for the warehouse, and a third for the sales office. The point is that throughout the presentation the circle will denote the same entity, the triangle another, and the square a third. Or perhaps the identification would be made by the use of three colored circles.

These are special-purpose symbols created for the restricted use of this particular presentation. In another presentation, the circle may be assigned to an entirely new idea.

Special-purpose symbols should use representations which have no strong association with existing symbolism. Usually, abstract shapes, colors, or alphabet letters are considered neutral, and can be used effectively as special-purpose symbols.

Color is especially useful as an "identifier" because it stands out so strongly from the usual black-and-white fare we are so accustomed to. And while color fills the world around us, it is nevertheless unusual to find it in written, and (less so) in visual, material. When it does appear, however, it delightfully adds an additional dimension to the communication.

6-48 Various Applications for Symbols

WORDS	PLANT	WAREHOUSE	OFFICE
LETTERS	P	W	O
SHAPES	●	▲	■
COLOR	●	●	●
PATTERNS	▨	▨	▨
TONES	▲	▲	▲
SIGNS	⊕	★	✕
PICTURES	🏭	🏢	🚢

7

The Dimension of Color

In 1939, Willard Brinton wrote: "It is believed that the evidence is conclusive that to get the maximum result in graphic presentation the question is not 'Can one not afford to use color?', but, 'Can one afford to omit color?' "

Today, three decades later, his opinion is even more pertinent and all the more worthy of our attention. Unfortunately, however, color, while filling the world around us, is an enigma to all but the color specialists — and even they are confused, at times, by its various phenomena.

Using various classification systems, color experts can identify and name about two or three hundred colors. Scientists have estimated that there are actually some ten million different colors. For all practical purposes, however, only a handful of colors can be precisely identified by the average viewer. To most people, red is red, regardless of differences in shade. Thus, to quibble about subtle distinctions, as far as charting is concerned, would be absurd. Color is a continuum, and the human mind can only make rather gross distinctions.

Color is an intricate science, replete with laws of physics in which only the scientist is expected to be proficient. Color has been subjected to extensive psychological testing (especially by the Gestalt school) to study human emotional and neurological responses. Color has also had its empiricists in the many artists who have propounded various theories concerning its paradoxes. In one way or another, these disciplines have attempted to explain color — the "how" and the "why" it affects us as it does.

Meanwhile, the viewer, unconcerned with explanations, continues to accept the presence of color and his reactions to it without serious question. His sole concern is that he likes, or dislikes, the color of a particular thing — and this he does for reasons he himself does not understand, nor cares about understanding.

The communicator, however, cannot be as complacent about color because he must use it — hopefully to his advantage. Obviously, he cannot hope to master the scientific aspects, and if he did, it would be of little relevance to his purpose; the science and theories of color may be of interest to the communicator, but they are almost impossible to use as working tools.

Simply, the communicator does need to understand the rudiments of color, with which he can unravel the mysteries of why some colors are easier to see; why some are more pleasing than others; and why the same color looks different at different times with different applications. The solutions to these questions are certainly within his understanding.

Nomenclature of Color

An investigation into color begins with its nomenclature. Color has three characteristics by which it can be described. The first is hue, the term used to describe a basic color. In most color systems,* hues are the primary (red, yellow, and blue) and binary (orange, green, and violet) colors.

The second term to describe color is value, which is the apparent lightness and darkness of a color. Often this relative lightness or darkness is referred to by the term "density." For instance: a color at 30 per cent of its value has a lesser density than it would have at 80 per cent of value.

137

---

* There is an inconsistency in the terminology of the characteristics used in the various systems. For instance, the term value in one system is synonymous with saturation in another. Likewise, brightness is another term for chroma.

7-4 The Larger the Sp
Between Color Inten
ties, the Greater t
Contrast

7-3 Colors of Different Value May Have the Same Intensity

The third term is *chroma,* which describes the brilliance or "intensity" of a color. Bright colors, such as yellow and orange have high chroma (i.e. intensity) while violet and blue, which are more muted colors, have a low chroma.*

Beyond these three characteristics any further delving into the classification and identification of colors, involving tints, tones, and shades (as used by the painter), would merely be academic to the communicator. His problem is not what a color is called, but rather how to use it. For the most part, the communicator's approach to the utilization of color should be instinctive — i.e. a color does, or does not, look good in a particular context. His aesthetic judgments are usually derived from these instinctive reactions. And thus, the empirical trial-and-error method formulates his judgment and sets his criteria.

---

* There are various systems which attempt to organize all colors logically. Probably the best known is the *Munsell Color System* worked out by the painter Albert H. Munsell (1858-1918). Also well known is the *Oswald Color System* devised by the German chemist Wilhelm Oswald (1853-1932). Most encyclopedias adequately describe these systems.

138

7-5 Contrast Is Minimized When Colors of the Same Intensity Categories Are Matched

PER CENT OF VALUE (DENSITY)

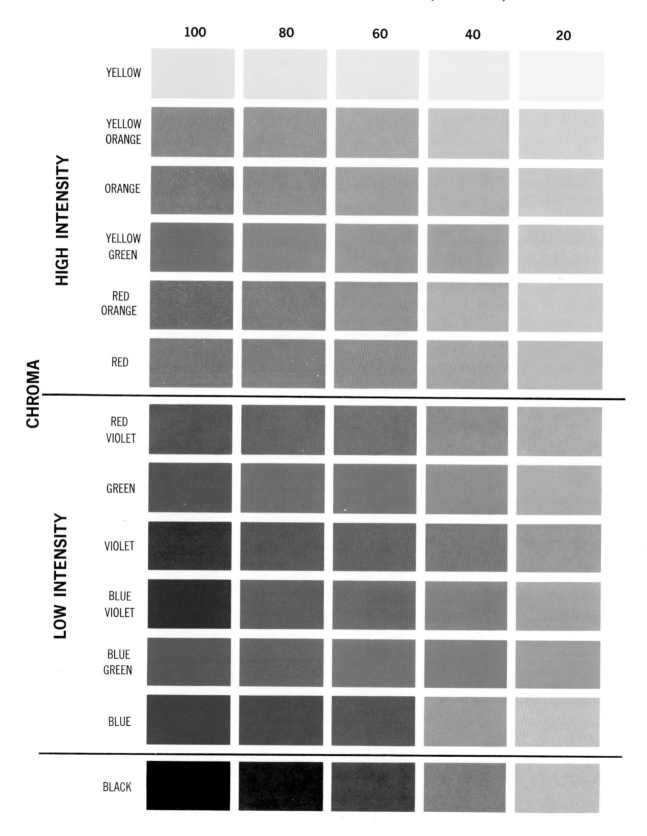

Stratification of Basic Colors

Empirically, we tend to distinguish the differences in color by chroma and value. Using this concept as a basis the chart in Figure 7-2 has been devised to show the relationships and interactions between basic color characteristics. The chart's vertical scale is a stratification of chroma (intensity) and the horizontal scale of value (density) for each color. Basic colors have been arranged on the vertical axis according to their apparent degree of brilliance, and are further segregated into two classes, high and low intensity. The high-intensity colors are yellow, yellow-orange, orange, yellow-green, red-orange, and red. The low-intensity colors are red-violet, green, blue-violet, violet, blue-green, and blue. In addition, at the bottom of the chroma scale is black.*

Using increments of 20% the horizontal scale stratifies the value (i.e. the lightness or darkness) of the colors. When color is at full strength it is said to be *pure*, and is rated at 100%. As the percentage of pureness decreases, the density of color lessens. Thus, blue, say at 60% of its value, appears to have more intensity than the more chromatic green that is at 100% of its value (Fig. 7-3). For this reason the relationship of colors tends to have one appearance in one situation and another appearance in another situation.

Guidelines to the Selection of Color

From Figure 7-2 certain guidelines can be formulated that may assist the communicator in his selection of color.

The larger the span between intensities, the greater the contrast. Since visual acuity relies on contrasting colors, the communicator should be aware of ways to maximize this effect. Black on yellow, for example, creates a very sharp contrast because of the large span between the intensities of these two colors on the vertical scale. On the other hand, pure red-violet on pure red is a poor contrast because their intensity span is shorter (Fig. 7-4). The communicator can thus achieve the degree of contrast he desires by manipulating the span of his colors.

Contrast is minimized when colors of the same intensity categories are placed adjacent to each other. This guideline is a corollary to the contrast-by-span above. When high-intensity colors are placed adjacent to other high-intensity colors, or low-intensity to low-intensity colors, contrast is minimized in almost direct relationship to the span separating the colors being juxtaposed.

In Figure 7-5, for example, the color orange is placed next to the basic colors as stratified in Figure 7-2, and as the orange moves downward, the contrast grows greater; but not until it leaves the high-intensity group does the contrast become significant. Blue moves in the opposite direction to demonstrate the same point.

In many cases, the communicator will find that low contrasting colors may well fit his needs best. For example, he may want to achieve a subtle effect on a printed cover, and so he will deliberately minimize the contrast between the colors used.

Differences in value will alter the effect of the "span of contrast." An understanding of this guideline will sharpen the communicator's judgment in selecting color.

For example, if the pure black on yellow (shown in Fig. 7-6) were modified by reducing the value of black to 20% and placing it on the 100% yellow, the contrast would lessen considerably; and, at 5% black, the contrast would be almost nullified.

Similarly, the poor contrast of pure red-violet on pure red can be modified by reducing the value of red-violet to say about 20%, which when placed on the 100% red would increase the contrast. The phenomenon that intensity is related to density allows the communicator greater flexibility in working with a limited number of basic colors.

The less chromatic colors have greater potential for value variation. This is a particularly important guideline to follow when preparing printed material. Color printing is expensive — the

---

* Two important "colors," which are not technically colors, are black and white. Neither of them appears in the color spectrum but both of them play an extremely important part in our concept of color. Actually, black, the darkest of all colors, is produced by complete absorption of all light — causing none of the spectrum to be reflected. White is black's opposite, in that no light is absorbed, and all of the spectrum is reflected. Technically then, black is the presence of all colors, and white is the absence of all color. Nevertheless, black and white are firmly implanted in our minds as specific colors — and are used as such.

more colors used, the more costly the job. Often, however, color halftones can be used in place of different colors. Halftones are percentage values of pure colors (e.g. 30% red). A printed piece, for example, can be planned in two colors — say, black and green. Yet, many variations are possible from just these two colors. Some of these variations are shown in Figure 7-7, where the top left bar is 100% black; the top right bar is pure green; the middle left bar is 20% black; the middle right bar is 40% green; the bottom left bar is 10% black and 20% green combined; and the bottom right bar is 60% green and 20% black combined.

With high-intensity colors the horizontal range of perceptible values is shorter; hence, fewer variations are possible.

Visual acuity of symbols is sharper when symbols, made of low-intensity colors, are placed on high-intensity backgrounds. Sometimes, to avoid a sense of monotony, light-colored letters are used on a dark background. This can be very effective, and a welcome change of pace. But visual acuity is at its highest when lettering and symbols are made of darker, low-intensity colors and placed on light, high-intensity backgrounds (Fig. 7-8).

An example of this guideline is the traffic sign that uses black lettering on a background of yellow — which, incidentally, is the point of highest visibility on the spectrum. This fact, however, is an apparent contradiction to the contrast-by-span guideline, since theoretically the span between white and black would be greater than that between yellow and black; nevertheless it is true. Reason would then follow that perhaps text matter should be printed on yellow stock rather than the conventional white. But this assumption is wrong. Although black on yellow is more legible, it is not logically the most readable. The difference is that the optic nerve is highly stimulated by sharp contrasts that literally explode in the viewer's mind. However, the eyes tire more quickly if subjected to prolonged periods of extreme contrast. Therefore, white, which causes less strain, is used more frequently as a background for reading purposes. The same point holds true for soft-copy visuals: too much contrast for long periods of time tires the eyes and enervates the viewer.

The density of color appears to vary depending on the size of the area it covers. The size of the area covered by a color has an effect on the density a color .appears to have. The smaller the area, the greater the density appears; and conversely, the larger the area, the less the density appears, although the value of the color remains the same.

This visual phenomenon occurs because the eyes focus on the area the color covers. If the focus is tight, as with small areas, the energy radiating from the color is concentrated, and if the focus is wide the energy is spread over the optic nerve and the density appears less.

The relevance of this phenomenon to the communicator is that he will often select a color based on a small color swatch, only to be disappointed when the color appears spread over a larger area in the end product. As a safety measure, the communicator should insist on seeing the color in the actual size it will cover. When printing is involved, a trial run should be made and examined only *after* the ink has dried.

Colors That Please

People's response to color is highly subjective. Everybody has a favorite color or colors, and many people have "hate" colors. For the most part, empathies and antipathies to different colors, while often strong, cannot be explained. Some psychologists claim that color preference is more like an involuntary reflex than a considered choice. While this may or may not be true, we do know that as a practical matter the choice of color — like politics and religion — is a very personal matter.

Color has always played a role in the culture and customs of people. The superstitions of the pagan and the language of heraldry are examples. But never has color been put to the pragmatic purposes that it has in our society: that of conditioning the psyche of "everyman" and motivating the consumer to impulse buying.

The function of color as a conditioner can be seen in the use of certain colors in factories and offices "to relieve tension." Color is also used to excite and stir the emotions, as in the make-believe world of the theatre and the festive environment of the amusement park.

141

7-6 Differences in Value Will Alter the Effect of the Span of Contrast

7-8 Low-Intensity Colors on High-Intensity Backgrounds Are Easier To See

7-7 The Less Chromatic Colors Have a Greater Potential for Value Variation

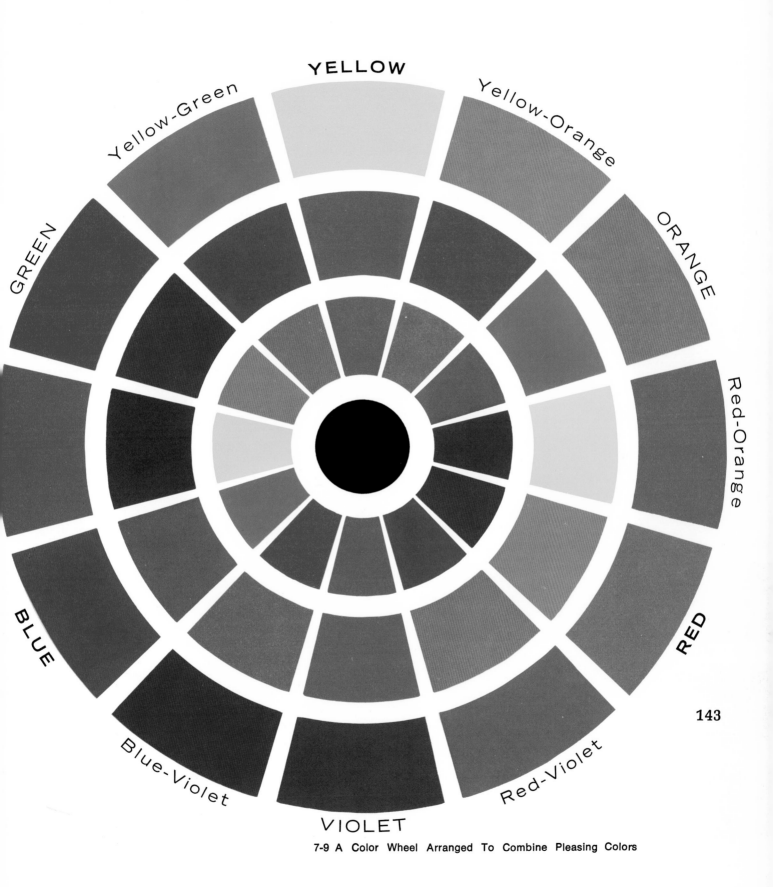

YELLOW

Yellow-Green

Yellow-Orange

GREEN

ORANGE

Red-Orange

BLUE

RED

Blue-Violet

Red-Violet

VIOLET

7-9 A Color Wheel Arranged To Combine Pleasing Colors

7-10 Color Used for Emphasis

7-11 Color Used To Differentiate

That color is a consumer persuader is evidenced by the proliferation of its use in packaging — today's silent salesmen in the competitive milieu of mass distribution. Without doubt, color has become the backbone of modern merchandising. Witness the fact that the automobile industry now makes available a wide choice of colors from which the consumer can have his pick. This is a far cry from the approach that Henry Ford took in marketing his Model T, which, he said, was available in any color of the rainbow, "so long as it's black."

Colors, like styles, pass through vogues. Ones that may have been popular yesteryear may today be regarded as unacceptable. In addition, technology is continually providing us with "new" colors that increase the range of preference and widen the diversity of opinion.

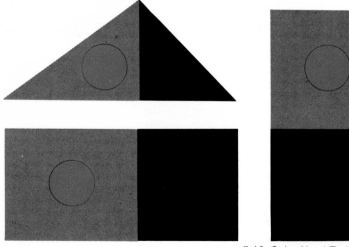

7-12 Color Used To Identify

The effect of color on people, however, should concern the communicator only obliquely, because his use of color is somewhat different. The use of color in charting is an impersonal use. Moreover, it is a transitory use, in that the same color is used over and over again without taking on a permanent meaning. And, also, the use of color in charting is functional, in that it plays a specific role in the communication (e.g., to emphasize, identify, or differentiate). Therefore, since color bias is usually limited to people paying attention to the color of the things they own and clothes they wear, it is unlikely that the communicator will encounter strong objections to the colors he selects in charting. Of course, this does not mean that color can be used indiscriminately.

By and large, the colors that the communicator selects must be pleasing. But colors that please cannot always be agreed upon. While we are aware that likes and dislikes are virtually impossible to fathom, we also know that certain color combinations are generally accepted as pleasing.

In their attempt to identify and describe these colors, and their combinations, researchers have created their own thesaurus: warm, cold, positive, negative, chromatic, achromatic, advancing, receding, complementary, near-complementary, adjacent, triadal, and so forth. Throughout the many systems, however, the underlying principle that determines pleasurable colors is "harmony." In one way or another, all terminology ascribed to color combinations depicts a harmonious relationship. And though many of these combinations will have their disputants and adherents, there are also many combinations that most people will agree are in harmony.

When the color expert speaks of color harmony he is referring to various color combinations, derived from the color wheel, that look well together. For example, on a conventional wheel complementary colors are opposing colors, such as yellow and violet, red and green, orange and blue, and so forth. Another example of harmony is the color triad, which consists of three colors on the wheel spaced an equal distance apart, such as yellow, blue, and red; or orange, violet, and green.

Figure 7-9 is a three-ringed color wheel. The outer ring is a "conventional" wheel, in that the color yellow is positioned at "12 o'clock" and the other eleven colors are placed in the standard sequence moving clockwise.* The other rings of the figure are variations on this outer ring: the middle ring has blue-green and the inner ring has red-orange in the 12 o'clock position. Except for these differences the colors on the middle and inner ring are in standard sequence and move in a clockwise direction.

This three-ringed color wheel was devised to assist the communicator in his selection of colors by providing him with predetermined color harmonies that are pleasing (although it is entirely possible that some readers may disagree). Initially, the combinations shown in Figure 7-9 were developed empirically; however, a subsequent examination revealed a very logical pattern. To explain: the combinations for yellow on the outer ring were found by moving three steps counterclockwise to blue-green (this was an arbitrary formula based on the observation that yellow and blue-green made a pleasing combination). Thus, blue-green was entered on the middle-ring, below and adjacent to yellow. Next, the complement of blue-green, which is red-orange (its opposite on the outer ring), was placed on the inner ring as being pleasing with both blue-green and yellow. The other combinations were found in the same way: three steps counterclockwise

---

* This color wheel contains twelve colors. However, many wheels contain a great many more variations and hence many more colors. Generally, all color wheels move in a clockwise direction.

for the middle ring, and a complement for the inner ring.

Many other pleasing combinations can be found by manipulating and juxtaposing the colors of a wheel. As another example, trial and error empirically found that yellow and orange was a pleasing combination, as were orange and red, red and violet, violet and blue, blue and green, and green and yellow. Note that the full circle was completed — beginning and ending with yellow. The pattern, or course, is a simple one that consists of alternating colors on the twelve-part wheel. Interestingly enough, these colors are primary and binary ones. The same alternating sequence using intermediate colors (i.e. yellow-orange, red-orange, red-violet, etc.) did not necessarily produce pleasing combinations.

There is little in the way of hard and fast rules to offer communicators who wish or need to use color. Many people (even those with considerable experience) are convinced that they use color "flying by the seat of their pants." This, however, is hard to believe. Chartists seldom arbitrarily pick colors — even though they may think they do. The instinct for selecting pleasing colors comes from years of experiencing colors in every facet of our lives. Without being fully aware, we have schooled ourselves to accept color combinations that have been prevalent and acceptable to our culture and generation. Except for the highly experienced practitioner, most chartists will select color by trial and error — i.e., first matching one set, then another, and so on, until he is satisfied that a particular combination looks best. Into this selection have gone all the color conditioning and exposure that have filled his past experience. And because he has been subjected to the same environment as his audience the chances are great that he will meet little or no opposition to his selections.

Thus, in using color the communicator should bear in mind that: (1) color bias, which usually applies to personal possessions, seldom enters into the selection of colors used in charting; (2) colors that please are founded on harmonies that are developed empirically; (3) instinctive color preferences are based on prior exposure and experience, and will most probably be common to an audience that has shared this background; and (4) the intent of using color in charting is not only to please visually, but to perform specific functions.

The Functions of Color

Color, used as a visual aid, adds a dimension to the visual that is impossible to achieve with any other kind of graphic adornment. Color attracts the reader; it excites his imagination and it pleases the eye. Yet the functions of color in charting reach beyond merely making a visual attractive. We know, for example, that color is an excellent means of creating *emphasis*. Colors of contrasting value can be used to arrest the eye of the viewer and cause him to focus his attention on a particular point of emphasis (Fig. 7-10).

Color *differentiates* more effectively than any other method. It can be used as a "label" that distinguishes one group from others (Fig. 7-11). Moreover, differentiation can be made rapidly and accurately. Consider, for example, a fast-moving game like football in which uniform colors allow the players to differentiate friend from foe instantaneously.

Color is used to *identify*. The green of the Irish and the red of the Communist are color suggestions that are used as identifications in the conceptual sense. Color, as an identifier, is commonplace in trademarks, for example. As such, it is symbolic.

Color-coding, or *color-keying*, is a technique used to identify by color. It is a simple device whereby a particular entity is assigned a color that represents it within the context of a presentation. Suppose, for example, we had a presentation in which Tom, Dick, and Harry were to be symbolically represented as squares. Color could be used to identify each of them: Tom, by a red square; Dick, a blue; and Harry, a green. Accordingly, the easy and rapid identification made possible by using color-coding is shown in Figure 7-12. In color-coding, colors take on a meaning assigned to them by the communicator.

The Meanings of Color

We see color everywhere. It is such a natural part of our experience that, aside from color preferences, we attach little significance to its presence in the things about us. At a more conscious level, however, color does have meaning. White,

for a bride; blue, for a boy; and pink, for a girl are common associations. Yet, the meanings of color are ambiguous, continually changing according to customs and cultures.

In ancient symbolism color played an important role in the lives of people. Their meanings were very practical ones based on visual experience. For instance, red was related to the blood of sacrifice that was the cornerstone of a religion to placate their omnipotent gods. Thus the color red had a profound significance to pagans. Similarly, yellow had a religious meaning connected to the sun — the granddaddy of all gods. So yellow symbolized strength and wisdom and most of all light — which drove away the demons of darkness.

Early Christianity brought a different interpretation to colors, based on mysticism. For instance, the red that had signified blood to the pagan now connoted heat to the Christian — and there was no place hotter than the netherworld of Hades. Yellow took on the meaning of earth, probably because the source from which Christianity sprung was the sun-baked land of the Bible.

A millenium later heraldry adopted red and yellow still differently. Color is important in the language of heraldry; its meanings are precise. For instance, red is for courage and zeal, and yellow for honor and loyalty. (Ironically, the present day attribute for yellow in connection with a warrior is diametrically opposite.)

Heraldry also used black for grief and penitence, and today we still regard black as a sign of mourning. Strangely enough, the origin of wearing black had nothing to do with demonstrating grief. It was born of fear. In pagan days people's dread of the dead far exceeded their respect. In order to escape being haunted by the spirit of the corpse they disguised themselves in black and hoped against hope that the ghost of the deceased would fail to recognize them.

Black, however, appears to be the absence of color, and since all living things have color, black was rationalized as the most appropriate to represent death.

Although the association is a strong one in Western civilization, black has never been a universal color of mourning. The Burmese use yellow; the Turks violet; some parts of China use white, while other parts use purple; and in the

South Seas some Islanders purportedly use black and white stripes. Thus the meanings of colors come and go and differ.

Color has also crept into our language and can be found in common sayings that have long since grown banal. The origins of most of these sayings are obscure, but a close examination reveals that a great many of them are based on what can be seen.

Take, for example, someone who is "in the pink": his complexion is one that radiates good health. Anger may cause him to become "purple with rage": his face reflects his mounting blood pressure. Or he may take on a sickly color when he becomes "green with envy." He may also "turn white" as fear drains the blood from his face. Fear may also give rise to a jaundiced pallor, branding him "yellow."

Meanings of color are also used in very practical ways. Signs of yellow and black warn us of danger. This combination of colors used as diagonal stripes is especially effective to identify hazardous areas. In industrial settings safety equipment is painted green, and dispensaries are identified by a green cross. Fire apparatus is usually colored red, and purple has become a warning signal in atomic energy complexes.

The meaning of any color is by no means precise, yet paradoxically its meaning can be unequivocal in a given context. For example, the red and green of a traffic light can only mean stop and go. But, as we have seen, red has many meanings — and yet no meaning in itself.

Thus, it is the context that determines the meaning of color. In most cases the communicator will have the prerogative of assigning particular meanings to the colors he uses. However, he should guard against picking colors that already have specific associations to his audience.

Color enhances a presentation, whether it be oral or printed. Its use, however, is expensive, and an extensive use of color — particularly in printed presentations — can be very expensive. The appropriateness of using color depends a great deal on the audience and purpose of the communication. It would, for example, be less than prudent to use profusely colored charts in a routine report to a management committee on cost reduction.

The economics of using color depend mainly on the vehicle used for the presentation — a fact which should be borne in mind in the selection of medium.

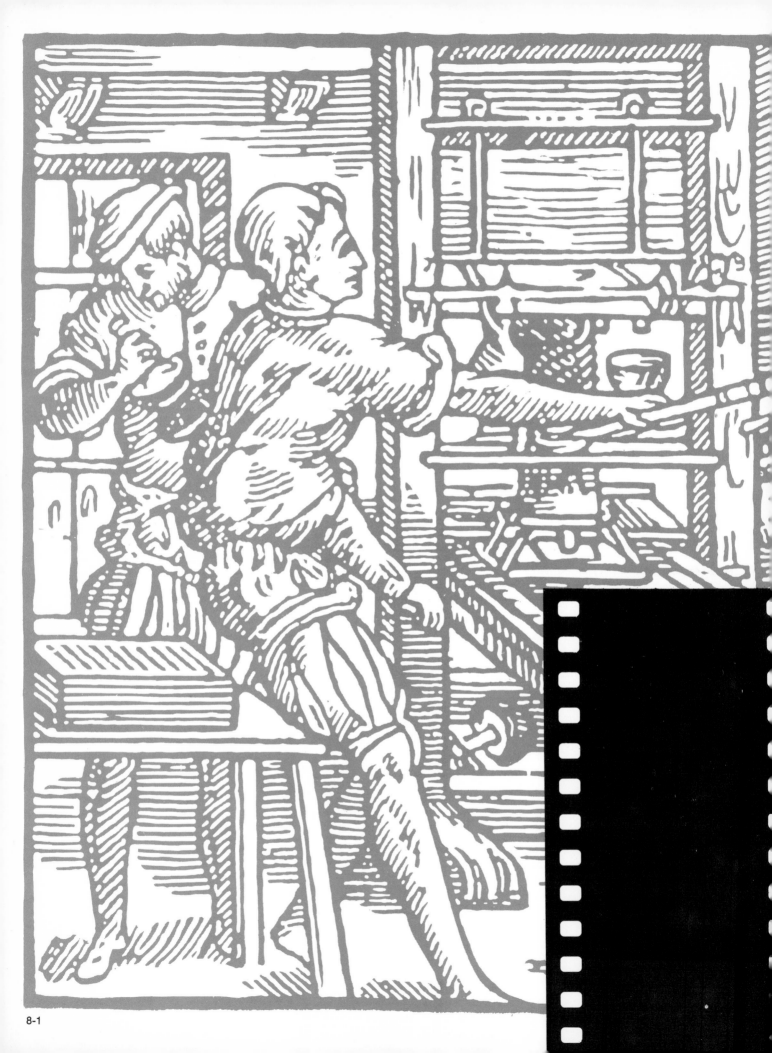

8-1

8

Selection of Medium

The medium of mass communication was baptized with ink in the fifteenth century, when Johann Gutenberg invented movable type and gave the printing press a new dimension. The apparatus was crude, and its meager output reached an audience limited to the very few who were literate. In the following 400 years the spread of printed matter gained momentum, and by the close of the nineteenth century its proliferation had generated an intellectual explosion that shaped the course of mankind.

The early part of our present century introduced another milestone in the evolution of mass media — the motion picture. Its flickering images with their staccato-like movement replaced the archaic lantern slide and ushered in a new era of visual communications. But it was not until Al Jolson stepped before the camera to become the Jazz Singer that sound was added to the projected image, and the modern "talkie" was born. With the addition of sound the silver screen became (and remains) the queen of the projection media. However, as a practical tool it was beyond the economic reach of the industrial and educational communicator, who needed a fast, flexible, and cheap means of projection, but at a lower cost than seemed possible in the motion picture field.

It took more than a decade, and another World War, to lift commercial projection media out of their infancy into adolescence. The mobilization of some fourteen million Americans into the armed forces required more rapid and efficient methods for orientation, indoctrination, and plain old-fashioned teaching. There was a lot to learn, and not much time in which to learn it. It was this necessity that spurred the development of projection media as training aids for large audiences.

During the postwar years many pioneers, armed with the knowledge of the potentials of audio-visual techniques, sought to introduce those concepts into the many facets of academic and business life. They were helped and encouraged by corporate giants like Eastman Kodak, which, pushing to make photography a household word, used their cost-saving technology and innovations to penetrate the sleeping commercial markets.

By the late 1950s their crusade was won, and the audio-visual presentation became an accepted means of modern communication. We know, even from our brief experience, that the combination of sound and sight has far-reaching effects on the minds of its audiences. Yet we also know that we have just begun to tap the potential that lies ahead.

Today most communicators subscribe to the concepts of the audio-visual presentation — if for no other reason than to cope with the information explosion spawned in the 1960s. Furthermore, the communicator is also aware that the choice of medium used as a communicative link between himself and his audience has a direct bearing on the success of his presentation. Thus, from the many media available to him, he is confronted with the task of selecting the one best suited to his purpose.

Basically, there are two types of media from which the communicator can choose: non-projected images, which are called *hard copy,* and projected images, which are called *soft copy.*

Hard and soft copy differ in two ways that can seriously affect the process of selection. The first difference is that soft copy can be projected, to magnify its image, whereas hard copy, for all practical purposes, cannot. Secondly, soft copy can be easily reproduced from a master copy, whereas each hard-copy reproduction requires the same amount of effort as did the original (except for mass reproduction by printing).

Within the hard and soft copy categories a number of media can be identified and described.

Hard-Copy Media

CHALKBOARDS   The chalkboard (better known as a blackboard, even though many are not black) is perhaps the oldest medium still in use. As students, all of us have seen how a chalkboard operates; probably we can even recall how the excruciating sound of squeaking chalk tingled our nerve ends.

Chalkboards are especially effective in classroom situations, where they can be used for impromptu visual explanations of points that are difficult to grasp. As a medium the chalkboard is inexpensive and easy to use. However, it has some rather unfortunate disadvantages. For one thing, the visual material recorded on the board has no permanence, since it must be erased in order to record subsequent material. Another disadvantage is that visual material drawn on the board tends to be extremely primitive, unless the presenter has unusual artistic skill. Even with skill it is difficult to draw detailed illustrations with chalk. The final disadvantage is the fact

that the presenter is forced to turn away from his audience each time he records something on the board. By having to do this continually, he breaks face-to-face contact and may lose control of his audience.

EASEL PADS   The easel pad, as its name implies, is a pad of inexpensive newsprint sheets mounted on an easel so constructed that the completed pages can be torn away or flipped over the top.

In concept, the easel pad is very much like the chalkboard, and except for two essential differences it has the same drawbacks. One difference is that the visual material is permanent; completed sheets can be flipped back and forth to recapture a point made at a prior time. The other is that the individual sheets of an easel pad are portable. (That is, sheets can be torn off and carried away conveniently to some other locations.) Both differences make the easel pad more flexible than the chalkboard.

Another advantage of the easel pad is that visual material can be made much more exciting, by using colored grease pencils and magic markers, than it can ever be on a chalkboard, even with colored chalk. Often the artwork can be prepared in advance, sometimes with a high degree of artistry — especially if it has been executed by professionals.

PANEL BOARDS   Conceptually, a panel board is any chart that is used in its original form and presented as an individual part of a series in a presentation.

Panel boards can be made from various materials, and they are usually identified by the material used. For instance, a *flannel board* is made by stretching a piece of flannel over a firm surface. The visual material added to this base is backed with nylon flocking or coarse sandpaper. The *magnetic board* is another type of panel. As one might expect, it is made by placing a metal sheet over a firm surface. The visual material is added by means of tiny magnets or magnetic rubber. There are also a number of plastic panel boards identified by the particular type of plastic used, for example, a *vinyl board*. The visual material added to these boards is backed with gummed adhesives. Other materials like paper, felt, wood,

8-2 The Chalkboard (Photo by Robert Muir)

cork, or even combinations of materials can also be used.

Many charts originally made for some other medium can also be used as panel boards. For example, sheets taken from an easel pad and used as individual units in a presentation no longer belong to the easel-pad medium, but are considered panel boards. Similarly, a piece of finished art that will subsequently be photographed as a 35mm. slide can be used as an individual unit in a panel-board presentation.

By and large, panel boards are not widely used as a presentation medium. The cost of materials for almost any type of panel board is nominal, but since they cannot be mass-reproduced like transparencies, the time to prepare them can be a real consideration in planning a budget. Of course, in cases where only one set of boards is needed, the cost will be little different from the preparation required for a soft-copy medium.

FLIP CHARTS Flip charts are a series of panel boards that are housed in a binder, hinged, or fastened together at the top, so that the presenter can progressively disclose his presentation by flipping one chart at a time.

Normally, the flip chart is put together from prepared charts made of lightweight material, or from photographs of such charts. Chart sizes are restricted to the sizes of the holders that are commercially available (with the maximum being about 18 by 24 inches).

The flip chart is widely used because it is convenient to carry around, it can be placed on a desk top, and it creates the impression of an intimate person-to-person presentation.

In most cases, flip charts are comparatively inexpensive to put together. However, elaborate artwork may drive the unit price for a single chart up to as much as $100.

Soft-Copy Media

OPAQUE PROJECTION Figure 8-3 illustrates opaque projection. The opaque object is brilliantly illuminated by a powerful lamp assisted by two reflectors. The light, reflected off the surface of the object, is directed to a mirror, which in turn channels it through a system of lenses. The result is an image of the object that is projected onto a screen.

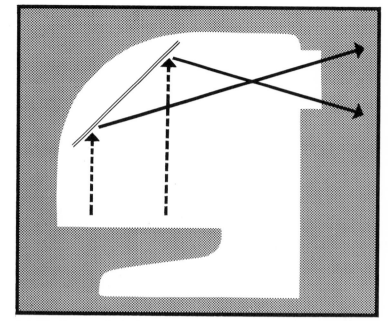

8-3 The Opaque Projector

As a method of projection it is unique because it is the only soft-copy medium that does not require a transparency as an intermediary step. As a matter of fact, opaque projection really projects hard copy as soft copy, and although it has the soft-copy characteristic of magnification, it lacks the essential characteristic of easy reproduction. Perhaps the singular advantage of opaque projection is that it makes possible the projection of printed matter and small three-dimensional objects *without prior preparation.*

Attractive as this possibility may be, opaque projection has some severe disadvantages. For example, the quality of the projected image is generally poor, because much of the illuminating light is absorbed by the object, and only a fraction of this light reaches the screen. Furthermore, the poor quality of the projected image limits the area of the audience viewing zone, and adequate viewing can only be achieved by completely darkening the room.

The powerful lamp required to illuminate the object is a further disadvantage because the lamp's heat may damage the object on the projection platform (as well as burning the fingers that remove the object). In order to dissipate the heat a powerful air blower, which makes an infernal racket, is required. And finally, opaque projectors are heavy, bulky, and difficult to transport. While opaque projectors are seldom used, there are other soft-copy media, like overhead projection, that are used quite extensively.

151

8-4 The Overhead Projector in Action (Photo by Robert Muir)

OVERHEAD PROJECTION The principle of overhead projection is illustrated in Figure 8-4. Basically, the machine is similar to a light table. A film transparency is placed on a surface (which is called a stage). Then, from below, a lamp throws light onto a mirror that reflects this light upward, through the film transparency and onto another mirror housed in a periscope-like device above the stage. In Figure 8-5 this second mirror redirects the light through a lens to project an image of the transparency onto a screen. In Figure 8-6 the lens is positioned between the stage and the second mirror housed in the periscope device above the stage.

As a training aid, overhead projection is considered the most versatile of the soft-copy media. The most common film transparency size is 10 by 10 inches; 5-by-5-inch and 7-by-7-inch sizes are also available, but not often used. The transparency can be constructed in single or multiple layers of film, and removable overlays can be effectively employed for progressive-disclosure techniques. Moreover, a good assortment of colors can be used to enhance the visual material.

Overhead projection has some distinct advantages that stem from the fact that the mirror system and the short-focal-length lens of the projector allow the projector to be located in front of the audience, and only a short distance from the screen. The picture in Figure 8-4 shows the position of the projector relative to the presenter and his audience. Because of this proximity the presenter can face his audience and simultaneously operate the machine, thereby controlling the pace of his presentation.

Since the presenter has access to the projector he can easily use a grease pencil or felt pen to revise or emphasize the material on the film transparency. These changes will immediately appear on the projected image that is located above and behind him. Similarly, he can write on a blank film transparency and create a visual on the spot.

In addition, the overhead projector can be operated in a fully lighted room — a distinct advantage over other soft-copy media. As a further advantage, transparencies are easy to make and comparatively inexpensive to process. The average cost of a transparency is quite nominal (exclusive of artwork time). Simple visuals are very inexpensive, and can be made in minutes by passing an original document, along with a sheet of transparency film, through office copying machines like Thermofax or Xerox. More complicated visuals, however, require considerable artwork that is subsequently passed through similar diazo-process machines. Complicated visuals, moreover, tend to have many overlays that restrict the amount of light passing through them, and consequently reduce the image brightness.

Overhead projection also has limitations. The larger model projector is bulky to transport and awkward to set up. And, finally, although overhead projection works well for informal training

152

sessions, the medium lacks the polish and sophistication necessary for more professional presentations.

In many instances the necessary polish required for a particular audience can be met by advancing a step beyond the overhead projector to slides.

SLIDES The term "slide" usually refers to smaller individual transparencies produced by photography and projected as still pictures. They can be photographed in black and white or color; the latter has much greater appeal and is, therefore, growing rapidly in popularity and usage.

although the term is seldom heard. These projectors actually take slides of several different aperture sizes, although the mount size remains 2 by 2 inches in all cases. The most common aperture is 23 by 34mm. (in Eastman Kodak mounts), and this is the standard and familiar "35mm." slide. Other aperture sizes are the Super slide, 38mm. square; the Instamatic slide, 28mm. square; and the "half-frame" 35mm. slide, which has an approximate aperture of 23 by 17mm. Since all these slides are mounted in 2-by-2-inch frames, they will fit into a 35mm. projector. But they may not all project equally well, and the user should test any projector he plans to buy

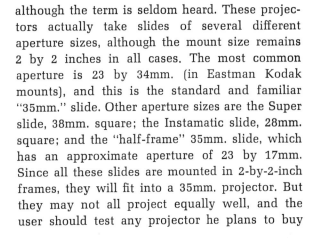

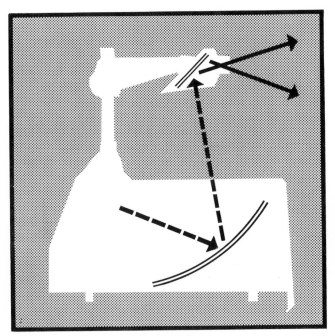
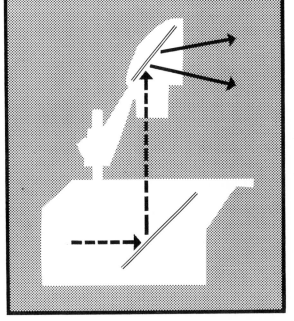

8-5, 8-6 Two Kinds of Overhead Projector

Slides come in various sizes, and can be classified (1) by the size of their mounts, (2) by film or camera size, and (3) by the actual transparency area size — which is referred to as the "aperture." There are three commonly used mount sizes: 2 by 2 inches, 2¼ by 2¼ inches, and 3¼ by 4 inches, the last generally called a lantern slide. Each size fits one of the three main projectors on the market: the 35mm. projector, the 2¼-by-2¼-inch projector, and the standard lantern-slide projector.

The 35mm. projector, however, is more accurately designated as a "2-by-2" projector,

with the slides he plans to use.

The 2¼-by-2¼-inch projector takes only slides mounted in that size frame, and the mounted slide has an aperture of 2-3/16-inch square. These slides are photographed with a "2¼" camera, like a Rolleiflex or Hasselblad.

The term "lantern slide" once referred to any still transparency used for projection, but now applies almost exclusively to larger transparencies having mounts of 3¼ by 4 inches and an aperture of 2¾ by 3 inches (Kodak mounts). The slides are traditionally made by contact-printing a negative on a lantern plate — a glass plate

153

with a photographic emulsion. If a full plate is to be used, the camera would have to be large enough to accept a 4-by-5-inch negative, putting it into the "press" or "view" categories. Smaller formats have been used, however, by masking out part of the plate area.

Recently the Polaroid company has introduced a film for its industrial camera that makes lantern-size transparencies directly on film—for which it supplies plastic mounts.

Projectors used for 3¼-by-4-inch mounts must be standard lantern-slide projectors, manufactured by such companies as Bausch & Lomb and Beseler. The projectors are naturally heavier and take higher-powered bulbs, which produce considerable heat. Some are adaptable to smaller slide formats, through the use of accessory lenses, slide carriers, and the like, but none, apparently, has the automatic capabilities of smaller-format projectors, and they are designed

primarily for auditorium use with a projectionist standing by.

Both 2¼-by-2¼-inch and lantern slides are occasionally used for presentations, but they are more expensive to photograph, process, and project. (Lantern slides, incidentally, are generally limited to black and white because of their method of production, although it is possible to mount a large color transparency in a lantern-slide mount.) Projectors for 2¼-inch slides are somewhat more versatile than lantern-slide projectors but still do not have the facilities available on 35mm. projectors, particularly the ease of loading, removing, and selecting individual slides of the Kodak Carousel, for instance.

The numbers and kinds of presentations using slides have expanded rapidly, primarily because this medium combines many of the separate advantages of other media. For instance, slides can be used in presentations to both large and

8-7 A 35mm. Projector in Action (Photo by Robert Muir)

small audiences. The 35mm. slide is considered effective for audiences numbering up to two hundred, while lantern slides can be used for audiences up to a thousand.

Actually, however, 35mm. slides can be equally effective with very large audiences, as long as the projection conditions are right. This is because the aperture size of the slide is not as important as the light output of the projector. In a fully darkened, properly set up projection room, 35mm. will do as well as the lantern slide, whose strength lies in its more powerful projector, not in its size. After all, many commercial movies are shot with 16mm. film, which is considerably smaller in area than a 35mm. slide.

Another reason for the increasing popularity of slide presentations is their professional appearance, which increases their versatility of application. They can be appropriately used for any kind of audience, from executive meetings to classrooms.

Slides also have the important advantage of timing control; that is, the presentation can be controlled and paced by the presenter to meet his needs. Moreover, because slides are individual frames they can be sequenced and resequenced in any order. This flexibility is invaluable in presentations which are modularly conceived to meet a variety of circumstances.

The portability of this medium is also beneficial. The equipment used for slide projection can be conveniently transported and set up. Peripheral equipment like remote control, tape recorder hookups, and dissolve devices are available readily and at moderate cost.

Finally, slides are easy to distribute, store, and retrieve, factors of importance with the increasing use of audio-visual presentations.

The economics of producing slides varies with the elaborateness of the artwork used. The slide transparencies themselves are relatively inexpensive to produce. The photography step of slide production is a nominal cost if in-house photography is available; commercial studio charges depend on local price structures, but should not cost more than $5.00 per first copy. Additional copies can be ordered at the same time at reduced rates, and duplicates can be made at a later date from an original slide also at a lesser cost.

Glass mounting, rather than the cardboard mounting used by the film processor, is desirable because it eliminates focus shift caused by projector heat and protects the slide from damage and soilage through handling. Glass mounting also prevents out-of-focus edges, which result from a curvature in the slide that is sometimes built in by the processer when he is mounting it. The purpose of the curvature is to avoid the focus shift that occurs when the slide "pops" under projector heat. But the curve makes the edges of the slide unusable since they are out of focus when the center is in focus.

The slide medium also has some limitations. For instance, slides cannot be projected in a fully lighted room (although a totally darkened room is not necessary). Also, any changes required in the slide cannot be made on the transparency. The change must be done on the original artwork, and a new slide photographed.

All in all, however, the slide medium is a versatile one in which the communicator can easily find the solutions to many of his media problems. Although slides are projected as individual units they are often "strung" together in a continuous strip. Once this is done, a filmstrip is created.

FILMSTRIP This medium is also known as a stripfilm, or slidefilm, and when used in conjunction with a sound track, a sound/slide film. A filmstrip is a continuous strip of slide frames that are projected as still images. The image area is usually about half that of 35mm. slides. Each frame in a filmstrip is photographed from a panel board or an individual original slide.

Because the production methods employed in making filmstrips are frequently more elaborate than in making 35mm. slide presentations, costs tend to run higher. For instance, in order to produce a highly polished soundtrack a professional narrator should be hired; to record him, studio time, along with its technicians, must be engaged; and to integrate his tape with the visuals, sound-synchronization equipment must be employed — all of which drive up expenditures.

Also, in-house photo setups are less likely to attempt filmstrips because of the need for continuous sequencing and because of other techni-

155

cal difficulties, such as color balancing and image-size uniformity. Moreover, the artwork used in filmstrips is usually more complex and elaborate in order to simulate animation—or at least stop-motion. Consequently, the usual in-house economies are not available. Given the higher costs, filmstrip presentations are more likely to be justified when a large number of copies is needed. With few exceptions, the economics of this medium requires quantity production and mass distribution to be practical.

The communicator has three options in making a presentation with a filmstrip. The first is a fully manual presentation: the oral part of the presentation is given "live" and a button is pressed to advance the frames on the strip. The second is partially manual: the sound part of the presentation is recorded and an audible beep signal is built into the recording. When the signal sounds, the operator advances to the next frame by manually pressing the button. The third is fully automatic: the presentation is recorded and a film-advance signal is built into the recording. The projector is placed on "automatic" and the frames are advanced by the inaudible advance signal.

The chief advantage of a filmstrip, when used with an oral or recorded presentation, is that the sequence of the slide frames will never be out of order, nor will the frames inadvertently appear upside down. In this respect the filmstrip is a fixed package that is convenient to handle (although the strip roll is subject to damage and soiling because it has no protective covering). The virtue of a fixed order, however, is also a disadvantage, since the inflexibility of frame sequencing does not allow editing, which is sometimes necessary to fit a particular situation.

Adding recorded sound to a filmstrip provides a uniformity of performance, which is considered an advantage. Communicators know that no two oral presentations—given either by the same person or by different persons—can ever be exactly the same. Obviously, some will be better than others. With the sound/slide technique a recording of the presentation can be perfected that will ensure a uniformity of performance. Thus, the quality of a sound/slide presentation will not vary from showing to showing. (A tape

recorder tied into a carousel projector will accomplish the same result, although the quality of the recording will not be as good as one made professionally.)

By and large the production of a filmstrip can be expensive, especially when the audio is built in as a record or tape. As in other media, the cost of the artwork will depend on its elaborateness.

Projection equipment for filmstrips is readily available. It is compact, lightweight, and easy to transport and set up.

Often the continuous movement the filmstrip medium tries to capture can only be accomplished by the medium of motion pictures.

MOTION PICTURES The motion picture is a moving record of an action captured on film. Although we are accustomed to thinking of motion pictures as a source of entertainment they also have applications in education, science, and business. Outside of the movie industry, 16mm. sound films are generally used, but in some cases 8mm. and/or silent films are sufficient.

The motion picture so closely simulates reality that it draws the viewer in to share the experience occurring on the screen. Accordingly, it is probably the most effective training tool we have. Not only do movies provide continuity of movement, but the rate of movement can also be varied. For example, the lengthy process of an egg hatching can be speeded up through photography and the entire process can be compressed into a few minutes. Conversely, actions that occur so rapidly that their movements defy the human eye can be shown in slow motion.

156

8-8 A Sound /Slide Filmstrip Projector (Photo Courtesy of Dukane Corp.)

The motion picture is probably the most complete audio-visual aid. It combines motion and sound to produce a credibility no other medium can achieve. To heighten the experience, color can be added, although most viewers, having been conditioned to black and white through years of movie-going, will not notice the absence of color.

The quality of presentation with this medium is as good as the movie itself is — it will never vary from showing to showing. Motion pictures, like filmstrips, have their sequences locked in place, and any change necessitates redoing the reel.

But the cost of motion pictures is high and the production time long. Movie-making is mostly beyond the capabilities of in-house personnel and equipment, and must be made in conjunction with a professional producer. The advantage of the motion picture is that it is a complete audio-visual package that is acceptable to the average viewer — even a bad movie will be tolerated. Its main disadvantage is the investment that is required in time and money. Furthermore, there are some situations for which the motion picture would not be a good choice, for example, a sales presentation; the chemistry between seller and buyer is so important that the impersonal nature of the motion picture would be an impediment.

Criteria for Selection

There are many considerations that enter into selecting the medium for a particular presentation. At first it may appear that a number of choices are possible, but subsequent investigation will reveal that many of these choices are eliminated, either by the nature of the presentation or by other limitations connected to it. For example, a presentation conceived as a client proposal may, in the eyes of the sales executive, rule out less sophisticated media like overhead projection or easel pads. On the other hand, a budgetary limitation might preclude the more expensive presentation media. Or perhaps the availability of certain equipment in particular locations may become the determining factor in selection.

There are a number of ways in which to approach selecting a medium. One way is to rely on prior experience; that is, to assume that what has worked satisfactorily before will, under similar conditions, work just as well again. (Another way, is to choose the medium that suits the production facilities available, but this approach can hardly be considered a selection process.)

Assuming that the various types of media are equally available, selection can be made easier if a logical approach is employed, one that systematically eliminates the inappropriate media so that only those eligible to meet the needs of the presentation can be concentrated upon.

Such an approach would examine the needs of a presentation, according to certain criteria for selection, and then evaluate the media according to ratings drawn from the criteria. The following discussion defines these criteria, which are then compared to the different media in Figure 8-9.

THE SIZE OF THE AUDIENCE Audience size is the first criterion in selecting a medium. Most soft-copy media can be used with almost any size audience, since the image size on the screen can be varied within wide limits by adjusting projector distances and/or focal lengths (page 172). Soft-copy media can accommodate large audiences, often numbering in the hundreds. On the other hand, opaque projection limits the size of the audience because its light output is poor and it produces a weak image. Hard-copy media are automatically eliminated when the number of the audience exceeds 15 to 20 people.

For rating purposes, on the chart in Figure 8-9 audiences that are considered *large* number over 50 people, *medium* from 20 to 50, and *small* fewer than 20 people.

THE CHARACTER OF THE AUDIENCE This criterion plays a subtle, (but necessary) role in media selection. Audience rank, in most cases, determines the degree of polish a presentation should have. For example, a presentation made to a large potential client generally requires a greater polish than one given to a class of trainees (Chapter 10).

Once the character of an audience is determined, it can be rated (in Figure 8-9) as: *first degree*, those which require the impact of a top-grade presentation; *second degree*, those which

157

need to be impressed by the presentation's form, but not overly so; and *third degree,* those for which content is important, and form merely secondary — such as in a classroom.

THE PRODUCTION LEAD TIME The amount of time provided to produce a presentation is a key criterion in selecting a medium. It is difficult to generalize on the length of time it takes to produce an audio-visual package. A long slide presentation, for example, may take as much time to produce as a short filmstrip. In addition, it is difficult to generalize on the amount of work that goes into making the individual pieces of artwork that go into a presentation. Some may be one-line Word charts, whereas others can be multicolored, complex pieces of artwork. Therefore, the amount of production lead time needed for any particular medium can vary with the circumstances involved.

However, some broad observations can be made (for instance, it is obvious that producing a motion picture will take substantially longer than a flip-chart presentation), and by using a reasonably paced presentation that runs about an hour as a frame of reference, some benchmarks can be established. The number of slide frames or film transparencies needed for an hour-long presentation averages about fifty, filmstrip frames about 200, panel boards less than fifty, and motion-picture footage infinitely more than 200 (1400 feet for silent and 2000 feet for sound).

Thus, from these approximations, production lead time can be rated (in Figure 8-9) as: *long,* being over six months; *medium,* less than six months but more than a month; *short,* less than a month; and *none,* which means that no production time is required prior to the presentation.

THE PRODUCTION BUDGET The amount of money allotted for a presentation will eliminate certain media from consideration. For example, the subject of a proposed presentation may lend itself ideally to a motion picture. However, the estimated cost of making a movie is $1,000 a minute for finished footage, and the total expenditure may exceed the amount budgeted for the presentation.

Cost depends on many factors; among others:

medium used, length of the presentation, its audience, and production lead time. Take the last as an example: the lead time may be such that in-house facilities cannot meet the imposed deadline, and the production must then be farmed out to a commercial studio — probably doubling, or tripling the out-of-pocket costs.

The production budget is a criterion that must be considered realistically before any commitment is made to begin work on a presentation. Hidden costs, which exist in virtually all media, must be rooted out and accounted for in the planning stages. Unfortunately, many cost factors are variables that depend on the specific circumstances surrounding the presentation. The range of prices is so large that it defies generalization. For rating purposes (in Figure 8-9) however, limits for production budgets for an hour-long presentation can be set as: *high,* over $3,000; *average,* approximately $1,000; *small,* less than $500; and *none,* which indicates that the investment is nominal and not worth considering.

THE NUMBER OF COPIES REQUIRED This criterion has a bearing on the selection of the medium insofar as some media do not permit the reproduction of many copies economically.

Except for printing, which involves very large quantities, the cost and time involved in the reproduction of hard copy is equal to the amounts required to produce the original. For example, to duplicate an easel-pad presentation takes the same effort as did the original. Of course, the easel-pad presentation can be copied by photography, but then the reproduction is in a different medium. Soft-copy media are mechanically reproduced at a fraction of the cost and time spent on the original.

Not only does the number of copies required affect media choice from the standpoint of reproduction possibilities and cost, it also affects distribution costs, in that, for some media, visuals are more expensive to ship than for others. For example, to send multiple copies of 10-by-10-inch transparencies to a number of locations around the country costs considerably more than sending comparable slides, filmstrips, or even a reel of a motion picture. Of course, unless many shipments are made, this cost factor is not significant.

Moreover, the number of copies required also affects storage and retrieval. A filmstrip, for example, is relatively easy to store and retrieve, whereas panel boards may present a space problem.

Essentially, the criterion of number of copies required is concerned with mechanically reproducing multiple copies from an original. Obviously, hard-copy reproduction is *impossible*, while soft-copy is *possible*.

THE PORTABILITY OF THE VEHICLE

The criterion of portability applies when the presentation vehicle must be transported to another location and set up. To some extent, it also includes the availability of the required equipment on a rental basis.

Generally, the portability of the media vehicles can be rated as *convenient* or *inconvenient* to transport and set up.

In all fairness, it must be noted that some media have a number of projection models that can be used. However, in establishing a rating for portability only a representative model was chosen. A case in point is the overhead projector, which is rated as "inconvenient" (on Figure 8-9), based on the large models used for 10-by-10-inch transparencies. This model was chosen as a representative because it is the one most commonly used. And yet, small portable models are now being manufactured that would be nearly as convenient as a 35mm. projector. The weight and bulk of the 10-by-10-inch transparencies, however, remain unchanged.

THE FLEXIBILITY OF SEQUENCE

This criterion looks ahead to postpresentation changes. Actually, it asks two questions: (1) is there the possibility that the order in which the visuals are presented will change, and (2) is there the possibility that some visuals may need modification in their visual content when the presentation is given again to a different audience? If the answer to either of these questions is "yes," then both filmstrips and motion pictures are impractical, because their sequences are locked in and changes in sequence or modifications of visual contents require making a new master film. In this respect, the material made into a filmstrip or motion picture must be carefully checked for errors that could make the entire presentation unusable.

The, the ratings for the flexibility of sequence are *flexible* and *inflexible* in Figure 8-9, the former indicating that the order in which the visual material appears can be manipulated easily, and the latter indicating that considerable cost is involved in changing the sequence of material.

THE CONTACT WITH THE AUDIENCE

This criterion takes into consideration three aspects of a presentation. The first deals with the pros and cons of a "canned" presentation. Any form of artificially reproducing voice — by tape, record, or film track — is a canned presentation. Movies, for example, use it almost exclusively.

Canned sound offers the advantage of allowing the voice part of a presentation to be perfected offstage. Using this technique, the speaker can try over and over again to achieve precisely what he wants to say in the manner he wants to say it. Thereafter, the quality of his performance is constant, no matter how many times the presentation is given. No doubt, the principal motive for using the sound/slide filmstrip medium is to achieve this uniformity in the audio part of the presentation. Tape recorders synchronized with a slide projector are used for the same reason. However, sometimes canned audio, because it lacks the warmth of human presence, becomes a disadvantage. A machine that talks rarely achieves the rapport of a human voice.

The second aspect of audience contact is lighting. An audience must see, as well as hear, a live presentation to come under its spell; a human voice in a dark room is just as impersonal as a loud-speaker spouting canned material.

Hard-copy media, of course, can be used in a fully lighted room. It is also possible to use overhead projection in a normally lighted room; however, its image becomes much more vivid as the room lighting is diminished.

At one time, slide projection required a room devoid of light, but advancements in screen technology and more efficient projector lamps now allow sufficient light to make audience contact. Filmstrips also limit the amount of light that can be permitted during projection. And an opaque

159

projector, to be effective, requires the room to be dark.

The third aspect of audience contact is continuity of attention. When a presenter must divide his attention between his audience and his medium, he invariably loses audience contact. For example, the presenter must turn his back on his audience to record material on the chalkboard or easel pad.

The ratings assigned to this criterion (in Figure 8-9) are: *good,* which indicates full contact with an audience; *fair,* which indicates an interrupted contact; and *poor,* which means that direct contact between presenter and audience is not present.

THE PACE OF THE PRESENTATION Presentation pace refers to the degree of control the presenter has in varying the time it takes to give his presentation. The pace of canned presentations, such as a sound/slide film, is fixed and cannot be varied. But live presentations are under the control of the presenter.

For instance, in giving a slide presentation, the presenter may decide to stop at a particular slide and devote as much time to it as he believes his audience warrants. With another audience, however, he may decide to hurry over the same slide, perhaps to concentrate his time on another slide.

Thus, pace is determined by the presenter best to suit the needs of his audience. Accordingly, presentations that normally take fifteen minutes to give could be shortened to ten, or expanded to twenty minutes.

Therefore, the pace of the presentation for the purpose of Figure 8-9 can be rated as: *controllable,* which permits a varying pace; or *uncontrollable,* which means that the presentation has a fixed running time from which there is no deviating.

THE CHANGEABILITY OF THE VISUAL The criterion of changeability pertains to whether or not the image of the visual can be modified while the presentation is in progress. For example, in overhead projection the image produced by the film transparency can be modified in writing on it with a grease pencil or magic marker *while* the image is being projected on the screen. Other soft-copy media (except opaque projection) are not alterable. In each case changes must be made on the original artwork and rephotographed.

All hard-copy media can be modified. A panel board, for example, can develop a visual, piece by piece, during the course of a presentation.

The ratings of *changeable* or *unchangeable* are applied to this criterion in relation to only those changes that can be effected while the presentation is in progress.

Evaluating Media

The final step in the selection of media is to apply the ratings, drawn from the criteria, to a proposed presentation. This evaluation will, at the very minimum, assist in eliminating the very obvious, and narrowing the range of choice to a few media.

There may be other criteria that you need, or wish to add, to those discussed above. For instance, the evaluation may indicate that overhead projection best suits the requirements of the proposed presentation. But perhaps an overhead projector is not available, or the facilities to produce 10-by-10-inch transparencies are inadequate — then it would be foolish to select this medium. Therefore, additional criteria may be used to eliminate those media that your operation cannot accommodate.

Figure 8-9 is a summary chart showing the criteria ratings applied to the presentation media. It should be remembered, however, that the assignment of these ratings are intended only as guidelines. They should help, but not necessarily determine, the presenter's selection of medium.

Once you have selected the presentation medium, you can put the wheels of production into motion and begin planning the facilities in which the presentation will be given.

	Chalkboard or Easel	Presentation Boards	Flipcharts	Opaque Projection	Overhead Projection	Slides	Filmstrips	Motion Pictures
Audience Size	small	small	small	medium	large	large	large	large
Audience Character	3rd degree	3rd degree	2nd degree	3rd degree	2nd degree	1st degree	1st degree	1st degree
Production Lead Time	none	short	medium	none	short	medium	medium	long
Production Budget	none	small	average	none	small	average	high	high
Number of Copies	impossible	impossible	impossible	impossible	possible	possible	possible	possible
Vehicle Portability	inconvenient	convenient	convenient	inconvenient	inconvenient	convenient	convenient	convenient
Sequence Flexibility	flexible	flexible	flexible	flexible	flexible	flexible	inflexible	inflexible
Audience Contact	fair	good	good	poor	good	good	poor	poor
Presentation Pace	controllable	controllable	controllable	controllable	controllable	controllable	uncontrollable	uncontrollable
Changeability	changeable	changeable	changeable	changeable	changeable	unchangeable	unchangeable	unchangeable

8-9 Media Selected according to Ten Basic Criteria

9-1 A View of a Communication Center or "Decision Room" Equipped with Screenwall for Double Image, Large Screen, Random-Access Display System (Courtesy of Information Management Facilities, Inc.)

9

Facilities-Planning

The planning of facilities requires a systematic, step-by-step procedure that begins when the telephone rings, and the voice on the other end says, "George, we're giving a presentation to the branch sales force on the fifteenth of the month; will you (please) make the arrangements." With this simple request begins an arduous task that will keep George busy (and worried) up to, and including, the day of the presentation.

The design, preparation, and execution of presentation material usually receive a good deal of planning. All too often, however, this planning excludes thoughtful consideration of the facilities in which the presentation will be given.

By and large, facilities are not planned — they are provided! The illusion that almost any room and setup will do is often deeply ingrained. But the question that George must ask himself is whether just any room will provide the maximum benefit from all the effort that will be put into planning the rest of the presentation. He knows from past experience that even the best of presentation will fail to be completely effective if the environment in which it is given is not suitable.

Facilities-planning is difficult because it involves a number of interrelated facets whose determinations are contingent upon each other. For example, the *size of the audience* determines the size of the room, which determines the screen material, which determines the seating arrangement, which determines the image size, which determines the projector distance, which determines the lens focal length, which determines the first- and last-row distance, which determines the viewing zone, which determines the unit space, which, on occasion, will determine the *audience size* that you can accommodate. And so it goes around and around like the age-old riddle of the chicken and the egg.

Facilities-planning is like putting together a huge jigsaw puzzle; each piece must fit into the right place or the piece next to it will be out of kilter. The exactitude of each piece, however, can never be calculated to the last inch. Facilities-planning must deal in approximations — its success depends on how sound the approximations are.

Many sources provide data on screen sizes, projector distances, aperture widths, formulas, rules of thumb, and other pertinent generalizations. But these data are rarely organized into a planning approach that can be applied to actual situations that confront those, like George, who must plan the facilities for a presentation.

When George (graciously) accepted the assignment, there was only one question he could ask: "How many people?" In almost every request to plan facilities this fact is basically the only information given (or known), and it is actually the only information needed to put the wheels into motion.

Let us now follow George through a step-by-step procedure that he will use to determine the facilities requirements for the planned presentation. And let us assume that when George asked, "How many people," he was told, "About 200."

Step One: Determine Size of Audience

The first step in the planning of facilities is to determine the size of the audience as exactly as possible. More often than not, the precise number of people who will attend a presentation is unknown. In such cases a working estimate — rounded off on the high side — should be made.

For instance, George might have been told, "We've invited about 200 but only expect about 180 or so to show up." As far as George is concerned, he had better plan for 200.

163

Obviously, with an audience this size the visuals must be projected, and since past presentations of this kind have used 35mm. slides, he will assume the same medium is desired for this one. In case he is in doubt, he can always check to be sure.

Having determined that the size of the audience will be 200, George moves to the next step.

Step Two: Determine Unit Space

How much space should George allocate for each member of the audience? He knows that if they are packed together like sardines they will become restless and inattentive. On the other hand, he realizes that the more room he allocates for unit space, the more total space he will need; and, the greater the amount of total space used, the greater the distance from the last row to the screen.

The space allocated to each viewer should allow him to move his arms and legs comfortably, without interfering with his neighbors' comfort. Generally, 6 square feet is considered adequate unit space (including aisle room). This figure, however, can be larger or smaller, depending on circumstances. For instance, 4 to 5 square feet may suffice for children, while 10 to 12 square feet may be necessary for a conference meeting that requires additional space for tables.

Other circumstances may also create considerations for using different unit spaces. For instance, a small audience can easily be afforded a unit space of 8 square feet without encountering visibility problems. Or perhaps the occasion calls for "the luxury of space" in entertaining important people.

Since George is dealing with a large audience of intracompany personnel, he determines that 6 square feet is a sufficient unit space.

Step Three: Approximate Room Size

At this point George must arrive at some idea of how much space he will need so that he can begin contacting facility-providers for a presentation room.

By doing a little arithmetic he calculates that his audience requires a seating area of at least 1200 square feet (6 square feet per person times 200 people).

This seating area, however, is the portion of a room that is the *viewing zone* — usually a trapezoidal area from which the image on the screen can be comfortably seen (Fig. 9-2). The remaining portion of the room is *dead space,* from which the image on the screen cannot be seen. Every presentation room has both a viewing zone and dead space; the apportionment of any room depends on its size, shape, and the type of screen material used.

Since the 1200 square feet that George has calculated represents only the viewing zone area, he must somehow add to it the area for dead space in order to arrive at an estimate of the total area needed. As a practical matter there is no formula that George can use in calculating the amount of dead space in an unknown room, so he chooses to rely on prior experience, which has taught him that only about 50 per cent of any given room is usable for viewing. Therefore, George applies an arbitrary factor of 2 to arrive at an approximate room size of 2400 square feet (2 times 1200; or, 50 per cent dead space and 50 per cent viewing zone).

Armed with this approximation, he begins shopping for presentation rooms having an approxi-

9-2 Relationship between Dead Space and Viewing Zone in a Typical Room

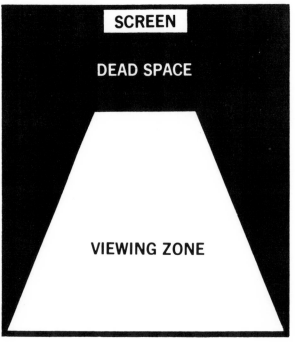

SCREEN

DEAD SPACE

VIEWING ZONE

164

mate area of 2400 square feet. He receives three replies: Room A at the Ritz is 50 by 50 feet (2500 square feet); Room B at the Savoy is 60 by 35 feet (2100 square feet); and Room C at the Carlton is 75 by 30 feet (2250 square feet). At first glance George thinks Room A at the Ritz looks good, but, realizing that he is dealing with an approximation, he knows that he had better check them all out. So, making no commitment, he turns to the next step.

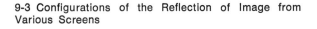

9-3 Configurations of the Reflection of Image from Various Screens

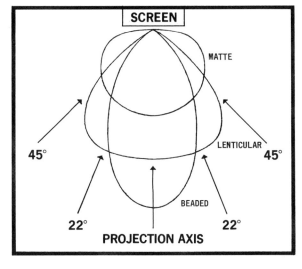

Step Four: Select Screen Material

For all practical purposes, screens may be divided into three basic types following the order of their development: *matte, beaded,* and *lenticular.* The types differ in the manner in which the light reflected from the image is directed back to the viewing audience. The concentrating effect of these various screen types is shown in Figure 9-3.

The matte screen diffuses light evenly in all directions; hence, an image appears equally bright from almost any angle. The lenticular screen is still more even in its distribution, especially over a fan-shaped beam, equally visible to angles of 40 to 50 degrees. The beaded screen is very efficient in concentrating the reflected light in a beam close to the projection axis. However, since a high gain is made along the axis, the light level drops off rapidly as the viewing angle

increases. The angles-of-visibility limits, formed by the various types of screens, determine the shape of the viewing zone in a room.

Each screen type has specialized uses that make it more desirable than others for specific conditions.

The matte screen, for instance, is the least efficient in concentrating light; this disadvantage turns into an advantage in situations where an even wider light distribution is useful, and reflected light intensity is not a problem. Also, for close (less than 10 feet) viewing distances, the beaded- and lenticular-screen surface structures (i.e. the beads and "lens") may be discernible, whereas the matte surface would appear smooth.

The lenticular screen has the great advantage of more light concentration than the matte screen. An image can be easily seen up to 50 degrees from the axis. Seating beyond these angles would yield too much distortion and practically no light. This relatively wide beam, however, can have an image brightness three or four times the one a matte screen has. On the other hand, if the room is narrow and deep, the rapid light falloff of the lenticular screen is a disadvantage. Moreover, lenticular screens are directional in their light spread; the angle of reflectance is wide horizontally but narrow vertically. Hence, if part of the audience were seated in a balcony, its viewing angle would be poor.

Beaded screens provide an even sharper (but narrower) concentration of the reflected image. Most of the light striking the glass beads imbedded in the screen is reflected back towards the projector, and a narrow-peaked beam is formed. On the projection axis the brightness is many times that of a matte screen, but at an angle of 20 degrees or 25 degrees, the beaded-screen image brightness would be about equal to that of a matte screen. Beaded screens can be useful for long narrow rooms where the brightness gain along the axis is needed to make up for an insufficient projector brightness.

Although the lenticular screen is generally more versatile, very often other factors influence the choice of screen. One common decisive factor is availability, and in George's case a beaded screen is probably the only type of screen available in a size large enough to accommodate a presentation for his large audience.

165

9-4 Seating-Capacity Chart

Distance to Last Row (feet)	Room Width (feet)																
	10	15	20	25	30	35	40	45	50	55	60	65	70	75	80	85	90
10	5	5	5	5	5	5	5	5	5	5	5	5	5	5	5	5	5
15	11	13	13	13	13	13	13	13	13	13	13	13	13	13	13	13	13
20	18	21	23	23	23	23	23	23	23	23	23	23	23	23	23	23	23
25	24	31	36	36	36	36	36	36	36	36	36	36	36	36	36	36	36
30	30	41	47	52	52	52	52	52	52	52	52	52	52	52	52	52	52
35	36	51	61	65	71	71	71	71	71	71	71	71	71	71	71	71	71
40	44	60	74	82	85	92	92	92	92	92	92	92	92	92	92	92	92
45	49	69	87	99	106	108	117	117	117	117	117	117	117	117	117	117	117
50	55	78	99	116	127	133	145	145	145	145	145	145	145	145	145	145	145
55	60	86	111	132	147	157	161	175	175	175	175	175	175	175	175	175	175
60	66	99	123	148	167	181	189	193	208	208	208	208	208	208	208	208	208
65	71	107	135	163	186	204	217	224	226	245	245	245	245	245	245	245	245
70	77	115	146	178	205	227	244	255	261	262	284	284	284	284	284	284	284
75	82	123	156	193	224	250	270	286	296	301	326	326	326	326	326	326	326
80	88	132	176	207	242	272	297	316	330	339	343	371	371	371	371	371	371
85	93	140	187	221	260	294	323	346	364	377	385	387	419	419	419	419	419
90	99	148	198	235	278	316	348	376	398	415	426	433	434	469	469	469	469
95	104	156	209	261	295	337	374	405	431	452	468	478	483	483	523	523	523
100	110	165	220	275	312	358	399	434	464	489	509	523	532	536	580	580	580
105	115	173	231	288	329	378	423	462	497	525	549	567	581	588	591	639	639
110	121	181	242	302	345	399	447	491	529	562	589	612	629	641	647	649	701
115	126	189	253	316	379	418	471	518	560	597	629	655	676	692	703	708	708
120	132	198	264	330	396	438	494	546	592	633	668	699	724	744	758	768	772
125	137	206	275	343	412	457	517	573	623	668	707	742	771	795	813	827	835
130	143	214	286	357	429	476	540	600	654	703	746	785	818	846	868	886	898
135	148	222	297	371	445	519	562	626	684	737	784	827	864	896	922	944	960
140	154	231	308	385	462	539	584	652	714	771	822	869	910	946	976	1002	1022
145	159	239	319	398	478	558	606	677	744	804	860	910	956	995	1030	1059	1084
150	165	247	330	412	495	577	627	703	773	838	897	952	1001	1045	1083	1117	1145

Seating Capacity with Beaded Screens

Section I

Section II

Section III

166

Room Width (feet)

Distance to Last Row (feet)	10	15	20	25	30	35	40	45	50	55	60	65	70	75	80	85	90
10	10	13	15	15	15	15	15	15	15	15	15	15	15	15	15	15	15
15	16	22	27	30	33	33	33	33	33	33	33	33	33	33	33	33	33
20	22	31	40	47	52	54	60	60	60	60	60	60	60	60	60	60	60
25	27	41	52	63	72	79	83	86	93	93	93	93	93	93	93	93	93
30	33	49	64	79	91	102	111	117	122	124	135	135	135	135	135	135	135
35	38	57	77	93	110	124	137	148	156	163	167	169	183	183	183	183	183
40	44	66	88	110	127	146	163	177	190	200	209	215	219	222	240	240	240
45	49	74	99	123	144	167	187	206	223	237	249	260	268	274	279	281	303
50	55	82	110	137	165	187	211	234	255	273	289	304	316	326	335	341	345
55	60	90	121	151	181	211	234	261	286	308	328	347	363	377	390	400	408
60	66	99	132	165	198	231	257	287	316	342	367	389	409	428	444	458	470
65	71	107	143	178	214	250	286	313	345	376	404	430	455	477	497	515	532
70	77	115	154	192	231	269	308	346	374	408	441	471	499	526	550	572	592
75	82	123	165	206	247	288	330	371	401	440	476	511	543	573	601	628	652
80	88	132	176	220	264	308	352	396	440	471	511	549	586	620	652	682	711
85	93	140	187	233	280	327	374	420	467	514	545	587	628	666	702	736	769
90	99	148	198	247	297	346	396	445	495	544	578	625	669	711	751	790	826
95	104	156	209	261	313	365	418	470	522	574	627	661	709	755	800	842	882
100	110	165	220	275	330	385	440	495	550	605	660	715	749	799	847	893	937
105	115	173	231	288	346	404	462	519	577	635	693	750	787	841	894	944	992
110	121	181	242	302	363	423	484	544	605	665	726	786	847	883	939	994	1046
115	126	189	253	316	379	442	506	569	632	695	759	822	885	948	984	1042	1099
120	132	198	264	330	396	462	528	594	660	726	792	858	924	990	1028	1090	1151
125	137	206	275	343	412	481	550	618	687	756	825	893	962	1031	1100	1138	1202
130	143	214	286	357	429	500	572	643	715	786	858	929	1001	1072	1144	1215	1252
135	148	222	297	371	445	519	594	668	742	816	891	965	1039	1113	1188	1262	1302
140	154	231	308	385	462	539	616	693	770	847	924	1001	1078	1155	1232	1309	1386
145	159	239	319	398	478	558	638	717	797	877	957	1036	1116	1196	1276	1355	1435
150	165	247	330	412	495	577	660	742	825	907	990	1072	1155	1237	1320	1402	1485

Section I · Section II · Section III

Seating Capacity with Lenticular Screens

167

Thus George decides to use a beaded screen, while continuing his further check on the available rooms.

Step Five: Select the Room

George now turns to his file and withdraws a "Seating Capacity Chart" (Fig. 9-4). This chart is a matrix on which the seating capacities for rooms of various sizes and shapes have been pre-calculated. To get the data for the chart, a computer was programmed to determine the area of viewing zones formed by the angles of visibility of beaded and lenticular screens. Within each viewing zone the computer calculated the seating capacity based on a unit space of six square feet.

The chart can also be used for unit spaces other than 6 square feet by dividing 6 into the desired unit space and using the result as a factor. Then multiplying the size of an actual audience by this factor produces an *adjusted* audience size that is then used in working with the tables.

For example, suppose the actual audience size were 200, and the meeting were to be conference style calling for a unit space of 12 square feet. The first step would be to create a factor: 6 divided into 12 is 2. The actual audience size is then multiplied by this factor: 2 times 200 equals 400, which is the adjusted audience size. According to the tables in Figure 9-4 the readings of the adjusted size of 400 would be used even though the actual audience size is 200.

The same procedure is followed if the unit space desired is less than 6 square feet. Suppose, for example, the unit space of 5 square feet was sufficient. 6 divided into 5 would result in a factor of 0.8, which, when multiplied by the 200 actual audience, will produce an adjusted audience of 160.

Using the tables in Figure 9-4 for a beaded screen, George finds, much to his surprise, that Room A (50 by 50 feet) seats only 145 people; Room B (60 by 35 feet) seats 181; and Room C (75 by 30 feet) seats 224. Neither Room A nor B will be large enough for his audience of 200, but Room C will do nicely. As a matter of fact, it is a little large.

A room that is too small is impossible to use, while a room that is too large may be imprudent to use. Of course, George's situation is not all

bad, but supposing he had only twenty people to seat in this room that will hold 224 people. Using a room too large for its audience is, in some strange ways, psychologically intimidating. Voices bounce off empty chairs and large walls. The ceiling — usually quite high — gives one a feeling of being dwarfed. The empty space seems to cause people to lower their voices as they would in religious or official buildings. All in all, it is not wise to use a room that is much too large.

George elects to take Room C at the Carlton and makes an appointment to visit the facility to plan the seating arrangement.

Step Six: Select Seating Arrangement

George looks at his "Seating Capacity Chart" again to determine how to seat his audience. The chart (Fig. 9-4) is divided into three sections: I, II, and III. There is a specific seating arrangement for each section, shown in Figure 9-5 as A, B, and C. Each of these arrangements has been designed to gain maximum seating capacity from the viewing zone produced by the room's shape and size and the screen material used.

Room C, which George has chosen, is 75 by 30 feet; this falls into Section II, and therefore B is the seating arrangement he will use.

Step Seven: Determine Last Row

One of George's main concerns is to have everyone in the audience see the images on the screen. It stands to reason that the closer they are to the screen, the better their visibility. With this in mind, he again consults the chart in Figure 9-4, and sees that, although Room C is 75 feet long, he does not really need all that length. Had the room been 70 feet long it would accommodate 205 people — still enough for his audience of 200.

Therefore, George decides to place his last row 70 feet from the screen and leave the remaining 5 feet of the room empty. He will use this adjusted room size (70 by 30 feet) for the remaining steps in the procedure. (George also checks to see if the adjusted length affects the seating arrangement in Step Six.)

Step Eight: Determine First Row

The chart in Figure 9-6 is also a result of a computer program that has taken various pertinent formulas (page 174) and expressed them as relationships to the distance of the last row from the screen.

Using the adjusted 70-foot room length, George consults the appropriate column and finds that the distance of the first row from the screen should be 23 feet.

Step Nine: Determine Image Size

If the last row is 70 feet from the screen, how large must the image be to provide good visibility? Obviously this is an important question for George to answer, since everyone in the audience must be able to see the pictures on the screen clearly in order to understand the presentation fully.

The appropriate column in Figure 9-6 indicates to George that the horizontal size of an image that can be seen from the last row is 140 inches.

Step Ten: Determine Minimum Symbol Size

In the event the presentation may use some hard-copy material (viz. panel boards, easel pads, or flip charts) in addition to the 35mm. slides, George must also concern himself with the size of the lettering in these non-projected visuals.

He knows, of course, that being able to see the copy and being able to read it are two different things. So, checking the column on Figure 9-6 labeled "Minimum Symbol Size," George finds that the minimum symbol size on any hard-copy (or projected soft-copy) should be 2.6 inches high so that those in the last row (70 feet back) will be able to see it.

Passing this valuable bit of information on to the chartist preparing the presentation, George returns to his study of the presentation needs.

Step Eleven: Determine Screen Size

The size of the screen must accommodate the required size of the image. In George's case the image is 140 inches across. The 35mm. medium he is using projects an image that is roughly a 2:3 relationship, with the longer dimension being the horizontal measurement. Thus, a 35mm. slide projected in a horizontal format would produce an image 140 inches long and about 93 inches

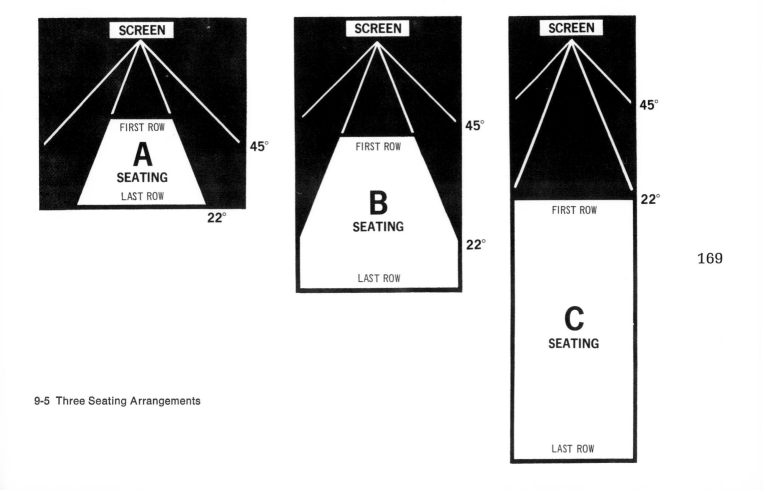

9-5 Three Seating Arrangements

169

Room Length	Last Row	First Row	Image Size	Minimum Symbol Size	Projector Distance	Bottom of Image	Top of Image	Projector Brightness Provided
10	10	3	20	0.4	8	4	5½/6	2
15	15	5	30	0.6	12	5	6½/7	4
20	20	6	40	0.7	16	5	8/9	8
25	25	8	50	0.9	20	6	9/10	12
30	30	10	60	1.1	25	6	10/11	18
35	35	11	70	1.3	29	6	11/12	24
40	40	13	80	1.5	33	7	12/14	32
45	45	15	90	1.7	37	7	13/15	40
50	50	16	100	1.9	41	8	14/16	50
55	55	18	110	2.0	45	8	15/17	60
60	60	20	120	2.2	50	9	16/19	72
65	65	21	130	2.4	54	9	17/20	84
70	70	23	140	2.6	58	9	18/21	98
75	75	25	150	2.8	62	10	19/22	112
80	80	26	160	3.0	66	10	21/24	128
85	85	28	170	3.2	70	11	22/25	144
90	90	30	180	3.3	75	11	23/26	162
95	95	31	190	3.5	79	11	24/27	180
100	100	33	200	3.7	83	12	25/29	200
105	105	35	210	3.9	87	12	25/30	220
110	110	36	220	4.1	91	13	26/31	242
115	115	38	230	4.3	95	13	27/32	264
120	120	40	240	4.4	100	14	28/34	288
125	125	41	250	4.6	104	14	29/35	312
130	130	43	260	4.8	108	14	31/36	338
135	135	45	270	5.0	112	15	32/37	364
140	140	46	280	5.2	116	15	33/39	392
145	145	48	290	5.4	120	16	34/40	420
150	150	50	300	5.6	125	16	35/41	450
Feet			Inches			Feet from the Floor		Rating
			Feet from the Screen					

170

9-6 Variables Determined from Room Length

high. In a vertical format the height of the image would be the 140-inch measurement.

Standard screens, however, are constructed primarily to accommodate the horizontal format. Consequently, if George selects the screen size based on the 140-inch image size, any slides made in a vertical format will bleed off the screen, and part of the image will be lost to the viewer.

In order to avoid this, George must provide a screen that is 140 inches or more in both its horizontal and vertical dimensions.

Another solution could be to use a zoom lens (see Step Thirteen) and, while projecting, reduce the image size for slides having vertical formats. However, the continual changing of image size and focus may have a disturbing effect on the audience. Furthermore, a reduction in image size may cause visibility problems for the rows farther

9-7 Projector Distance Factor Determined from Lens Focal Length

Projector Type	Aperture Width	Lens Focal Length (inches)							
		1	1½	2	2½	3	3½	4	5
8 mm. Movies	.172	1.10	1.65	2.21	2.76	3.30	3.85	4.42	5.51
16 mm. Movies	.380	.50	.75	1.00	1.25	1.50	1.75	2.00	2.50
35 mm. Single Frame Filmstrip	.885	.22	.32	.43	.54	.64	.75	.86	1.07
35 mm. 2″ x 2″ Slides Double Frame	1.34	.14	.21	.28	.35	.42	.50	.57	.72
Super Slides 2″ x 2″	1.50	.13	.19	.25	.32	.37	.44	.51	.63
2¼″ x 2¼″ Slides	2.1875	.08	.13	.17	.22	.26	.30	.35	.43
3¼″ x 4″ Slides, Lantern	3.0	.06	.10	.13	.16	.19	.22	.25	.32
Overhead Projection	5.0	.04	.06	.08	.10	.12	.14	.16	.20
	7.0	.03	.04	.05	.07	.08	.09	.11	.13
	10.0	.02	.03	.04	.05	.06	.07	.08	.10
Opaque Projection	10.0	.02	.03	.04	.05	.06	.07	.08	.10
	(inches)	Projector Distance Adjustment Factor							

Projector distance adjustment factors for lens focal lengths not listed may be found by adding entries for those listed focal lengths totaling the needed lens focal length. For example: the adjustment factor for a 7″ lens focal length can be found by adding entries for 3″ and 4″, or 2″ and 5″; (similarly a 40″ focal length can be determined by multiplying the 5″ entry by 8).

back. And finally, zooming must be controlled at the projector position, thus ruling out remote control.

Step Twelve: Determine Approximate Projector Distance

George's next step is to determine the distance his projector must be placed from the screen in order to get the 140-inch image required. Again, looking at the appropriate column in Figure 9-6, he sees that the approximate distance of the projector from the screen is 58 feet.

This, however, is not the actual distance, although in some cases it could be. This figure is used as a base from which the actual distance is adjusted according to the aperture size of the slide (i.e. the slide mask's opening) and the focal length of the lens.

Therefore, George must now determine the actual projector distance from the screen. To accomplish this he moves to the next step.

Step Thirteen: Adjust for Actual Projector Distance

Using the chart in Figure 9-7, George must determine the proper *adjustment factor* and multiply the approximate distance (from Step Twelve) by this factor to arrive at the actual distance the projector must be placed from the screen in order to produce a 140-inch image. But in order to know which adjustment factor to use, the slide-frame aperture and the focal length of the projector's lens must be known.

The projector George has available to him is a Kodak Carousel Model 800 with a 5-inch lens. The Carousel is designed primarily for 35mm. slides, so George looks for this equipment category on the chart in Figure 9-7. He finds the adjustment factor for his five-inch lens is 0.72. Thus George multiplies the approximate distance by this adjustment factor (58 feet times 0.72) and arrives at an adjusted projector distance of 41¾ feet. When focused from this distance the projector will show the required 140-inch image on the screen.

If for some reason, the projector cannot be moved to the 41¾-foot mark, George has the option of simply removing the projector's 5-inch lens and replacing it with a lens having a 7-inch focal length. In this event the 58-foot approximate distance is multiplied by an adjustment factor of 1.00, and the projector need not be moved at all to produce a 140-inch image from a distance of 58 feet.

If George wanted more flexibility and did not want to bother with changing lenses with every presentation, he could equip his projector with a zoom lens, which adjusts for a range of focal lengths. Kodak makes a four- to six-inch lens for the Carousel, providing a 140-inch screen image, for example, for any distance from 33 to 49 feet, with 35mm. slides.

Step Fourteen: Determine Screen Mounting

The mounting of the screen is crucial to proper viewing. Screens that are set too low will cause the audience in the back rows to have difficulty in seeing the projected image over the heads of those in front of them. On the other hand, the higher the screen is set, the more difficult it will be to avoid keystoning.* Keystoning is caused when the screen is set higher than the projector — so that the plane of the screen is not perpendicular to the center beam from the projector — thereby projecting an image that is narrower at the bottom than at the top.

George decides to tackle the problem of back-row visibility first (as he should). He consults the column "Bottom of Image" (Fig. 9-6) and finds that, when the last row is 70 feet from the screen, the bottom of the projected image must be 9 feet from the floor.

Similarly the column "Top of Image" indicates the distance that the top of the image must be from the floor. Thus at the 70-foot level the chart reads 18 feet/21 feet, the 18-foot distance accommodating slides in the horizontal format only, and the 21-foot distance accommodating vertical formats also.

Therefore, George will mount his screen so that the bottom of the projected image will be at least 9 feet and the top of the image at least 21 feet from the floor. Having determined these distances, he must now take steps to avoid keystoning.

---

* The term "keystone" comes from the architectural term for the stone used in the top of arches that completes the arch and holds the other stones in place. It has a trapezoidal shape.

Material Type	Lighting	Projector Lumen Output							
		50	100	200	400	800	1000	2000	4000
Pictures	Dark Room	5	10	20	40	80	100	200	400
	Shaded Room						2	4	8
	Daylight						1	2	4
Diagrams	Dark Room	20	40	80	160	320	400	800	1600
	Shaded Room				4	6	8	16	32
	Daylight				2	4	4	8	16
Text	Dark Room	100	200	400	800	1600	2000	4000	8000
	Shaded Room	2	4	8	16	32	40	80	160
	Daylight		2	4	8	16	20	40	80
		Brightness Provided							

Brightness provided for lumen outputs not listed may be found by adding the entries for those lumen outputs totaling the desired lumen output. For example: brightness provided for 600 lumen projector can be found by adding the entries for 200 and 400 lumen outputs.

9-8 Brightness Provided by Projector Lumen Output

He can achieve this in two ways. He can either mount the projector high enough so that it need not be tilted, and so projects flat onto the screen. Or he can tilt the screen forward at the top to bring the screen into a parallel position with the projected slide. In a large audience such as this, however, George may very well find that keystoning is not a serious problem. Given a projection stand 6 feet or so high, with the projector set back, say 40 feet or so, the angle of projection will be flat enough that keystoning, although present, will not be disturbing. It is worth noting, by the way, that longer-focal-length lenses will tend to minimize keystoning simply because they permit the projector to be set further back, thus "flattening" the projection angle.

Step Fifteen: Check Ceiling Height

At this point George makes a note to check the ceiling height of Room C to be sure that it is at least 21 feet high, with no obstructions, like beams or chandeliers, in the way. (He remembers that a prior presentation was ruined because the room it was given in had an Early American décor with a lovely chestnut cross-beamed ceiling that unfortunately interfered with back-row visibility.)

Step Sixteen: Determine Projector Brightness Rating

George is aware that the quality of the projected image depends a great deal on the light output of the projector he uses. If this output is insufficient for the kind of visuals and/or the room conditions planned, the projected image will diminish in visibility.

The last column in Figure 9-6, "Brightness Required," tells him that at the 70-foot level his projector should have an approximate brightness rating of 98.

George then turns to Figure 9-8 to compare his plan with this rating requirement. He knows, for instance, that his Carousel has a lumen output of

The charts in this chapter were derived by calculating the mathematical relationships between unknowns in a variety of circumstances and certain "established" rules of thumb which served as given. The resultant figures can be labeled "accurate" within the limits of the purposes they will serve.

● **Seating Capacity.** The seating capacity in Figure 9-4 was computed by a geometrical calculation of the viewing zone (i.e. the seating area) and dividing by the unit space (i.e. required area per person). Defining L = Length of Room, W = Room Width, and S = Screen Angle, the following equations were used to determine the sections of the viewing zone:

Section I: $Area = \frac{8}{9} \times tanS \times L^2$

Section II: $Area = L \times W - \frac{W}{4 \times tanS} - \frac{tanS \times L^2}{9}$

Section III: $Area = 2 \times \frac{L \times W}{3}$

The angle of 22° (tan .4040) was used for beaded screens and 45° (tan 1.0) for lenticular screens. Equations derived for sections I, II and III of Figure 9-4 representing the seating capacity the three shapes of viewing zone in Figure 9-5 were:

For beaded screens

Shape A: $Capacity = .058 \times L^2$

Shape B: $Capacity = .16 \times L \times W - .105 \times W^2 - .0073 \times L^2$

Shape C: $Capacity = .11 \times L \times W$

For lenticular screens

Shape A: $Capacity = .15 \times L^2$

Shape B: $Capacity = .16 \times L \times W - .041 \times W^2 - .017 \times L^2$

Shape C: $Capacity = .11 \times L \times W$

In Figure 9-4 the unit space of 6 square feet was chosen. To determine seating capacities for unit spaces other than 6 the correction factor: Unit Space divided by 6, can be used.

First Row. The distance of the first row to the screen is given, in feet, by:

$First\ Row = \frac{Distance\ of\ Last\ Row\ to\ Screen}{3}$

Source: an established rule of thumb

Note 1: Distance of last row to screen will hereafter be referred to as "Last Row Distance."

● **Image Size.** The Image Size of the projected image *(always* measured by its horizontal, or long dimension) is given, in feet, by:

$Image\ Size = \frac{Last\ Row\ Distance}{6}$

Source: an established rule of thumb

The image size converted into inches is found by multiplying the above equation by 12, which results in,

$Image\ Size = 2 \times (Last\ Row\ Distance)$

Minimum Symbol Size. As a rule of thumb, the minimum size of any symbol (be it a letter, number, sign or whatever) should be approximately 1/40 the size of the image's height (i.e. its *short* dimension). This guideline holds true regardless of the medium used. A Flipchart which is 20" high x 25" long, for example, should use symbols no smaller than 1/2" — since 1/40 of its image's 20" height is .5". Because the image's long dimension is used to define its size, this Flipchart has an Image Size of 25"; 1/2" symbols can be seen on it from a distance of approximately 12½ feet back. This is determined by substituting in the equation:

$Image\ Size = 2 \times (Last\ Row\ Distance,\ in\ feet)$, or

$25 = 2 \times (Last\ Row\ Distance)$

$Last\ Row\ Distance = \frac{25}{2}$, or

$Last\ Row\ Distance = 12½'$

If this Flipchart were photographed as a 35mm slide, for instance, and projected, its symbol size would be magnified in proportion to the magnification of the image size. Suppose the 20" x 25" image size was projected up to 20' x 25' — then the symbol size would correspondingly increase from 1/2" to 1/2', and would still be 1/40 of the projected image height.

Thus, the minimum symbol size on *original* artwork, for both hard copy and ultimate soft copy, should be 1/40 of that artwork's *height*.

The value of $\frac{1}{40}$ is given, in inches, by

$Symbol\ Size = \frac{1}{40} \times \frac{3}{4} \times (Image\ Size,\ in\ inches)$ or,

$Symbol\ Size = \frac{1}{40} \times \frac{3}{4} \times 2 \times (Last\ Row\ Distance)$

Restated,

$Symbol\ Size = \frac{(Last\ Row\ Distance)}{27}$

Note 2: Whereas Image Size is always defined as its long dimension, image height (i.e. its short dimension) is defined as 3/4 Image Size. This ratio of 3:4 is used in order to accommodate the various ratio aspects produced by the different apertures in soft copy media.

Note 3: The ratio of 1/40 was selected as a compromise between 1/30, maintained by some sources as the correct ratio, and 1/50, insisted on by other sources as the better ratio.

● **Projector Distance.** Projector distance from the screen is given, in feet, by:

Projector Distance =
(Focal Length Constant) x (Image Size, in feet)

Source: "Audiovisual Projection", Pamphlet S3, Eastman Kodak Company, Rochester, New York.

Substituting for Image Size in the equation,

$Projector\ Distance = \frac{(Focal\ Length\ Constant) \times (Last\ Row\ Distance)}{6}$

The Focal Length Constant is used to allow the equation to serve for any focal length. For example, in Figure 9-6 the focal length of 7 inches was used *(Source: ibid),* and the Focal Length Constant was defined as 5. Hence,

$Projector\ Distance = \frac{5 \times (Last\ Row\ Distance)}{6}$

Figure 9-6 gives the Projector Distance for Last Row Distances when the focal length = 7. Figure 9-7 gives a correction factor for different focal lengths (i.e. when a focal length is other than 7).

● **Bottom of Image on the Screen.** The measurement of the Bottom of the image (on the screen) from the floor, is the distance which allows a line-of-sight view of the image Bottom by the viewer in the last row over the top of the heads in the preceding row (as shown in the diagram).

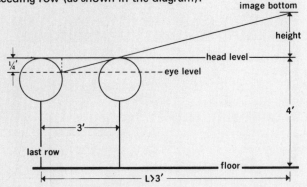

Assuming that (1) the top of the head level of a person seated to the floor is 4 feet, (2) the eye level of the viewer is 1/4 foot below that, and (3) the row separation (i.e. distance between rows) is 3 feet, then the distance of the Image Bottom from the floor can be found by similar triangles:

$$\frac{\text{(height from head level to image bottom)}}{\text{(Last Row Distance)} - \text{(row separation)}} =$$

$$\frac{\text{(head level)} - \text{(eye level)}}{\text{(row separation)}}$$

Substituting from the diagram above,

$$\frac{\text{height}}{\text{(Last Row Distance)} - 3} = \frac{\frac{1}{4}}{3}$$

Restating the equation,

$$\text{height} = \frac{\text{(Last Row Distance)} - 3}{12}$$

However, the distance of the Image Bottom, measured from the floor, is given by:

Image Bottom =

height from head level to Image Bottom +

distance of head level to floor, or

Image Bottom = height + 4

Therefore, by substituting,

$$\text{Image Bottom} = \frac{\text{(Last Row Distance)} - 3}{12} + 4$$

● **Top of the Image on the Screen.** The distance of the Top of the image (on the screen) from the floor, is found by adding the height of the image to the value of "Image Bottom" above. When the image is projected in a horizontal format (i.e. the long side of the image parallel to the floor):

$$\text{Image Top} = \text{(Image Bottom)} + \frac{3}{4} \times \text{(Image Size)}$$

Or, by substituting,

$$\text{Image Top} = \frac{5 \times \text{(Last Row Distance)} + 90}{24}$$

When the image is in a vertical format (i.e. the long side of the image perpendicular to the floor):

Image Top = (Image Bottom) + (Image Size)

Or, by substituting,

$$\text{Image Top} = \frac{\text{(Last Row Distance)} + 15}{4}$$

See Note 2, above

● **Projector Brightness Provided.** The projector Brightness check, to determine the light output a projector must have so that the image on the screen can be adequately seen from the last row, is performed by comparing two quantities in the following manner:

(Brightness Provided) must exceed (Brightness Required)

The "brightness required" is defined as:

$$\frac{\text{Projector Lumen Rating}}{\text{Image Area}}$$

Note 4: The lumen rating for any projector can be secured from a supplier or manufacturer.

The "brightness required" is defined as the image brightness equal to

(Background Brightness) x (Material Type Correction Factor)

Background brightness is considered to be the lighted condition of the room — sometimes referred to as *ambient* light. For measurement purposes the following three conditions will suffice:

Background Brightness
$$\begin{cases} \text{Dark Room} & - & 0.1 \text{ Foot Lamberts} \\ \text{Shaded Room} & - & 5.0 \text{ Foot Lamberts} \\ \text{Daylight} & - & 10.0 \text{ Foot Lamberts} \end{cases}$$

Source: "Audiovisual Projection", op cit.

This background brightness is corrected by a factor dependent upon the type of material to be projected. Basically, the three types are:

Correction factor
$$\begin{cases} \text{Pictures} & - & 100 \\ \text{Diagrams} & - & 25 \\ \text{Text} & - & 5 \end{cases}$$

Source: "Audiovisual Projection", op cit.

Therefore,

$$\left(\frac{\text{Projector Lumens}}{\text{Image Area}}\right) \text{must exceed} \left(\begin{array}{c}\text{Background}\\\text{Brightness}\end{array}\right) \times \left(\begin{array}{c}\text{Correction}\\\text{Factor}\end{array}\right)$$

This may be rearranged as:

$$\left[\frac{\text{Projector Lumens}}{\left(\begin{array}{c}\text{Background}\\\text{Brightness}\end{array}\right) \times \left(\begin{array}{c}\text{Correction}\\\text{Factor}\end{array}\right)}\right] \text{must exceed (Image Area)}$$

The left hand side of the inequality is read from Figure 9-8 knowing the projector lumens, the room lighting, and the type of material being projected. This number must *exceed* the value for image area listed (for each Last Row Distance) in Figure 9-6 as the "Projector Brightness Required."

600, and in Figure 9-8, by adding the lumen output columns of 200 and 400 lumen, he can determine the brightness provided by his Carousel. In this case, the brightness would be 240 for diagrams and 1200 for text in a darkened room. Both values are more than enough. In fact the excess in brightness for the text material may be easily tempered by increasing the ambient room light.

Experience tells George that his room need not be totally darkened. For instance, some side lights, and certainly the lectern light, can be on without impeding visibility. As a matter of fact, he will review all the lighting requirements as his next step.

Step Seventeen: Check Lighting

Unless a room is especially tailored for presentations, proper lighting will be a headache to facilities-planning. The lighting arrangements in most rooms in which presentations are given were designed merely to illuminate the room. Many of the fixtures — chandeliers, as an example — are primarily for decorative purposes. Consequently, optimum lighting conditions rarely exist, and since little can be done to alter them in a temporary room, George has had to learn to improvise the best he could. There are some requisites, however, that he has established, so as not to have lighting become detrimental to a presentation:

A room should never be completely darkened for a live presentation. Canned presentations like motion pictures or sound/slide films can work with the lights out, but the chemistry that occurs between speaker and audience needs illumination. At a minimum there must be a non-glare light at the lectern so that the speaker can be seen and so that he can see his notes. However, more than this minimum is desirable.

The projected screen image should be brighter than any other surface within the spectators' view. With this as a gauge, there should be enough light left in the room for the audience to take notes and feel as though it is part of a group.

There should be no light source reflected directly onto the surface of the screen. The areas above and to the side of the screen should be

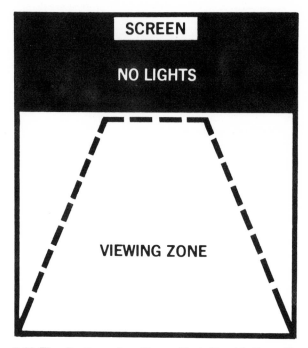

9-10 The Portion of a Room That Should Have No Lighting

darkened (Fig. 9-10). Often the lighting arrangement is set up in alternate banks, so that the lights in that part of the room in which the screen is located can be turned off independently. Some rooms have dimming rheostats that allow the light output to be reduced to the minimum desired. When these alternates are not possible, a desperate measure may be to unscrew the bulbs from fixtures that cause unwanted lights. Another solution is to place a cowling around the screen. For temporary rooms, however, this solution is rather costly, bothersome, and therefore impractical.

Sources of stray light should be eliminated. Tests should be made for light leaks that come from sources other than the projector, lectern, or lighting planned for the sake of the audience. Typically these sources are windows or corridors that, when the door is opened, allow light to enter the room. To exclude daylight entering from windows, drapes, venetian blinds, opaque shades, or makeshift devices can be used. Windows that are contiguous to the screen must have opaque coverings because venetian blinds alone will not keep out the sunlight. As for the door, keep it closed once the presentation has started.

All light switches should be located, and their use checked and labeled. Most presentations are given in unfamiliar rooms, such as the one George is renting. Therefore, he will have to learn in advance what each switch controls, and label it accordingly (usually by writing its use with a magic marker on a piece of masking tape). Although this procedure might seem overly elaborate, George has learned never to trust his memory, especially when it is under the pressure of a presentation in process. He will also make a separate point of checking whether the switch that turns off the lights does not turn off the source of power for the projector at the same time.

Step Eighteen: Check Acoustics

George has found (through some rather unfortunate experiences) that if a listener cannot hear, or hear properly, he will close his mind — for nothing is as disturbing as straining to hear, or clearly understand, the speaker.

The audio part of a presentation can usually be regulated by adjusting the volume controls of the microphones or loudspeakers. Acoustical tests made in empty rooms, however, will give different results than when the room is occupied, because human bodies absorb sound. Hence, proper audio levels cannot be determined until the last minute, when the room is filled. At that time, George will make these tests as inconspicuously as possible.

There are, however, some acoustical tests that he always makes prior to any presentation:

The room is checked to find any "dead spots" from which the audio cannot be heard clearly. If such spots fall in the viewing zone the loudspeakers will be repositioned to eliminate them.

The room is checked to find any annoying echo that would interfere with the listening comfort of the audience. Simple tests for determining reverberations are made by a sharp clap of the hands or a loud sound. Generally, all empty rooms will produce an echo, and if the reverberations are not severe they can probably be ignored, since slight echoes will be deadened when the room is filled with people. If the feedback is a harsh echo, then some sound-absorbent material (like drapes or carpets or padded screens) should be placed in positions to eliminate it. In cases where the room is temporary (like Room C, which

George will rent) and it is not convenient to provide these remedies, the room should be abandoned and another one selected — it would be a mistake for George to do otherwise. A presentation given in a room where sound waves bounce around will irritate the listeners and demoralize the speakers.

The room is checked for potential outside noise. Outside noise is difficult to control, but if the facility is properly surveyed, George will be in a position to prepare against it, and it will not come as a devastating surprise. In surveying the presentation room it is wise to find out what other activities will be going on during the time of the presentation in the areas contiguous to the room. For example, the rattle of dishes is a terribly distracting noise. It often happens that meetings are plagued with the rattle of preparations for the morning coffee break, then lunch, and again for the afternoon coffee break. Invariably, these operations are done just outside the door of, or even inside, the presentation room itself. Thus, George will make arrangements ahead of time to avoid these distractions by using a soundproof room, or by having the group enjoy their repasts somewhere away from the presentation room. Also, many facilities-providers have a series of adjacent rooms in which meetings of all sorts are run on a production-line basis. If this is the case at the Carlton, George will find out what his "neighbors" will be doing at their meetings. It may be his misfortune to have a convention of square-dance callers in an uninsulated room next to him.

Finally, it may be wise for George to survey the area outside the building. He may find, for example, that a construction project is in full swing, and his speakers will have to compete with pneumatic hammers and riveting machines to be heard.

A room is checked for internal noises. The noises from projectors and air conditioners do not come into being until the audience is seated and the presentations are in progress — then it may be too late. Therefore, George will test all equipment beforehand, but under simulated actual conditions, to determine its noise level and compensate for it by adjusting seating arrangements and audio volume levels.

177

Step Nineteen: Check Ventilation

Audience comfort contributes greatly to the success of a presentation. Hardly any room used today for presentation purposes is not equipped with systems capable of providing adequate ventilation. In arranging the facility George must furnish the provider with the number of people who will attend, how long the presentation will last, and whether or not smoking will be permitted. With this information the provider should be able to calculate the supply and turnover of fresh air needed.

Hot, stale air causes discomfort. It makes people drowsy and heady, distracting them from the speaker's presentation. Being comfortable, however, does not mean being cold, and George will have to guard against giving his presentation in an icebox. Nevertheless, a colder room is preferable after a heavy meal, or late in the day when fatigue sets in.

Usually, ventilation presents no problem in a commercial facility. Nevertheless, it cannot be taken for granted. Many office buildings, for example, turn off air-conditioning systems after hours, and an audience can find itself in a hot stuffy room midway through a presentation that went beyond the normal working-day hours.

Step Twenty: Check Electrical Outlets, Equipment, and Cords

George will check to insure that adequate and coveniently located electrical outlets are available. If extension cords are necessary they will be arranged as neatly as possible, and preferably taped down to the floor. Wires that need to cross aisles will be flagged in some manner to avoid people tripping over them.

In addition, George will check:

The electrical outlets — to determine whether or not they are compatible with the equipment that will be used. Occasionally movie- and some larger projectors are equipped with a three-pronged grounded plug. If the wall outlets accept only two-pronged plugs, George will be sure to get an adater from a local hardware store.

The projection equipment — to detect any shorts, defects, or frayed wires that may lead to shorts. This checkout is done before every presentation.

That replacement bulbs and/or stand-by projector are ready as a safety measure. The usual Carousel bulb — DEK — has a twenty-five-hour life. Also available is a DAH bulb with a 200-hour life.

Projector bulbs are often hard to remove, and if they burn out during a presentation, they will be doubly difficult to get out because they will be very hot. In the event one does burn out, George will have some sort of protection handy so he doesn't have to wait until the bulb cools to remove it. A cardboard cylinder that fits snugly is a good device. It protects the hands and gives additional leverage for wiggling out the bulb. Some professional projectionists use sections of automobile radiator hose. (Incidentally, toilet paper cords work fine on Carousel bulbs.)

George has learned that all these checks are well worth the trouble.

Of course, in preparing for this presentation George has the advantage of controlling the selection and setting up of the facility. But suppose the presentation had to be given in a strange location like a customer's conference room or a client's office. George has run into these situations and knows that they are difficult to deal with. In such cases George gives the advice to his people to try, in advance, to get some idea about the location of outlets, the size of the room, the lighting arrangements, and so forth. Above all, he counsels, avoid the "show me where the outlet is" syndrome — ask to be allowed to set up before the audience is invited in for the presentation.

The steps that George has just gone through have all been necessary in properly planning the ideal facilities he will require. Of course, some of the amenities remain to be looked after, such as providing paper and pencils, ashtrays, coffee breaks, refreshment bars, and other similar details. He will see to it that the facility-provider will attend to them — always, however, keeping a close watch over what is happening.

Basically, however, the hard core of the planning is done, and George can rest assured that he has selected and prepared the room that ideally suits the prevailing needs. This assignment is one more notch on his belt of experience. The next one may go even more smoothly. Or perhaps the next will have certain real-life circumstances that will force him to compromise the ideal — as he has had to do on occasions in the past.

As George gains more experience he may ask himself, "Need I go through this procedure every time?" The answer must be, "Yes!" The procedure, all twenty steps of it, is like a countdown. It is a form of discipline that helps avoid error and fosters thoroughness. At some point it will become somewhat automatic, and he may take a less formal approach, but the essence of the checklist must never be abandoned.

George is satisfied with his efforts, as he should be. All he needs to do now is to sit back and wait for the fifteenth to come around — and hope that nothing goes wrong.

There are other factors beyond George's control, however, that enter into the probable success of the presentation. The most important of these factors is, by far, the audience. Without a true understanding of the audience's character, and an accommodation to it, a presentation can be neither properly conceived nor implemented, and thus, the chance of success is vastly diminished.

10-1 Photos Courtesy of American Telephone & Telegraph

10

Relating to the Audience

If Mark Twain had thought about it, he might also have said, "Everybody talks about the audience, but nobody does anything about it."

In practice, the fact that it takes two (at least) to communicate has generally not been given the attention it deserves, perhaps because it seems so obvious. Yet, the other half of the communication relationship, the audience, requires a more careful analysis than any of the other elements of the presentation is granted.

The science of psychology has taught us that our experience is a bipolar relationship of subject to object; this applies more concretely to the art of communications than to many other more, or less, esoteric fields. Those who talk to themselves may have money in the bank, but they are not communicating.

For communication to be effective, both poles must be in harmony. The subject is, of course, the communicator; he must select that form of presentation best suited to elicit response from the object, his audience.

Behind this simple premise is hidden the most critical step in formulating a graphic presentation: relating to the audience. Often the communicator is so beset with the techniques and mechanics of the presentation that he gives this step only his cursory attention; sometimes it is overlooked altogether.

Actually, to relate properly to an audience involves a pretty thorough evaluation of the audience as a first step.

There are six primary characteristics of an audience that are essential to its evaluation: size, level, rank, background, exposure, and bias. This is not to say that additional characteristics cannot be included. Particular circumstances may well make the inclusion and measurement of other, more refined, characteristics desirable. But no evaluation can be considered complete without these six.

Although these characteristics can be found in every audience, their relative importance varies in different situations. Since these characteristics are variable, audience evaluation becomes a product of a multivaried analysis. The analysis of each variable produces a factor; the weighing of all the factors determines the ability of the audience to grasp the concepts being transmitted, and to understand the form which the transmission takes. For example, the level of the audience influences the complexity of the presented concepts; audience exposure dictates the sophistication of the chosen tools; the size of the audience determines the presentation medium, and so forth.

The order in which these variables are examined follows no particular sequence. Each variable can be weighed independently of the others, but its result must continuously be integrated with the concomitant results of the other factors, since no one factor can precisely describe the character of an audience. For example, the variable "background" can be weighed independently. But background only describes one audience characteristic. The form and content of the presentation is equally dependent on how large, how important, how sophisticated, and how mature the audience is. Concurrently, its attitudes, interests, and expectations must be cranked into the evaluation.

Thus, the evaluation of an audience can begin with the analysis of any variable and proceed in any sequence, but a thorough determination of the character of the audience cannot be arrived

10-2 Photo Courtesy of American Management Association

at until all the variables have been tested and their factors weighed.

Audience Size

The factor of audience size is the crucial determinant in the planning of printed or oral presentations.

In printed presentations, audience size is determined by the circulation of a publication. Circulation can be broadly categorized as *limited* or *open.*

In a limited circulation, the size of the audience is generally known. For example, a publication may be distributed to the stockholders of a company, the employees of an organization, or to a small audience like a Board of Directors. In each case the audience size is restricted. This fact has a direct bearing on the production economics of the printed presentation. For example, the unit cost for using color may be prohibitive in small printing runs; typewritten copy may have to replace type setting; multilith printing may be a necessary substitute for commercial printing processes.

In open circulation, the size of the audience is generally unknown, except that it is usually much larger than a limited one. A specific size estimate is quite difficult to arrive at. Books, magazines, and periodicals fall into this category. While circulation figures may be available, they are not really representative of a readership because not every recipient actually reads them; and conversely, they are passed around and seen or read by many people in addition to the recipient.

Large audiences permit greater economic flexibility in the production of a printed presentation. For instance, the use of color is more feasible in

large printing orders. On the other hand, while the size of the audience then allows the communicator the opportunity to make a finer printed presentation, it also imposes the obligation to achieve an excellence that warrants the greater expenditure. Since the excellence of a printed presentation is as dependent upon its form as upon its content, various production problems like design, typography, printing quality, and binding will arise to plague him.

Thus, the production requirements of both limited and open circulations are directly related to the size of the audience.

In an oral presentation, audience size is a prime factor in selecting the presentation medium. The consideration of visibility is the first determinant. For instance, a flip-chart (hard-copy) presentation is convenient for small groups sitting around a conference table. Obviously, the same presentation medium cannot be made to an audience of two hundred. Large audiences require soft-copy media like vugraphs, or some other projection method. The media used for an oral presentation must, therefore, be selected to accommodate the size of the audience. While there are no rigid rules in this regard, audience size will determine which media alternatives are possible and which are automatically excluded (Chapter 8).

In turn, the choice of medium determines production methods. For example, soft copy in 35mm. requires copy camera work, while overhead projection requires a diazo process. The manner in which artwork is prepared can also differ according to the medium chosen.

The size of the audience also largely determines the physical facilities required. For example, seventy-five people obviously cannot be herded into a room with a seating capacity of fifty. It is equally disastrous, though not as obviously so, to put five people in a room that seats 105.

The size of the audience has another effect on an oral presentation and, though subtle, it is a very real one to the communicator. In most people's minds size is equated with importance — and the communicator is sometimes psychologically intimidated by a large audience. This is not as much the case with printed presentations because, though the audience may be infinitely larger, the author is in a remote position. But the communicator giving a "live" presentation stands face-to-face with his audience, and audience size may then become a negative factor to him. On the other hand, some speakers thrive on large audiences; to them, the bigger the audience, the greater the challenge and the better the presentation.

In sum: the factor of audience size is an important characteristic that determines the medium, the production methods, the facilities, and even the choice of communicator.

Audience Level

An audience can also be characterized by its level. Taken as a group, every audience has a particular level, which the presentation must aim to reach. This level can usually be identified by reference to the group's experience in a field of specialization, the extent of schooling it has had as a group, or the range of its intellectual capacity. Often more than one of these "measures" must be used.

In many instances, the levels are fairly simple to determine. For example, a presentation to children is obviously made at a quite different level than one for mature adults on the same subject. If they were not different, the communicator would either be "talking down" to the adults or "up" to the children. In this case the sophistication of ideas is the key difference in setting the presentation's level.

To determine level on the basis of the audience's intellectual capacity is difficult because that characteristic is harder to discern. Of course, there are some obvious cases. A presentation geared to average college students would probably bore a gathering of Phi Beta Kappas, who have the potential to comprehend the given subject matter in greater depth — or, in other words, "on a higher level."

The measure of intelligence level is, of course, a sensitive issue. Generally, people dislike being classified by "how smart" someone else may think they are. (Understandably, they resent being classed with twelve-year-olds by media-raters, and any approach that makes this obvious will incur their enmity — even though the classification may often be justified.)

It is a fact, nonetheless, that in every audience some members will be intellectually superior to others, and, therefore, be capable of grasping

more material more quickly than their colleagues. This, of course, makes the determination of an audience's specific level of intellectual capacity much more difficult. In such cases the communicator has little choice. He must seek what he knows, or assumes, to be the *predominant* level, but he should also keep in mind some sort of "averaging" approach that will capture the interest of virtually all of his audience. It is a sad observation, however, that many communicators mistakenly construe the averaging approach to mean the banalization of their material, and thereby unnecessarily emasculate their presentations.

The level of expertise that an audience possesses is primarily a product of experience. At one end of the experience range is the newly graduated trainee; at the other end is the seasoned professional. Homogeneous groups of new graduates and seasoned practitioners are of course infinitely less difficult to handle than the heterogeneous groups in between, in which experience varies widely. But here again the communicator must pitch his presentation at a level that would not exclude members of the audience at either end of the experience range.

Using the measure of experience to determine audience level, the communicator must also consider the extent of familiarity an audience may have with related disciplines. By doing so, he

10-3 Photo Courtesy of United Nations

will be able to broaden the conceptual scope and approach of his presentation. For instance, a financial man is in his element when the presentation deals with financial data — but less so when manufacturing data are the subject. Nevertheless, because of the related nature of manufacturing and finance, and because of his training, education, and general business experience, he will understand the manufacturing data with greater ease than will a college professor of English Literature.

Audience level is not an easy evaluation to make. By and large, most of the audience levels that a communicator will need to identify are of a subtle nature. For the most part, the audience level is a broad evaluation of the audience based on what the communicator knows of its members' experience, schooling, and intellectual capacity. He may know his audience well enough so that such determinations present no problems. At other times he may have to assume, surmise, or just plain guess. But in every case he must determine, to the best of his ability, the level at which he will make his presentation. And, in any case, a wrong determination is better than no determination.

Audience Rank

The rank of audience refers to the importance that a particular audience has for the communicator. Accordingly, rank is relative: a vice-president is as important to a manager as the chairman of the board is to the vice-president. Curiously, though, it is a human vanity for a presenter to overrate the rank of his audience; but this tendency seldom does any harm and often is a positive factor.

Rank is an important audience characteristic because it influences the presentation in two ways. The first is psychological: the desire to make an impression. It is only natural that a communicator should want to put his best foot forward to impress an audience of importance to him. Often such audiences are the communicator's superiors, and the recognition of a job well done is a reward we all need. Audience rank, then, is a motivating force that spurs one to superior performance.

The second influence of audience rank is its ef-

fect on the conceptual approach to a presentation. For example, the higher the audience's rank is within an organization, the less detail is needed in reporting to it. Top echelons, usually the decision-making people, resort to exception-reporting techniques to gain an overview of their operation.

Thus the factor of rank in determining the character of an audience plays an important role in the manner a presentation is conceived and delivered.

Audience Background

The background of an audience is a factor that decides the depth in which the subject of a presentation can be treated. Generally, audiences are either *homogeneous* or *heterogeneous* by nature. An audience at an American Bar Association meeting would be considered homogeneous. On the other hand, an audience at a local Rotary Club luncheon can usually be considered heterogeneous.

For communications purposes, however, an audience is either homogeneous or heterogeneous in relation to the subject matter being presented and the technical complexity of its treatment. An audience may be heterogeneous in nature, but it will become hogomeneous in its need for interpretation of technical material with which it is unfamiliar as a group. Conversely, a homogeneous audience can become heterogeneous when the subject matter being presented is familiar to part of the group only.

Suppose, for example, that an audience of lawyers were exposed to a presentation on "Negotiable Instruments." The audience would be considered homogeneous because each member is thoroughly familiar with the subject matter. If the same audience were exposed to a presentation on "Nuclear Physics" it would again be homogeneous — this time because it would know little or nothing about the subject matter. However, if the same group were exposed to a presentation on "Playing Golf," it would probably be a heterogeneous audience, since some of the members would be golf "experts," some slightly familiar, and others totally unfamiliar with the game.

Thus, the factor of audience background sets the parameters of the technical depth that can be incorporated into a presentation. It also defines the limits of using technical jargon and/or sophisticated concepts in the presentation. For instance, to a homogeneous audience that is very familiar with the subject, concepts can be presented in their advanced stages. When, on the other hand, an audience is heterogeneous in its knowledge of the subject, or homogeneously uninformed, the same concept will have to be developed step by step, perhaps using ideas analogous to the audience's background and experience.

Audience Exposure

An analysis of audience exposure produces a factor that indicates the extent of experience an audience has had with "sophisticated" graphics. This evaluation is extremely important because it is the actual communication link between the communicator and his audience. The degree of complexity in which a graphic device can be executed is largely dependent on the extent to which the audience has been exposed to visual material of a similar nature.

Comprehension is not only a function of the ideas expressed, but also of the physical forms in which these ideas are presented. For example, a sociologist may want to chart the results of a study and present it in simple terms to a lay audience. The study involves all sorts of chi-squares and probability curves. But if his audience does not know chi-square from Times Square it will be impossible to communicate with it via the traditional forms of charting statistical data. Therefore, the idea must be "spoon-fed" to it in terms and with analogies it understands, and this information must be translated into conventional graphic forms commonly used.

Invariably, the degree of sophistication that can be incorporated into the design and execution of a presentation depends mainly upon the extent of experience the audience has in understanding and interpreting graphic forms without too much effort and without conceptual distortion.

Thus, the audience's ability to translate graphic materials into usable information is predicated on prior exposure to them. Selecting the graphic forms best suited to an audience is indeed a difficult task because communicators persist in as-suming that other people are as well versed in charting as they are. This erroneous assumption can ruin the best presentation. The generalizations shown in Figure 10-4 are some guidelines that will indicate the different degrees of complexity of graphic forms.

Audience Bias

The most elusive audience characteristic is its bias. The communicator can never be sure of the attitudes, interests, and expectations of his audience, but he knows that they are a factor in the success of his presentation.

While favorable reactions are usually shown openly, the decorum of most audiences masks their displeasure. The hostile audience is difficult to deal with. The audience that is coerced into attendance, for instance, is understandably hostile, and inevitably closes its mind. The audience that is burdened with unwanted printed matter wreaks its vengeance by tossing the material away unread. These are unfortunate facts of life, and when these situations cannot be avoided, they must be coped with as best one can.

There is another audience attitude that must be met with care—apathy. This state can have a negative effect on the communication disproportionate to the amount of negativism actually felt by the audience. Apathy is an involuntary state of indifference usually caused by lack of concern. For instance, the financial man is primarily interested in rates of return, the manufacturing executives in units of productivity, the marketing man in comparative distribution costs. With the same set of statistics, the emphasis can be shifted to the area that interests a particular audience the most. It is not that the audience members are not interested in anything but their own bailiwick, but that other areas are of secondary interest to them. In order to reach a particular audience, the communicator must "speak its language," and offer a meaningful presentation within its sphere of interest—or apathy may set in.

The factor of audience bias, then, also contributes to the identification of audience character. It is not the most important factor, nor the least important, but it can be the crucial determinant in preventing a beautifully designed presentation from falling flat.

185

Easily understood by those with little or no prior exposure	Requires some explanation to be understood by those with little or no prior exposure	Requires prior exposure to be understood properly
Simple Bar, Column, Line, or Surface	Subdivided 100% Bar or Column	Bar & Symbol
Grouped Bars or Columns	Paired Bars or Columns	Deviation Bar or Column
Subdivided Bars or Columns	Progressive Bar	Range Bar or Column
Single Step Line or Surface	Area Bar	Sliding Bar
Pictogram	Multiple Lines or Surfaces	Floating Column
Word Chart	Multiple 100% Lines or Surfaces	Band Chart
	Pictograph	Intersecting Chart
	Maps	Flow Chart
	Process Chart	Multiple (Double) Amount Scales
	Organization Chart	Ratio Scale Chart
	Third Dimensional Chart	Index Chart
	Circle Chart	Charts in Perspective
		Proportional Representational Chart
		Rates-of-Change Comparisons
		Scale Breaks

10-4 Graphic Forms Listed according to Ease of Audience Comprehension

Taken all together, then, the characteristics of audience — size, level, rank, background, exposure, and bias — form the character of an audience, and this character is an important — if not the key — element used in conceiving, designing, and implementing a graphic communication. In fact, as shown in the next chapter, the character of the audience influences almost all the decisions made in developing the tenor and direction of the final presentation.

11

The Presentation

The term "presentation," in the idiom of visual communications, has been given more than one meaning. To wit: the visual aids that are shown as a package (e.g. a group of slides) are called a "presentation," while the act of showing them is called a "presentation," and the conception, preparation, and execution of the various steps that produce a presentation are also called a "presentation." This last meaning is the subject of this chapter. Actually, it is a summing-up chapter—which refers to the material of previous chapters, and together with some new material, directs it to, and ties it in with, the formulation of a visual presentation.

Figure 11-2 is a graphic conceptualization of a presentation, showing its component steps. The chart, in which each circle represents a discrete activity, is a modified "network analysis"; though it may seem formidable at first, it can prove to be a valuable planning, scheduling, and progress-control tool for the communicator. Perhaps a few words of explanation will be useful before we begin to follow the chart, activity by activity, toward the final making of a presentation.

Note that the discrete activities in the chart proceed from left to right, and resultant activities do not begin before requisite activities have been completed. Medium, for example, cannot be selected until the size and character of the Audience is determined, and the Budget fixed; similarly, Facilities cannot be planned until the Audience is identified, the Budget fixed, and the Medium is selected. Some activities, however, like fixing the Budget and determining What to Chart, can begin concurrently, since neither is a prerequisite of the other.

The most valuable information provided by this chart is the relationships the activities have to each other. The Audience, for example, has a bearing on determining What to Chart, Organizing Ideas, Visualizing Ideas, selection of Medium, planning of Facilities, and the fixing of a Budget. Accordingly, each of these activities must take into consideration one (or more) audience characteristic in its execution.

Activity One: Receive Request

Upon receiving a request to make a presentation —from either an internal or external source— some basic information is immediately needed: (1) date, time, and place of the presentation, (2) time allowed, (3) subject matter, (4) size and general description of the audience, and (5) funds available.

The initial parameters of the presentation are set by this information. Most likely, some of it—like date, time and place, and audience—is unchangeable, but others—like subject matter and funds—can often be modified.

With this basic information in hand the communicator can begin to develop the rest of his network analysis.

Activity Two: Identify Audience

Primary attention should be given to this activity because so much of the subsequent planning for the presentation is based on the character of the audience. There are six primary audience characteristics essential to its identification: size, level, rank, background, exposure, and bias. Each of them is described in detail in Chapter 10, and when they are properly evaluated (in light of the audience described in the request), these characteristics will have a critical bearing on decisions which must be made in other activities of the network.

11-1 Photo Courtesy of American Telephone & Telegraph

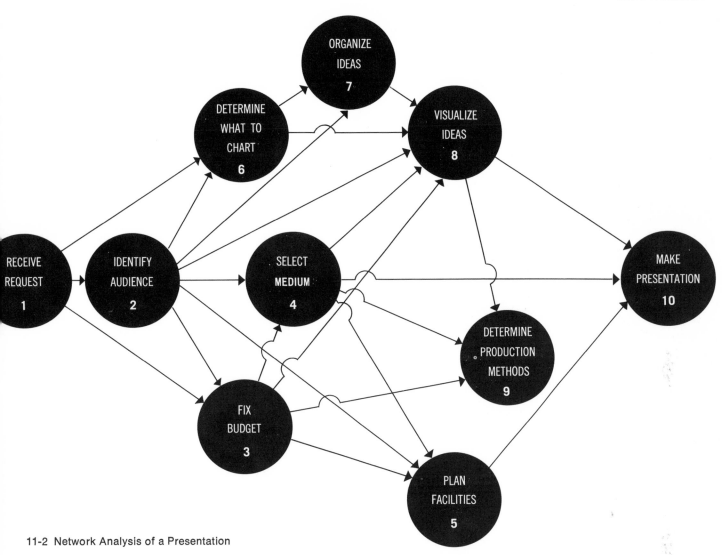

11-2 Network Analysis of a Presentation

Activity Three: Fix Budget

There are a number of factors that have an effect on fixing a budget for a presentation. All of them, however, are motivated, in some way or other, by an anticipated return on investment. (What is it worth to us? — and that "worth" cannot always be measured in dollars and cents.)

The cost of preparing and making a presentation, like any other expenditure, must be analyzed and evaluated to determine whether its return is worth the effort and expense. Cost factors are produced, for instance, by the audience; its characteristics of size and rank have a strong influence on determining the budget. Size, for example, will affect the choice of media and facilities. Rank will often dictate the extent of graphic elaborateness warranted in preparing visual material and the facilities in which the presentation will be given.

Once the cost has been estimated, the subsidy

(if any) authorized by the request in the form of a fee or honorarium is normally treated as an offset against the proposed expenditure. A deficit will require an appropriation that the communicator's firm, for reasons of its own, must decide whether or not to make. The budget, however, must be fixed before proceeding further.

Activity Four: Select Medium

Media for oral presentations and the criteria for selecting one are covered in Chapter 8. The different types of hard- and soft-copy media are discussed, with their attendant advantages and disadvantages. The chapter also establishes criteria by which each medium is evaluated, and from this evaluation the medium best suited for a particular oral presentation can be selected.

When, on the other hand, the presentation will appear as a printed piece, this activity in the network should be used to select the printed medium that will be used. Media for written pre-

189

11-3 Photo by Robert Muir

sentations are many: periodical placements, trade journals, direct-mail pieces, annual reports, house organs, professional magazines, research studies, management reports, proposals, newsletters, newspapers, advertising circulars, and sales brochures are some examples of generic groups.

Activity Five: Plan Facilities

The size of the audience is of primary consideration in the planning of facilities. The presentation room selected must be big enough (or small enough) to house the audience comfortably.

Audience rank is another important consideration. There are many grades of facilities, and to some degree the rank of the audience will influence the type chosen. Its relative luxury, however, depends on the provisions made in the budget.

The medium selected for the presentation also has an effect on the choice of room. A daytime presentation using a soft-copy medium, for instance, cannot be given in a room having windows that cannot be covered.

These and other factors that go into planning a facility for an oral presentation are discussed in Chapter 9 (Facilities-Planning).

In the case of written presentations this activity of the network should be utilized to select the supplier services needed to produce a printed piece. Among these are: typography, printing, paper, binding, mailing or distribution, postal requirements, photography library, and addressing and labeling.

Activity Six: Determine What To Chart

To some extent the request usually specifies the subject matter of the presentation. But the material actually charted is left to the judgment of the communicator.

From Activity Two the audience characteristics of level, rank, background, and bias provide him

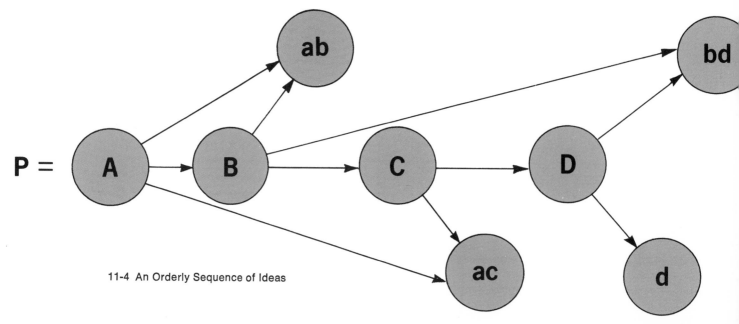

11-4 An Orderly Sequence of Ideas

with some guidelines in determining what to chart.

In addition, Chapter 2 (To Chart or Not To Chart) and Chapter 3 (Cornerstones, Pillars, and Pitfalls of Charting) discuss the kinds of material that lend themselves to charting, material that should not be charted, criteria for charting, and the advantages and disadvantages of charting.

Activity Seven: Organize Ideas

In the organization of ideas the communicator attempts to structure his subject matter in an orderly sequence that clearly, simply, and logically develops his thoughts, and that provides a cohesive thread of continuity for his text.

The words "orderly sequence," unfortunately, tend to be ambiguous; this is unavoidable because there is really no way to preorganize ideas in a manner suitable for every situation. Consequently, an "orderly sequence" becomes a variable factor, dependent on the purpose, subject matter, and audience of the communication.

Take the communication's purpose as an example. It has a considerable bearing on the presentation approach in that presentations that are designed to inform have different points of departure and certainly different ends than those meant to sell, and both are different from those designed to educate. The overall character of the audience also influences the organization of ideas, because even superb ideas of genius, brilliantly organized — but wrongly so for a particular audience — will merely become a series of frustrating question marks to it.

The ordering of parts is the wellspring from which come the clarity, simplicity, logic, and continuity of a presentation. By and large, the more creative facets of what is said, and how it is said, tend to overshadow the more prosaic need for organization. The most difficult task for the writer is the one of mechanics. Various attempts have been made to construct a methodology for the organization of ideas, and in the hands of some it has done good; for many users, however, who have used it as a crutch, it has become their Frankenstein.

Without demeaning the creative process, it can fairly be said that the organization of ideas is essentially mechanical. And, therefore, useful tools can be provided, which, when used with discretion, can assist the organizer in "thinking through" the arrangement of his material.

Accordingly, the following guidelines are offered as an approach to facilitate the organization of ideas into an orderly sequence:

(1) Make a rough outline of the key ideas, and their subordinates, that the text will cover.

(2) Fortify and amplify these ideas with the material derived from Activity Six.

(3) Build homely examples to illustrate abstruse points.

(4) Arrange the ideas in a sequence so that one main point leads logically into the next.

(5) Structure the logic into a presentation framework that suits the purpose of the message.

Let's take the last two steps through some more specific mechanics, using the letter "P" to signify the communication's principal message, capital letters to indicate key ideas, and lower case letters to represent subordinate ideas. Theoretically, then, the rough outline in Step 1 (above) could be symbolized as: $P = A + ab + ac + B + bd + C + D + d$.

This is an orderly series of ideas, but not necessarily an orderly sequence. The subordinate idea ab, for example, follows directly after A, but the audience is unfamiliar with b, as they are with c. Therefore, confusion is likely to set in unless B and C are explained before ab and ac are introduced. A network analysis (like the one this chapter is built on) will help avoid this confusion.

Figure 11-4 is a network analysis that shows the series in an orderly sequence. Note that each point leads logically into the next, and the subordinate ideas are not introduced until the audience is prepared to understand them. From techniques like this one the interaction of ideas can be readily visualized, and a logical integration can be effected.

Step 5 of the above, which is the framework encompassing the presentation, is shown in Figure 11-5 as either a pyramid form or an inverted pyramid form. The pyramid form presents its supporting argument first and slowly narrows to its principal message. (This technique is referred to as a "Punch Line.") The inverted pyramid form states its principal message at the very beginning

191

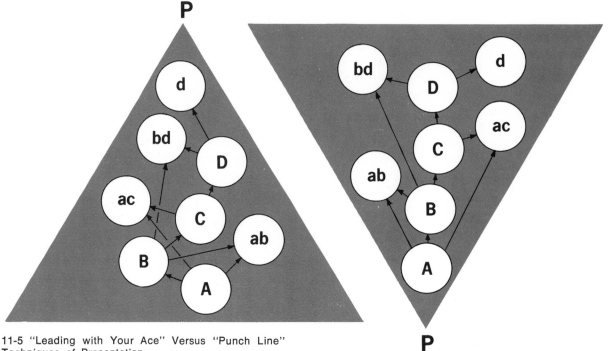

11-5 "Leading with Your Ace" Versus "Punch Line"
Techniques of Presentation

and then gives the argument to support it. (This technique is often referred to as "Leading with Your Ace.")

Either structure is generally suitable, but in some instances one or the other is more effective. In a budget request, for instance, the inverted pyramid form is psychologically superior, because, by telling the audience at the outset how much is requested, you remove them from tenterhooks, and for the balance of the presentation its attention will be focused on what is being said, rather than anticipating how much will be requested.

Activity Eight: Visualize Ideas

Problems that arise in the visualization of ideas invariably stem from a popular misconception that visual aids are strictly aids for the person making the presentation. They are not! He already knows the material being presented. Visual aids are aids for the audience to understand what is being communicated. Consequently, they should be conceived with only that thought in mind.

The most prevalent fault in conceiving visuals is the tendency to pack too much information into a single chart. It is a compulsion, especially in technical areas, and particularly with those who have little or no experience in using visuals as aids. The use of visual aids can be easily overused or misused, causing visual redundancies and irrelevancies — (both very common mistakes discussed in Chapter 2).

In conceiving visuals, the communicator must bear in mind that charts are used to communicate quickly, clearly, and memorably — and should be prepared for these purposes alone. (Being imaginative and inventive is not a license to be "arty," or to lose sight of the communication's purpose and audience.)

The visualization of ideas for an oral text is somewhat different than for a written text. The essential difference is the matter of continuity. In an oral presentation the viewer's attention is primarily attracted to the visual material. Occasionally he may glance at the speaker, but after a while the physical appearance of the speaker almost disappears — only his voice remains. This is especially true if the room is in semidarkness — which most projection media require. The viewer, in a sense "hypnotized" by the charts he is viewing, needs movement, or he will be lulled into inattention and will no longer absorb the words being spoken.

Thus, an oral presentation has got to march along. Visuals must be changed frequently. While it is true that an experienced speaker can some-

192

times compensate for insufficient visuals by hastening the pace of his delivery of "non-visualized" text, or by dwelling on particular points of a visual to "kill the clock," or even by going off on interesting tangents designed to "overpower" the lack of visualization, it is more often the case that none of these ploys relieve the hypnotic effect of a single, simple, silent visual floating in space for any considerable length of time—especially so, if the visual is no longer relevant to the text.

In more sophisticated oral presentations techniques of progressive disclosure are being widely used to avoid static visualization. In progressive disclosure the subject matter is broken down into small and simple bits. Each bit occupies a chart. A single idea may be composed of a number of bits that are presented additively. Suppose, for instance, an idea were made of bits A, B, and C. The first chart in the series would present only bit A. The second chart would retain A and add B. The third chart would retain A and B and add C. By using this technique a number of ends are accomplished: (1) three charts rather than one chart create a sense of movement by frequently changing; (2) presenting an idea in smaller bits increases the opportunity for the audience to grasp it more easily; and (3) the audience's attention is focused on one bit at a time rather than three bits all at once. This latter point is important because, if a complex idea is presented on only one chart, the viewer often attempts to search the chart to uncover its meanings before the speaker has a chance to explain them. In doing so, the viewer cuts himself off almost completely from the speaker.

In a written presentation, however, the need for visual movement hardly exists. The text is the vehicle of continuity. Since the viewer—or, in this case, the reader—is occupied with the text, the visuals can afford to be static. Moreover, they can afford to be more involved, and the communicator can pack more into them. He can double the scales. He can use multicomparison. He can use copious labeling and explanatory notes.

Thus, when the text demands, or refers to, a visual, the reader can turn to it. He can study it, muse over it, interpret it at will, and, in general, take his own sweet time. The ticking clock makes no demands on his attention.

If there is any key word that describes the process of visualization it is simplicity. Visuals should be kept simple in content as well as in design. (Being simple, of course, should not be confused with being simple-minded.)

In an oral presentation, simplicity can be achieved by breaking up complex information into a number of charts, with each chart serving as an uncluttered building block that carries forward the points and theme of the message.

In a written presentation simplicity may be achieved by showing a central idea in chart form, and supplementing the idea with short tables showing details. Wordiness in both types of visuals should be minimized. In fact, as a rule of thumb, if a chart is to be projected its text should comfortably fit on a 3-by-5 card when typewritten in capital letters. If the chart is to be printed, the use of less than 8-point type should be avoided.

In the translation of ideas into visuals the communicator should take full advantage of the many graphic devices available to him. Chapter 4 (Basic Charting Devices) and Chapter 6 (Pictorial Charts) hold a great many graphic ideas that can be effectively utilized in the visualization process. Chapter 5 (Mechanics of Charting) will help in putting the devices into their proper formats.

Before he begins, however, it is well for him to remember that the difference between successful graphics and those that are not successful—or at best, ordinary—depends on the application of the basics in an inventive and imaginative way, and never allowing the basics to become a strait jacket. On the other hand, art for art's sake has no place in charting.

Activity Nine: Determine Production Methods

The medium selected generally prescribes methods of production. A vugraph presentation on an overhead projector, for instance, is produced by a diazo process; 35mm. slides require camera work and film processing; opaque projection requires little or no production. In Chapter 8 (Selection of Medium) the various media are described.

The extent of elaborateness of the artwork for any medium, of course, is a budgetary matter. The use of color or outside services and the number of pieces produced are affected by the amount of money earmarked for the production of the presentation material. Therefore, when entering into the production phase, price quotations should be secured and checked against the estimates in the budget. If the quotations are higher than the budget estimates, the communicator will have to seek additional appropriations or backtrack through the network to effect cuts. Perhaps he can reduce the number of visuals planned, or perhaps he may chose to downgrade the medium originally selected. In addition, or as an alternative, he may seek economies in his production methods: perhaps by eliminating some color, or dropping planned illustrations, or perhaps by taking production short cuts that would eliminate elaborateness and yet not greatly impinge on the stature and quality of the finished product.

There are many, many methods and techniques used to produce visual aids — too many to describe or enumerate. It suffices, however, to point out that technology in this field is moving so rapidly that we can all learn something from opening our doors to the vendors who are eager to introduce their products and innovations.

The section "Sources and References" at the back of this book contains an extensive listing of vendor sources that can furnish up-to-date information on particular methods of production.

Activity Ten: The Presentation

The final activity in the network is the presentation — the last port of call, so to speak. The structured outline in its orderly sequence (Activity Seven), with its ideas visualized (Activity Eight), is now ready to have "meat put on its bones."

In a written presentation it is, of course, necessary to write out the text, but in an oral presentation it is better to leave the text in outline form so that spontaneity (during the presentation) will not be inhibited by reading the text aloud, or attempting to memorize it verbatim. Many speakers, however, make the mistake of writing out their text and reading it aloud — a procedure that rarely succeeds in stimulating an audience, regardless of the speaker's skill.

Each medium has its own mode of expression that must be taken into consideration when preparing the presentation text. They have in common the use of language, but their grammatical structures, rhythms, and rules of syntax are considerably different. (For instance, oral presentations that are translated verbatim into written prose usually read like the dialogues from some unfortunate TV drama.)

The communicator using the written word is in many ways more fortunate in that his presentation can be edited by others until a polished product is produced. However, written text is more demanding in its execution — poor writing is a great deal more obvious than a poor talk.

The fact is that, of the countless oral presentations given, very few of them are blessed with outstanding speakers (who can usually get by with the poorest of material). The average speaker, however, can be acceptable if his material is well

11-6 Photo by Robert Muir

planned, well prepared, and well executed. Quality control in giving presentations is a ticklish business, which is probably why the sound/slide films are so widely used.

For most people, getting up before an audience is a terrifying experience, and by and large the audience is sympathetic to a speaker who is obviously suffering. Perhaps it is precisely because an audience is willing to make such allowances for an oral presentation that its standards of quality are less demanding.

Speakers are usually chosen by virtue of their position or technical acumen. Generally, they are not trained speakers, and if they had their way, would choose not to give an oral presentation at all. If, for example, a company official had to write a presentation, he could employ a ghost writer and none would be the wiser. But when he must give an oral presentation, only he can get up before the audience and deliver his message. (For many, a maiden speech is the moment of truth.)

Gaining proficiency in giving oral presentations is, for the most part, a matter of practice. Many individuals have become better than average speakers by continual exposure to audience situations. Many organizations go to great lengths to train their executives in the art of public speaking, and many are rewarded for their efforts. It is not the intention of this chapter, however, to examine these programs. But for those individuals who find themselves apprehensive in having to give an oral presentation, this friendly advice can be given: *know your material, practice your presentation, and check your facilities in advance.*

More explicitly, the following suggestions are offered:

Type the outlined text with lots of space around it, and make it large enough to see.

Mark in pauses.

Use mnemonic devices (like color-coding) on your script to tip you off to what's coming next.

Edit visuals beforehand to make sure you have the right ones.

Arrange your visuals in their proper sequence and *do not* tamper with this order until the presentation is over. (If a chart is repeated in the course of the presentation, use multiple copies of it.)

Practice handling your visuals. If remote control is used, become accustomed to how to advance, reverse, and focus the projector.

Study both your charts and text beforehand for hidden implications you may have missed in designing them — don't wait until you are up before your audience to stammer through trying to answer a question on some overlooked facet of your material.

Practice your presentation as an integrated whole — the audio and visual will be presented together and must be learned together.

Explain your visuals fully — don't leave the audience to try to figure out points made either superficially or not at all.

Keep visuals covered until they are ready to be shown.

Don't use terms in your text that conflict with terms on the visuals.

Read key words from the visual, but don't read every bit of text on the visual.

Don't read your text and don't memorize either — work in ideas and explain them in your own words of the minute.

Prepare for emergencies. Be able to break into your presentation at any point and then resume it again smoothly.

Vary your introduction to each new visual.

Smoothen your transitions between visuals so that one chart leads into the next chart logically and evenly.

Change your pace from time to time during the presentation.

Check out facility arrangements in advance.

Check lectern for proper lighting so that notes can be read.

Make sure that everybody will be able to see.

Arrange yourself so that you will stand close to your visuals and become a part of the presentation.

Put some real enthusiasm in your voice.

Rehearse, rehearse, rehearse.

195

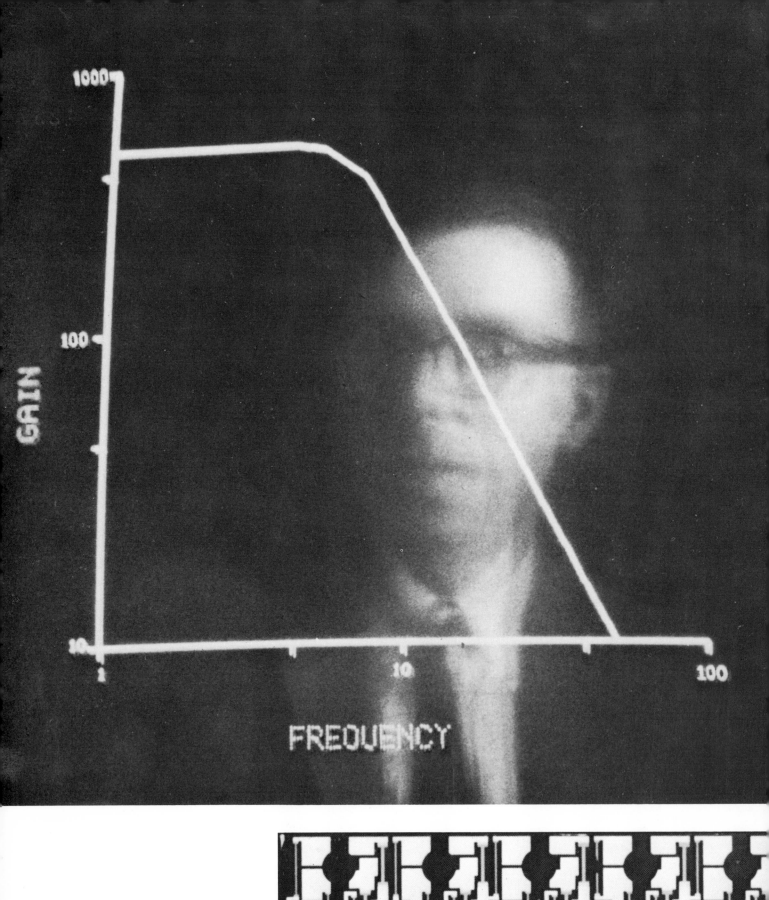

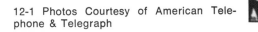

12

Tomorrow the Tube

The Evolution of Charting

It was less than 200 years ago that William Playfair developed his method of visually depicting, by lines, forms, and symbols, certain relationships in quantitative data.

"The advantage proposed by this method," he wrote, "is not that of giving a more accurate statement than by figures, but it is to give a more simple and permanent idea of the gradual progress and comparative amounts, at different periods, by presenting to the eye a figure, the proportions of which correspond with the amount of the sums intended to be expressed."

Playfair called his system *lineal arithmetic,* and in 1786 published a work entitled *The Commercial and Political Atlas,* which is acknowledged as the origin of statistical charting techniques as we know them today.

Playfair was wholly aware of the value of his innovation. Concerning his new ingenious technique he wrote, ". . . as much information may be obtained in five minutes as would require whole days to imprint on the memory, in a lasting manner, by a table of figures."

Thus, at the close of the eighteenth century a remarkable communication tool was made available to the world. Actually, it is a wonder that it took as long as it did for someone to formulate and apply the concepts of charting. The mathematical bases for Playfair's lineal arithmetic can be found long before the eighteenth century. Descartes' work in analytical geometry, with his methods of establishing rectangular coordinates, for instance, dates as far back as 1637. Leonardo da Vinci, in 1560, used the x-y axes in his experiments with gravitation, while intrepid explorers of the Old World sailed the unknown seas by longitudes and latitudes invented by astronomers long before the birth of Christ. In the eleventh century the renowned Persian poet-mathematician, Omar Khayyam, used graphs to combine algebra and geometry. In fact, it can be said that the possibility to develop charting has existed since 300 B.C., when Euclid organized the random principles of geometry into a logical system — some 2,000 years before Playfair came onto the scene.

The explanation for the long delay, however, is simple enough: until the eighteenth century the need for charting simply did not exist. Until then, the tempo of the times was comparatively slow. Communications sometimes took weeks, months, and even years to reach their destination. Economies were agrarian, mercantilism was rampant, the artisan supreme, and the entrepreneurs isolated into microcosmic pockets of provincialism. And so there was little reason for an orderly accumulation of quantitative data to exist. Furthermore, few people could read.

The eighteenth century, however, brought forth two significant developments that made the time right for the introduction of charting.

The first of these was the Industrial Revolution, which began in England about 1750. It signaled the birth of modern industrialism by altering the economic structure from its former basis of agriculture and mercantilism to one of technology and capitalism. With it came concepts like production, sales, inventories, receivables — all of which are *quantitatively* related.

Parallel to this dramatic change came the introduction of the science of statistics, developed in Germany about the same time that the Industrial Revolution was irrevocably altering English

197

society. In its early use, statistics dealt with the collection, classification, and discussion of facts bearing on the condition of the State (hence, the name *statistics*); the application of its methods to business and industry soon became apparent.

Thus, industrialism gave rise to a wealth of numerical facts, and statistics provided methods for their orderly accumulation. The stage was set for William Playfair.

Once introduced, it would seem reasonable to assume that charting would take hold as a powerful communication device. But it didn't happen that way. Charting remained dormant throughout the nineteenth century, its potential inert. What was needed was a new pioneer to begin the task of implementation. This pioneer arrived on the scene in the person of Willard Brinton, who published his milestone, *Graphic Methods for Presenting Facts,* in 1914. Despite Brinton's efforts, however, an additional catalyst was needed for charting to take permanent root. The First World War provided the needed impetus.

In 1939 Brinton acknowledged this fact, writing, "Probably the feverish demand for prompt and reliable data during war times did more to stimulate the use of graphic chart technique than anything that has happened since 1920."

It was not solely the war that stimulated the use of charting; another factor, an important one, had a good deal to do with lifting charting out of its obscurity. In 1938 The American Society of Mechanical Engineers published a Standards Manual that provided a uniform approach to the concepts and presentation of charting techniques. Prior to this the graphic language of charting lacked the commonality necessary for dependable communication.

The project for standardization had begun shortly before World War I, when the Society sponsored Willard Brinton as organizer and chairman of a Joint Committee on Standards for Graphic Presentation. The committee was charged with the task of laying the groundwork for standardizing the nomenclature and meanings of charting. It was on the recommendations of their report that the Standards Manual was based.

Ironically, its publication came just in time for another world war; like the First, the Second gave charting another tremendous boost. When industry went to war, so did charting. The monumental quantifications produced by our "Arsenal of Democracy" found their way onto charts, charts, and more charts. So, in those frantic days of massive production the value of charting became apparent. Charting had arrived. The lessons taught by the speed and conciseness of reporting via graphic techniques should have been indelible. But many lessons, those of war and others, seldom remain learned for long. It's somehow the human way.

Carried by the momentum of its wartime role, charting became an accepted communicative device — yet, not with the fervor and pervasiveness it should have had.

Nevertheless, today, charting techniques are familiar forms of communication. They are common enough to be found in many technical books, magazines, newspapers, annual reports, and many other sources. And it can be truly said that if communication graphics is never developed beyond its present state, or applied beyond its present uses, it can still be considered a powerful and valuable communications tool. *But its potential has not yet been fully realized!*

The Information Explosion

The tempo of our busy, bustling world is becoming irrefutably faster. The need to know is virtually an instantaneous need, and the amount to know is virtually an insurmountable amount. One hardly needs to be told that we are being burdened with more and more information; we are experiencing it daily.

Yet, what each of us experiences is only an infinitesimal part of the information presently being generated and accumulated at a startling rate. Indeed, some observations can be made that dramatize the magnitude of the communication problem faced by virtually every user of information. For example:

Starting with the birth of Christ, the first doubling of knowledge occurred by 1750, the next doubling by 1900, the third by 1950, the fourth by 1960, the fifth by 1966, and, in all probability, the sixth doubling is on its way to completion.

Business and government employ two million clerks who file 1,500 trillion pieces of paper annually at an estimated cost of $39 billion. Each year sixty-two million filing cabinets are made to meet the need for additional filing space. In government alone, two million employees annually write a billion letters and cause to be printed some eighteen billion different forms.

A reader determined to keep abreast in only the natural sciences would have to be aware of what is being said in over a half-million articles and papers appearing in some 100,000 journals in sixty languages. More than that, he would have to find his way among some forty million volumes already on the shelves.

In technology the paper used to design a jet bomber outweighs the plane itself. The data generated from a single satellite launched and in orbit for a few months filled 700 miles of magnetic tape, which, if analyzed manually, would require five men and 500 years to turn it into useful information.

By the early 1970s nearly one out of every two people who graduates from college in the United States will have to adopt teaching as a profession in order to maintain our present teacher-student ratio, which is hardly sufficient to meet the demands of imparting new knowledge at rates somewhere near those at which it is being accumulated.

This astonishing deluge of the written word is properly labeled the Information Explosion. Certainly the volumes of information pouring forth from pens, typewriters, and presses are alarming — and if they aren't, they should be. The trouble is that the figures involved tend to be beyond our grasp (like the national debt). The complacent, however, need only reflect upon this sobering thought: ". . . it has been estimated that during every sixty seconds of the twenty-four-hour day more than two thousand pages of text are published throughout the world. Hence, if an indvidual with an average reading speed . . . were foolish enough to attempt to read this entire

output, even though he devote the entire twenty-four hours of the day to his reading, he would fall behind some billion pages a year" — and this was written in 1960!

So we have a problem — a real one, which becomes more onerous as the minutes tick by, depositing in their wake thousands more pages of text — all in the name of knowledge. But it a kind of knowledge unlike that which the Enlightenment thirsted for: a *desire* to know. Ours is a *need* to know. It is a means, just as a technique is a means. It is a raw material (a most vital one) that forms the bases of our decision-making processes.

Knowledge, in the contemporary sense, is information, in its most basic sense: a compendium of facts. It does not follow, moreover, that if information is knowledge, more information is more knowledge. Unstructured information leads to chaos, massive amounts of unbridled information lead to intellectual indigestion.

199

12-2, 12-3 Photos by Ted Russell (From *Machines*. TIME-LIFE BOOKS, Time Inc. © 1964)

We face a challenge: to be masters or be mastered. Obviously, not all information is of primary value. Much of it is redundant or superfluous. It has been claimed, for example, that business has created a file drawer full of paper on each of the 67,000,000 workers in American industry, 95 per cent of which is never referred to again. Also, much of the information produced is buried and obscured in the estimated 288,000 pages published daily. Researchers, for example, often find it easier to repeat an experiment or a test than to search the literature to find if it had been performed previously.

The struggle of harnessing information is not being regarded lightly. In all sectors of our literate community people are becoming vitally concerned with the clarification, unification, and integration of information storage and retrieval. Industry, institutions, and government are giving high priorities to pioneering efforts in data retrieval because it is the most significant technological development in our struggle to master the

galloping data and information accumulation threatening to smother us. Beneath the darkened clouds of the paper plague the battle is joined.

But the clouds, however dark, have a silver lining. A major step in coping with the information explosion has been the development of the electronic digital computer. Technological advancements are occurring so rapidly in this field that the vast potentials, popularly ascribed to the machine in its embryonic stages, may one day soon become more fact than fantasy.

For instance, compared with machines of the first- and second-generation computers, today's third-generation computers are purported to be a hundred times faster, their electronic makeup (by virtue of the silicon chip) ten times smaller, and, in the all-important terms of economics, they are probably 1,000 times less expensive.

We need not recite, here, the role that computers play in handling data; enough is said elsewhere. Our concern is the communication role that charting can play in conjunction with the

200

12-4 Photo Courtesy of General Electric

computer. Both charting and computers use the same mode of expression: quantification. Anything that can be shown in numbers and symbols can be charted. Likewise, anything shown in numbers and symbols can be stored in a digital computer. The compatibility of computers and charting, therefore, is apparent.

For the past two decades, those who have utilized a computer for charting have had to convert manually raw information, produced from the computer in tabular form, into graphic form in order to produce a chart. With more up-to-date equipment, raw information can be easily converted into graphic form directly *from* and *by* computers.

Digital Plotters

In recent years computer-controlled digital plotting has taken root in many industries, businesses, and government agencies to solve problems and to generate charts. A commonly recognized use is the meteorological maps of the Weather Bureau.

Plotters are being used when the volume of computations of data makes manual operations either uneconomical or impossible. Digital plotting systems provide an efficient, flexible means of producing high quality ink-on-paper plots of computer output data, with unvarying accuracy. The format possibilities of plotters are many; a pictorial representation, for example, may include a combination of axes, lines, letters, and symbols, with a wide range of scale increments, and letter and symbol sizes.

The plotting is produced by the movement of a pen on the surface of the recording paper in much the same manner as the familiar electrocardiogram. (These systems are used both off-line and on-line.) In short, any computer-output data that could be reduced to graphic form manually can also be plotted automatically with a digital plotter — certainly faster and with greater precision, and, in most cases, at a lower unit cost.

Plotters, for example, are credited with being able to produce charts that normally take 150 hours of hard meticulous manual work in about eight hours. A marvelous achievement — but not enough, by any means.

To meet the challenge of exploding information a fantastically more rapid device is needed merely to cope with the needs of today, and certainly

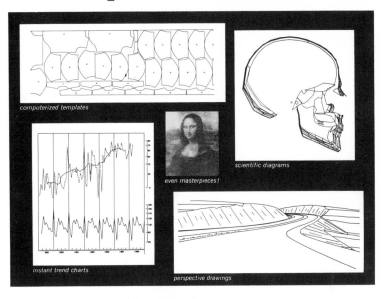

12-6 Illustration Courtesy of California Computer Products, Inc.

12-5 Photo Courtesy of Electronic Associates, Inc.

201

with the demands of tomorrow.

Such a device exists; it is the CRT (Cathode Ray Tube).

Computer Graphics

The CRT is an evolutionary new tool for the communicator. Visually, this device looks like a TV set mounted on top of a typewriter-like key-

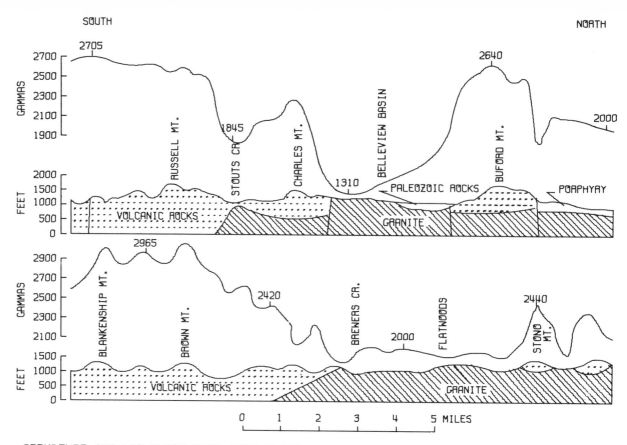

STRUCTURE AND LITHOLOGY FROM AEROMAGNETIC PROFILES OVER THE ST. FRANCOIS MOUNTAINS

12-7 A Configuration Drawn by a Digital Plotter (Illustration Courtesy of California Computer Products, Inc.)

12-8 Photo Courtesy of International Business Machines

board. With the aid of a sensor called a lightpen (a gadget that actually produces no light although it is shaped like a flashlight pen), the information on the CRT screen can be manipulated in accordance with stored programs.

Magic? Not in the least. With CRT as the medium, we enter an era of "computer graphics," a term referring to the concept of man communicating directly with the computer by means of graphic symbols (lines, symbols, points, etc.). Sometimes called man-machine dialogue, this concept of information display technology promises to provide its users with information in graphic form that the user can manipulate in a variety of exciting ways.

Basically, computer graphics works like this: information is stored in the computer's system, retrievable and formatted by program. Requests for information are entered directly onto an input panel by pressing the appropriate button(s). The program is activated, and the information stored in the system is called forth in the form of graphic and alphanumeric displays on the CRT screen. Alterations are then made by keyboard and lightpen. When a reformatting of the information is desired, the on-screen format is returned to storage (as altered), and a new (preprogrammed) format is called up.

In addition to the wide range of flexibility, the CRT has amazing speed—a key factor in coping with the information explosion. Drawings, for example, that might take five hours to do manually, and fifteen minutes to do with a digital plotter can be handled in seconds on a CRT.

The application possibilities of computer graphics are vast. Yet, so new is it in its development that at this stage only the corporate giants can afford to use it. Even they have limited its application mainly to engineering design. For instance, computer graphics can conceivably decrease the design time for a new automobile from its present two to three years to some four months; a Navy ship detail design from eighteen months to two to four weeks. In large scale projects such as these, computer graphics is economically feasible.

But it's only a matter of time before the price is right for many other applications. One of these will surely be charting. In anticipation, let us take a sneak preview of the effects computer

graphics, and its CRT, might have on some of the aspects of charting.

The gruesome paper handling now required for charting will be eliminated. The communicator will have instant access to stored data in visual form.

Information could be "massaged" to produce charts that will forecast, by simulation, the outcome of various alternative courses of action. Such comparative analyses will facilitate sound decision-making.

Data could be manipulated into different formats; the selection of scale ranges and intervals will be virtually infinite; color will become a routine matter.

For instance, the stored data could be called up as a Bar chart with a selected scale; the scale could then be changed, and the picture will instantly change to show the chart revamped with its adjusted scale. Or, data could be reformated

12-9 Photo courtesy of American Stock Exchange

as a Pie chart, converting the absolute numbers into percentages. Or, a trend line could be created and projected by pressing a button.

Information "in depth" will be available for analyzing the backup of charted material. For example, the chart may be shown having an increment in years. By pressing a button, any or all years can be exploded into months, or weeks, or even days (if the information were stored in daily increments).

Another example is the establishing of upper and lower limits on a given chart; supporting detail data to explain variations from these limits can be called up for examination.

CRT will become a medium allowing direct on-line reporting, and off-line mass presentations will be possible. Instant reporting from branches or locations, or even from departments, could be made in graphic form at any time. Since the system is on-line the information will always be timely and comprehensive.

Mass presentations could be simultaneously given a diverse geographic location, somewhat like a closed-circuit television setup with the computer acting as chartist.

Charting will become "personalized." Individual queries from desk-top units could be made that will produce chartings of information that will interest the requestor. This could be done without requiring the large graphics department that is presently needed to render similar service.

All these and many other possibilities are in store for us through computer graphics and CRT. Of course, many of them are still a long way off from the average communicator. While many of the pieces for such a system exist today — in some feasible form or other — the big problem is the immense amount of programming that has yet to be mastered. Programming for computer graphics is a comparatively new field, though some "primitive" examples are in use. The stockmarket CRT devices for price quotations are an example of what has been accomplished so far.

There is no denying the complexity and difficulty of implementing computer graphic systems, given the present state of the art. But the state is advancing so rapidly that any such observation is doomed to obsolescence.

We have come a long way from William Playfair's lineal arithmetic. In the eighteenth century the time was right for his development. In this latter part of the twentieth century the information explosion has created the need for computer graphics. And we are steadily moving toward meeting that need.

The machine alone is not enough. The art of data retrieval (a software problem) must be brought up from its lag behind computer technology, before many of the new concepts become practical. We must learn means and techniques to edit, classify, store, manipulate, and retrieve information. As a tool the computer is capable of processing monumental amounts of data; it has enabled us to record information in a condensed form, which has facilitated the art of charting. To go further, this art must be programmed, a task still beyond our capabilities, and, at present, beyond our ability to afford; the cost must be lowered.

Probably the most dramatic advancements in computer graphics will occur within the next decades when concepts like computer utility and time-sharing move out of their experimental stages and become available on a wide scale. The computer utility, much like the electric and telephone utilities of today, will offer computer services to individual subscribers who will share the time and cost of the facility. Utilities, with computers having speeds even greater than present-day systems, will allow each of their individual users almost instantaneous access to the complex, thereby affording him service equivalent to having his own computer — and at a fraction of the cost. Considering the incredible progress computer technology is making almost on a daily basis, the day that the utility becomes a reality may be rapidly approaching.

Lord Kelvin is supposed to have said, "When you can measure what you are speaking about and express it in numbers, you know something about it."

It is in this quantitative expression that graphics can play a key role. We have not as yet tapped all of the potentials of charting; as we combine it with the computer we open new vistas: *tomorrow the tube.*

12-10 Photo by Arthur Lavine (Courtesy of Chase Manhattan Bank)

Sources and References

A principal problem in the communications field, today, is that the many sources and references that could help the communicator do his job better are not adequately communicated. With this thought in mind the following listing has been prepared as an aid in locating those many sources and references.

In order to give them some semblance of order, however, ten categories were established. And where a source or reference is pertinent to a category it is so indicated. To facilitate retrieval the ten categories are defined as follows:

Charting Forms & Devices: Basic charting devices as covered in Chapter 4, and pictorial forms as covered in Chapter 6. In addition, other more unusual forms and devices are included.

Charting Mechanics: Primarily the material covered in Chapter 5, but also including subjects such as layout, sizing, composition, and generally "how to" construct a chart.

Media & Facilities: The material covered in Chapters 8, 9, and 12, and detailed descriptions concerning the utilization and maintenance of the various media.

Production Methods & Techniques: Detailed descriptions of the methods and techniques used in chart-making — the diazo process, for instance. Also included is the production of films, slides, and printed matter. This subject is not covered in this book.

Production Materials: Sources for the myriad of materials used in chart-making.

Photography: Some of the literature available on a subject worthy of a book in itself.

Typography: Informative material on methods and techniques of entering text onto a chart.

Color: Some of the practical aspects which augment and supplement Chapter 7.

Audio-Visual Equipment Manufacturers: Makers of various equipment, such as projectors and screens, used in audio-visual presentations.

Film & Photo Libraries: Valuable sources for picture material used in chart-making, and for training material in learning how films are made. Also, a treasury of interesting prepared material for countless other uses.

The literature listed herein that is published by suppliers and manufacturers can be readily obtained upon request. Much of it is furnished at no charge or at a nominal cost.

	Char-ting Forms & Devices	Char-ting Mechan-ics	Media & Facil-ities	Produc-tion Methods & Tech-niques	Produc-tion Mate-rials	Photog-raphy	Typog-raphy	Color	Audio-Visual Equip-ment Manufac-turers	Film & Photo Li-braries
ACS Tapes, Inc. Newton, Massachusetts					●			●		
Advance Products Co. Wichita, Kansas									●	
Airequipt, Inc. New Rochelle, New York									●	
Allied Impex Corp. New York, New York									●	
Amateur Filmstrip Production. N. Woefel. Columbus: Ohio State University, 1958.			●	●		●				
American Felt Company Chicago 6, Illinois			●		●					
American Management Association New York, New York										●
American Marketing Association Chicago, Illinois										●
American Optical Company Buffalo, New York									●	

	Charting Forms & Devices	Charting Mechanics	Media & Facilities	Production Methods & Techniques	Production Materials	Photography	Typography	Color	Audio-Visual Equipment Manufacturers	Film & Photo Libraries
American Standard Specification for Slidefilm Projection. New York: American Standards Association, 1945.			●							
Annotated Bibliography of Audio-Visual Aids for Management Development Programs. New York: Research Service.			●						●	●
The Annual Report. Boston: S. D. Warren Company.			●	●						
Annual Technical Bulletin Guide. New York: Industrial Photography.			●						●	
Applied Color Photography Indoors. Rochester: Eastman Kodak Company, E-76, 1966.						●		●		
H. Armstrong Roberts Philadelphia, Pennsylvania										●
Artificial Light Photography. Ansel Adams. Hastings, New York: Morgan & Morgan, Inc.						●				
Artype, Incorporated Crystal Lake, Illinois				●	●		●			
Artwork for Photofabrication. Rochester: Eastman Kodak Company, P-1-63-2, 1963.				●	●	●				

	Charting Forms & Devices	Charting Mechanics	Media & Facilities	Production Methods & Techniques	Production Materials	Photography	Typography	Color	Audio-Visual Equipment Manufacturers	Film & Photo Libraries
Artwork Size Standards for Projected Visuals. Rochester: Eastman Kodak Company, S-12, 1966.	●									
Association Films New York, New York										●
Audicon Corp. Ann Arbor, Michigan									●	
Audio-Visual Education. A. J. Cross and Irene F. Cypher. New York: Thomas Y. Crowell Co., 1961.			●							
The Audio-Visual Equipment Directory. Fairfax, Virginia: National Audio-Visual Association, Inc.			●						●	
Audio-Visual Guide to Better Projection. Morton Grove, Illinois: Radiant Manufacturing Corp.			●						●	
Audio-Visual Materials and Devices. Ben F. Holland, Horace C. Hartsell, and Raymond L. Davidson. Lubbock, Texas: Rodgers Litho, 1958.			●		●					
Audio-Visual Materials and Techniques. 2nd ed. James S. Kinder. New York: The American Book Co., 1959.			●	●	●					
Audio-Visual Materials: Their Nature and Use. 3rd ed. Walter A. Wittich and Charles F. Schuller. New York: Harper and Row, 1962.			●	●	●					

	Charting Forms & Devices	Charting Mechanics	Media & Facilities	Production Methods & Techniques	Production Materials	Photography	Typography	Color	Audio-Visual Equipment Manufacturers	Film & Photo Libraries
Audio-Visual Methods in Teaching. Rev. ed. Edgar Dale. New York: The Dryden Press, 1954.			●							
Audiovisual Planning Equipment. Rochester: Eastman Kodak Company, S-11, 1966.				●						
Audio-Visual Procedures in Teaching. Lester B. Sands. New York: The Ronald Press Co., 1956.			●							
Audiovisual Projection. Rochester: Eastman Kodak Company, S-3, 1966.			●							
Audio-Visual Source Directory of Educational Sound Filmstrips. St. Charles, Illinois: Dukane Corp., 1967.										●
Authenticated News International New York, New York										●
AV Instructional Material and Methods. 2nd ed. James S. Brown, Richard B. Lewis, and Fred F. Harcleroad. New York: McGraw-Hill Book Co., 1964.			●	●					●	●
AV Instructional Materials Manual. 2nd ed. James W. Brown and Richard B. Lewis, eds. New York: McGraw-Hill Book Co., 1964.			●	●					●	●
AV Materials Handbook. 2nd ed. Bloomington: Indiana University Audio-Visual Center, 1960.			●	●	●		●			

210

	Charting Forms & Devices	Charting Mechanics	Media & Facilities	Production Methods & Techniques	Production Materials	Photography	Typography	Color	Audio-Visual Equipment Manufacturers	Film & Photo Libraries
Basic Color for the Graphic Arts. Rochester: Eastman Kodak Company, Q-7, 1964.				●		●		●		
Basic Copying. Rochester: Eastman Kodak Company, AM-2, 1966.				●		●				
Basic Photography for the Graphic Arts. Rochester: Eastman Kodak Company, Q-1, 1967.						●				
Basic Titling and Animation. Rochester: Eastman Kodak Company, S-21, 1965.				●	●	●				
Bausch and Lomb Optical Company Rochester, New York									●	
Beckley-Cardy Company Chicago, Illinois			●	●	●					
Bell and Howell Photo Sales Co. Chicago, Illinois									●	
Charles Bessler Corporation East Orange, New Jersey									●	
The Bettmann Archive, Inc. New York, New York										●

	Charting Forms & Devices	Charting Mechanics	Media & Facilities	Production Methods & Techniques	Production Materials	Photography	Typography	Color	Audio-Visual Equipment Manufacturers	Film & Photo Libraries
Black Star Publishing Company New York, New York										●
The Blue Book of Audio-Visual Materials. Chicago: Educational Screen and Audio-Visual Guide.										●
Arthur Brown & Bro., Inc. New York, New York					●					
Brown Brothers New York, New York 10036										●
Brumberger Co. Maspeth, New York					●					
Charles Bruning Co., Inc. Mount Prospect, Illinois				●	●				●	
Business Charts: A Clear Explanation of the Various Types of Charts Used in Business, and of the Principles Governing the Correct Facts by Graphic Methods. T. G. Rose. London: Sir Isaac Pitman & Sons, Ltd., 1949.	●	●								
Business Education Films Brooklyn, New York										●
California Computer Products, Inc. Anaheim, California			●						●	

	Charting Forms & Devices	Charting Mechanics	Media & Facilities	Production Methods & Techniques	Production Materials	Photography	Typography	Color	Audio-Visual Equipment Manufacturers	Film & Photo Libraries
Camera Copying & Reproduction. O. R. Croy. Focal Press, Ltd.				●		●				
Cello-Tak Company New York, New York				●	●			●		
Central Press Association Cleveland, Ohio										●
Charting Statistics. Mary E. Spear. New York: McGraw-Hill Book Co., 1952.	●	●								
Chart-Pak, Inc. Leeds, Massachusetts				●	●			●		
"Check Your A-V Plans," David H. Curl, *Photo Methods for Industry* (July, 1965).			●							
Close-up Movies. Rochester: Eastman Kodak Company, AD-30, 1966.				●		●				
Color: A Guide to Basic Facts and Concepts. R. M. Burnham, R. M. Hanes and C. J. Bartleson. New York: John Wiley & Sons, 1963.								●		
Color Aid Company New York, New York					●			●		

213

	Charting Forms & Devices	Charting Mechanics	Media & Facilities	Production Methods & Techniques	Production Materials	Photography	Typography	Color	Audio-Visual Equipment Manufacturers	Film & Photo Libraries
Color as Seen and Photographed. Rochester: Eastman Kodak Company, E-74, 1966.						●		●		
Color, Form and Space. Faber Birren. New York: Reinhold Book Corporation, 1961.								●		
Color in Business, Science and Industry. 2nd ed. Deane B. Judd and Gunter Wyszecki. New York: John Wiley & Sons, 1963.								●		
Color Vu Chicago, Illinois					●			●		
Colotone Overlay Sheets New York, New York					●			●		
Communication for Modern Management. J. Barron Wiley. Elmhurst, Illinois: The Business Press, 1966.			●			●				
The Company Publication. Boston: S. D. Warren Company.			●	●						
Composition. Rochester: Eastman Kodak Company, AC-11, 1966.						●				
Computer Graphics: A Revolution in Design. R. A. Siders et al. New York: American Management Association, 1966.			●							

214

	Charting Forms & Devices	Charting Mechanics	Media & Facilities	Production Methods & Techniques	Production Materials	Photography	Typography	Color	Audio-Visual Equipment Manufacturers	Film & Photo Libraries
"Concept of the Profit/Volume Graph Applied to Capital Investment Planning," C. L. Moore, *Accounting Review* (October, 1966).	●	●								
Concord Electronics Corp. Los Angeles, California									●	
Contak Transograph Company Leeds, Massachusetts				●	●			●		
Controlling Two or Three KODAK CAROUSEL Projectors with a Single KODAK CAROUSEL Sound Synchronizer. Rochester: Eastman Kodak Company, S-58, 1966.			●							
Copying. Rochester: Eastman Kodak Company, M-1, 1965.				●		●				
Copying Method Manual. Chicago: The American Library Association.			●	●						
Cords, Plugs and Receptacles for KODAK CAROUSEL Projectors. Rochester: Eastman Kodak Company, S-54, 1965.			●							
"Corporate Projection Facilities," *Industrial Audio-Visuals* (January, 1967).			●							
Crafting Manufacturing Co. Cleveland, Ohio					●			●		

	Charting Forms & Devices	Charting Mechanics	Media & Facilities	Production Methods & Techniques	Production Materials	Photography	Typography	Color	Audio-Visual Equipment Manufacturers	Film & Photo Libraries
Creating Visuals for TV. John Spear. Washington: National Educational Association, 1962.	●	●	●							
Creative Color. Faber Birren. New York: Reinhold Book Corporation, 1961.								●		
Creatron, Inc. Floral Park, New York									●	
Culver Pictures, Inc. New York, New York										●
Da-Lite Screen Co., Inc. Warsaw, Indiana									●	
Decisions Systems, Inc. Teaneck, New Jersey									●	
Department of Audio-Visual Instruction National Education Association Washington, D.C.			●							
Design by Photography. O. R. Croy. New York: Hastings House, Publishers, 1964.	●	●		●			●			
Diazochrome Projectuals for Visual Communication. Holyoke, Massachusetts: Tecnifax Corp., 1964.			●	●	●			●	●	

	Charting Forms & Devices	Charting Mechanics	Media & Facilities	Production Methods & Techniques	Production Materials	Photography	Typography	Color	Audio-Visual Equipment Manufacturers	Film & Photo Libraries
Draper Shade & Screen Co. Spiceland, Indiana									●	
Dukane Corporation St. Charles, Illinois									●	
Eastman Kodak Company Rochester, New York									●	
Easy Slidemaking with a VERIFAX Copier. Rochester: Eastman Kodak Company, S-23, 1964.				●	●					
Educational Displays and Exhibits. J. Preston Lockridge and Greda G. Murray. Austin: Visual Instruction Bureau, University of Texas, 1960.			●							
Educational Exhibits: How to Prepare and Use Them. H. W. Gilbertson. Washington: United States Government Printing Office, 1948.	●		●	●	●					
Educators' Guide to Free Films. Randolph, Wisconsin.										●
Effective Business & Technical Presentations. George L. Morrisey. Reading, Massachusetts: Addison-Wesley Publishing Co., 1968.			●							
Effective Lecture Slides. Rochester: Eastman Kodak Company, S-22, 1966.		●		●			●			

217

	Charting Forms & Devices	Charting Mechanics	Media & Facilities	Production Methods & Techniques	Production Materials	Photography	Typography	Color	Audio-Visual Equipment Manufacturers	Film & Photo Libraries
Elco Optisonics Corp. Willow Grove, Pennsylvania									●	
Embosograf Corp. of America New York, New York									●	
Employee Communication: Policy and Tools. Geneva Seybold. New York: National Industrial Conference Board, Inc., 1966.			●							
European Picture Service New York, New York										●
Exhibition Techniques—Traveling and Temporary. James H. Carmel. New York: Reinhold Book Corporation, 1963.		●		●	●					
Film and Its Techniques. Raymond Spottiswoode. Berkeley: University of California Press, 1953.			●	●		●				
Film and the Director. Don Livingston. New York: The Macmillian Company, 1958.			●	●		●				
Film Guide for Marketing Executives. William Wachs, ed. New York: Research Division, Sales & Marketing Executives Institute.										●
Film Making from Script to Screen. Andrew Buchanan. New York: The Macmillan Company, 1951.			●	●		●				

	Charting Forms & Devices	Charting Mechanics	Media & Facilities	Production Methods & Techniques	Production Materials	Photography	Typography	Color	Audio-Visual Equipment Manufacturers	Film & Photo Libraries
Films Relating to Printing and Graphic Arts. Midland: Michigan Industrial Education Society, Inc.										●
Foot-High Letters: A Guide to Lettering. Matlack Price. New York: Dover Publications, 1961.							●			
Freelance Photographers Guild New York, New York										●
Grace Letter Company New York, New York					●		●			
Graflex, Inc. Rochester, New York									●	
Graphic Charts Handbook. Anna C. Rogers. Washington: Public Affairs Press, 1961.	●	●								
"Graphic Displays: Help for Middle Managers." *The Metal Working Weekly.*			●							
Graphic Methods for Presenting Facts. Willard C. Brinton. New York: McGraw-Hill Book Co., 1914.	●	●		●						
Graphic Presentation. Willard C. Brinton. New York: Brinton Associates, 1939.	●	●	●	●				●		

	Charting Forms & Devices	Charting Mechanics	Media & Facilities	Production Methods & Techniques	Production Materials	Photography	Typography	Color	Audio-Visual Equipment Manufacturers	Film & Photo Libraries
Graphic Presentation. Francis J. McHugh. Holyoke, Massachusetts: Tecnifax Corp., 1956.	●	●	●							
Graphic Presentation Simplified. R. P. Lutz. New York: Funk and Wagnalls Co., 1949.	●	●	●	●	●					
Graphical Analysis—Understanding Graphs and Curves in Technology. Philip Stein. New York: Heyden Book Co., Inc., 1964.	●	●								
M. Grumbacher, Inc. New York, New York					●			●		
A Guide for Preparing Technical Illustrations for Publication and Projection. New York: American Society of Mechanical Engineers, ASA Y15.1-1959.	●	●		●	●		●			
Guide to Audio-Visual Presentations. J. M. Dugan, J. S. Jones, S. A. Hawk, and L. E. Walkup. New York: Wolf Business Publications, Inc., 1964.	●	●	●							
Handbook for Production of Filmstrips and Records. John Lord and Robert Larson. St. Charles, Illinois: Dukane Corp., 1962.			●	●		●				
Handbook of Basic Motion Picture Techniques. Emil E. Brodbeck. New York: McGraw-Hill Book Co., 1950.			●	●		●				
Handbook of Graphic Presentation. Calvin F. Schmid. New York: The Ronald Press Co., 1954.	●	●	●	●	●					

	Charting Forms & Devices	Charting Mechanics	Media & Facilities	Production Methods & Techniques	Production Materials	Photography	Typography	Color	Audio-Visual Equipment Manufacturers	Film & Photo Libraries
Handbook of Graphic Reproduction Processes. Felix Brunner. New York: Hastings House, Publishers, 1962.				●						
The Handling, Repair, and Storage of 16mm Films. Rochester: Eastman Kodak Company, D-23, 1967.			●							
Heat-set Web Offset. K. Wallace. Neenah, Wisconsin: Kimberly-Clark Corporation, 1961.				●						
Historical Pictures Service Chicago, Illinois										●
Holiday / Glossary for Planning Business Meetings. New York: Holiday Magazine.			●							
Honeywell Denver, Colorado									●	
How to Check Your Exposure Meter and Camera. Rochester: Eastman Kodak Company, AF-8, 1966.						●				
How to Do Paste-ups & Mechanicals. S. R. Maurello. New York: Tudor Publishing, 1960.				●						
How to Lithograph Coated Offset Paper. Neenah, Wisconsin: Kimberly-Clark Corporation.				●						

	Charting Forms & Devices	Charting Mechanics	Media & Facilities	Production Methods & Techniques	Production Materials	Photography	Typography	Color	Audio-Visual Equipment Manufacturers	Film & Photo Libraries
How to Organize and Operate Photographic Service Departments. Rochester: Eastman Kodak Company, P-17, 1961.						●				
How to Prepare Artwork for Letterpress. Eugene M. Ettenberg and Ralph E. Eckerstrom. Neenah, Wisconsin: Kimberly-Clark Corporation.				●	●					
"How to Read an Organization Chart for Fun and Survival," Donald Winks, *Harper's Magazine* (January, 1967).	●	●								
How Will It Print By Offset. Boston: S. D. Warren Company.				●						
Hudson Photographic Industries, Inc. Irvington-on-Hudson, New York									●	
The Imperfect Miracle. Ulric Meisel. Dallas: Meisel Photochrome Corp.						●		●		
Industrial Motion Pictures. Rochester: Eastman Kodak Company, P-18, 1966.				●		●				
Instant Artwork. Rochester: Eastman Kodak Company, P-1, 1964.				●	●					
Institute for Visual Training New York, New York										●

	Charting Forms & Devices	Charting Mechanics	Media & Facilities	Production Methods & Techniques	Production Materials	Photography	Typography	Color	Audio-Visual Equipment Manufacturers	Film & Photo Libraries
Instructo Products Co. Philadelphia, Pennsylvania									●	
Integrated Teaching Materials. R. Murray Thomas and Sherwin S. Swartout. New York: Longmans, Green and Company, 1960.			●							
International Audio Visual Ltd. New Westminster, B.C., Canada									●	
July Company Minneapolis 1, Minnesota			●		●					
Kalart Co., Inc. Plainville, Connecticut				●	●	●			●	
Keufell & Esser Co. Chicago, Illinois					●					
Kimpressions (series). Neenah, Wisconsin: Kimberly-Clark Corporation.				●	●			●		
Kodak Artwork Template. Rochester: Eastman Kodak Company, S-25, 1966.		●		●	●					
Harold M. Lambert Studios, Inc. Philadelphia, Pennsylvania										●

223

	Charting Forms & Devices	Charting Mechanics	Media & Facilities	Production Methods & Techniques	Production Materials	Photography	Typography	Color	Audio-Visual Equipment Manufacturers	Film & Photo Libraries
Legibility Standards for Projected Material. Rochester: Eastman Kodak Company, S-4, 1965.		●			●		●			
E. Leitz, Inc. New York, New York									●	
Let's Stop Calling It Portable. Raymond Wyman. Holyoke, Massachusetts: Tecnifax Corp., 1962.			●							
Library of Congress Printed Cards for Motion Pictures and Filmstrips Card Division, Library of Congress Washington, D. C.										●
Library of Congress Prints and Photographs Division Washington, D. C.										●
Magnetic Visual Control Systems. New York: Methods Research Corp., 1964.			●	●	●					
Magphoto/Chicago Chicago, Illinois										●
Mailing Lists and Regulations. Boston: S. D. Warren Company.				●						
Making Black-and-White Transparencies for Overhead Projection. Rochester: Eastman Kodak Company, S-7, 1967.				●	●					

	Charting Forms & Devices	Charting Mechanics	Media & Facilities	Production Methods & Techniques	Production Materials	Photography	Typography	Color	Audio-Visual Equipment Manufacturers	Film & Photo Libraries
Marsh Stencil Marking Pens Belleville, Illinois					●					
Mast Development Co. Davenport, Iowa			●							
Mercury Archives Hollywood, California										●
A Method for Editing Your Movies. Rochester: Eastman Kodak Company, AD-26, 1966.				●		●				
MGM Studies Research Department Culver City, California										●
Minnesota Mining and Manufacturing St. Paul, Minnesota			●	●	●				●	
Morgan Sign Machine Co. Chicago, Illinois					●					
Motion Picture Production for Industry. Jay E. Gordon. New York: The Macmillan Company, 1961.			●	●		●				
Movichart: Graphic Chart Systems. Chicago: Pryor Marketing Products, 1963.			●	●	●					

225

	Charting Forms & Devices	Charting Mechanics	Media & Facilities	Production Methods & Techniques	Production Materials	Photography	Typography	Color	Audio-Visual Equipment Manufacturers	Film & Photo Libraries
National Archives Audio-Visual Records Branch Washington, D. C.										●
The New Art of Color Printing. Neenah, Wisconsin: Kimberly-Clark Corporation.				●	●			●		
"New Management Reporting Systems," Richard G. Canning, *EDP Analyzer* (January, 1967).	●									
New York Daily News New York, New York										●
The New York Times New York, New York										●
Nikon, Inc. New York, New York									●	
Opaque Projection. J. Y. Taylor. Buffalo: Scientific Instrument Division, American Optical Co., 1941.			●							
"Opaque Projector," T. C. Arthur, *International Journal of Religious Education* (November, 1957).			●							
The Opaque Projector. Kenneth L. Bowers. Austin: Visual Education Bureau, University of Texas, 1960.			●							

	Charting Forms & Devices	Charting Mechanics	Media & Facilities	Production Methods & Techniques	Production Materials	Photography	Typography	Color	Audio-Visual Equipment Manufacturers	Film & Photo Libraries
Operating Audio-Visual Equipment. Sidney C. Eboch. San Francisco: Chandler Publishing Company, 1960.			●							
Ozalid Division, General Aniline & Film Johnson City, New York			●	●	●			●	●	
Pantone Matching System Pantone, Inc. New York, New York								●		
Paper in the Making. International Paper Company, Southern Kraft Division.				●						
Papers and Their Uses. Boston: S. D. Warren Company.				●						
Paste-Up Drafting. Rochester: Eastman Kodak Company, P-1-63-1, 1963.		●		●		●				
Photographic Materials for the Graphic Arts. Rochester: Eastman Kodak Company, Q-2, 1967.					●					
Pictographs and Graphs. Rudolph Modley and Dyno Lowenstein. New York: Harper & Row, 1952.	●	●								
Picture Book of Symbols. Ernst Lehner. New York: Tudor Publishing, 1960.	●									

227

	Charting Forms & Devices	Charting Mechanics	Media & Facilities	Production Methods & Techniques	Production Materials	Photography	Typography	Color	Audio-Visual Equipment Manufacturers	Film & Photo Libraries
Picture Sources. Celestine G. Frankenberg, ed. New York: Special Libraries Association, 1964.										●
'Piggyback' Stand for Two-Screen Projection with Two CAROUSEL Projectors. Rochester: Eastman Kodak Company, S-55, 1965.			●							
Planning and Producing Visual Aids. Rochester: Eastman Kodak Company, S-13, 1966.				●	●	●				
Planning a Slide Presentation. Rochester: Eastman Kodak Company, P-100-4, 1967.				●						
Planning Schools for Use of Audio-Visual Materials. Washington: Department of Audiovisual Instruction, National Education Association, 1952.			●							
Planoscope Corp. New York, New York				●	●		●	●		
Polaroid Corporation Cambridge, Massachusetts				●		●			●	
Practical Audio-Visual Handbook for Teachers. Herbert E. Scuorzo. New York: Parker Publishing Co., Inc., 1967.			●	●	●					
Practical Rules for Graphic Presentation of Business Statistics. L. Edwin Smart and S. Kramer. Columbus: Bureau of Business Research, Ohio State University, 1951.	●	●		●						

	Charting Forms & Devices	Charting Mechanics	Media & Facilities	Production Methods & Techniques	Production Materials	Photography	Typography	Color	Audio-Visual Equipment Manufacturers	Film & Photo Libraries
Preparation and Use of Audio-Visual Aids. Kenneth B. Haas and Harry Q. Packer. Englewood Cliffs, New Jersey: Prentice-Hall, Inc., 1955.	●	●	●	●	●					
Preparation of Inexpensive Teaching Materials. John E. Morlan. San Francisco Chandler Publishing Company, 1963.		●	●	●	●		●	●		
"Preparing Opaque Projection Materials," Sam Blanc, *Teaching Tools* (Fall, 1956).			●	●						
Pre-printed Pictorial Symbols. Washington: Division of Extension Information, U.S. Department of Agriculture.	●			●	●					
Prestype, Inc. New York, New York				●	●		●			
"Printing—The Essential Aid to Management," Booklet No. 4. Boston: S. D. Warren Company.			●	●						
The Processes of Reproduction. Boston: S. D. Warren Company.				●						
Producing Slides and Filmstrips. Rochester: Eastman Kodak Company, S-8, 1966.			●	●		●				
Programmed Learning and Computer-Based Instruction. John E. Coulson, ed. New York: John Wiley & Sons, 1962.			●							

229

	Charting Forms & Devices	Charting Mechanics	Media & Facilities	Production Methods & Techniques	Production Materials	Photography	Typography	Color	Audio-Visual Equipment Manufacturers	Film & Photo Libraries
Projection Distance Tables for KODAK CAROUSEL Projectors. Rochester: Eastman Kodak Company, S-41, 1967.			●							
Publix Pictorial Service Corp. Chicago, Illinois										●
Radio Times Hulton Picture Library London, England										●
RCA Victor Division Radio Corporation of America Camden, New Jersey									●	
Rear-Projection Cabinet. Rochester: Eastman Kodak Company, S-29, 1967.			●						●	
Redi-Art, Inc. New York, New York	●			●	●					
"ROP (ColoROPtics) Color and Its Effect on Newspaper Advertising," Burleigh B. Gardener and Yehudi A. Cohen, *Journal of Marketing Research* (May, 1964).								●		
The Sales Catalog. Boston: S. D. Warren Company.			●	●						
San Francisco News Call Bulletin San Francisco, California										●

	Charting Forms & Devices	Charting Mechanics	Media & Facilities	Production Methods & Techniques	Production Materials	Photography	Typography	Color	Audio-Visual Equipment Manufacturers	Film & Photo Libraries
School Pen Co. Chatham, New Jersey					●					
Selected References on Audiovisual Publications. Rochester: Eastman Kodak Company, S-10, 1966.										●
"Selecting the Proper Screen," *Industrial Audio-Visuals* (March, 1967).			●							
A Simple Wooden Copy Stand for Making Title Slides and Filmstrips. Rochester: Eastman Kodak Company, T-43, 1964.				●		●				
Simplified Techniques for Preparing Visual Instructional Materials. Ed. Minor. New York: McGraw-Hill Co., 1962.	●		●	●	●					
16mm Sound Motion Pictures: A Manual for the Professional and Amateur. William H. Offenhauser, Jr. New York: Interscience Publishers, 1958.			●	●		●				
Slides and Movies for Service Groups. Rochester: Eastman Kodak Company, AT-10, 1964.										●
Slides: Confusing or Clear? B. A. Jones. Detroit: The Ethyl Corp., 1952.			●							
Some Sources of 2x2-Inch Color Slides. Rochester: Eastman Kodak Company, S-2, 1966.										●

	Charting Forms & Devices	Charting Mechanics	Media & Facilities	Production Methods & Techniques	Production Materials	Photography	Typography	Color	Audio-Visual Equipment Manufacturers	Film & Photo Libraries
Sources of Motion Pictures and Filmstrips. Rochester: Eastman Kodak Company, S-9, 1966.										●
Sources of Motion-Picture Services and Equipment. Rochester: Eastman Kodak Company, AD-20, 1966.										●
Spindler & Sauppe, Inc. Glendale, California									●	
Standard Projector & Equipment Co., Inc. Glenview, Illinois									●	
Standards of Statistical Presentation (chapter on Graphic Presentation). Office of the Comptroller of the Army. Washington: Department of the Army, 1955.	●	●								
Studio Lighting for Product Photography. Rochester: Eastman Kodak Company, O-16, 1965.						●				
Successful Movie Projector Operation. Rochester: Eastman Kodak Company, AD-36, 1965.			●							
Suggestions for Loading and Handling 35mm Cameras. Rochester: Eastman Kodak Company, AE-46, 1966.						●				
Symbology. Elmwood Whitney, ed. New York: Hastings House, Publishers, 1960.	●									

232

	Charting Forms & Devices	Charting Mechanics	Media & Facilities	Production Methods & Techniques	Production Materials	Photography	Typography	Color	Audio-Visual Equipment Manufacturers	Film & Photo Libraries
Synchronizing Slide Change for Two or More Projectors. Rochester: Eastman Kodak Company, S-15, 1965.			●							
The Technique of the Sound Studio. Alec Nisbett. New York: Hastings House, Publishers, 1962.				●						
Techniques of Magnetic Recording. Joel Tall. New York: The Macmillan Company, 1958.				●						
The Techniques of Special Effects Cinematography. Raymond Fielding. New York: Hastings House, Publishers, 1965.				●		●				
Tecnifax Corporation Holyoke, Massachusetts									●	
Time Saving Specialties Minneapolis, Minnesota					●					
Time-Series Charts. New York: American Society of Mechanical Engineers, ASA Y15.2-1960.		●		●						
Trouble Shooting for Printers. Neenah, Wisconsin: Kimberly-Clark Corporation, 1962.				●						
Type and Its Relation to Paper. R. Hunter Middleton. Neenah, Wisconsin: Kimberly-Clark Corporation, 1959.				●			●			

233

	Charting Forms & Devices	Charting Mechanics	Media & Facilities	Production Methods & Techniques	Production Materials	Photography	Typography	Color	Audio-Visual Equipment Manufacturers	Film & Photo Libraries
Type and Typography—The Designer's Type Book. Ben Rosen. New York: Reinhold Book Corporation, 1967.							●			
Types & Typography. Boston: S. D. Warren Company.							●			
Typography: A Manual of Design. Emil Ruder. New York: Hastings House, Publishers, 1967.							●			
Typography: Basic Principles. John Lewis. New York: Reinhold Book Corporation, 1964.							●			
United Nations Photographic Department, Room 994 New York, New York										●
United Press International News Pictures New York, New York										●
United World Films, Inc. New York, New York										●
"The Use of Colors to Improve Operating Efficiency," Allen Weiss, *The New York Certified Public Accountant* (October, 1965).								●		
"Use of Graphs in Internal Reporting: A Summary of Practice, *NAA Bulletin* (October, 1961).	●	●								

	Charting Forms & Devices	Charting Mechanics	Media & Facilities	Production Methods & Techniques	Production Materials	Photography	Typography	Color	Audio-Visual Equipment Manufacturers	Film & Photo Libraries
Using the Opaque Projector. Raymond Denno. Dallas: Squibb-Taylor, Inc., 1958.			●							
Varityper Corporation Newark, New Jersey									●	
Visual Art for Industry. George Magnan. New York: Reinhold Book Corporation, 1961.	●	●		●						
Visual Presentation of Invisible Processes. Anton Stankowski. New York: Hastings House, Publishers, 1967.	●	●	●	●						
Visualizing the Abstract. Patrick H. Beatts. Holyoke, Massachusetts: Tecnifax Corp., 1956.	●	●								
Visucom-Equipment and Materials Catalog. Holyoke, Massachusetts: Tecnifax Corp., 1964.			●	●	●			●		
Vu-Graphics: A Manual on Vu-Graph Projection. East Orange, New Jersey: Charles Bessler Company, 1952.			●							
"What's Behind the Growth of Color?" Ann R. Lyon, *Printers Ink* (September 13, 1963).								●		
Wide-Screen/Multiple-Screen Showmanship. Rochester: Eastman Kodak Company, S-28, 1966.			●	●						

	Charting Forms & Devices	Charting Mechanics	Media & Facilities	Production Methods & Techniques	Production Materials	Photography	Typography	Color	Audio-Visual Equipment Manufacturers	Film & Photo Libraries
Wide World Photos, Inc. New York, New York										●
H. Wilson Corp. Chicago, Illinois			●							●
Workbook for Planning Printing. Boston: S. D. Warren Company.				●						
Carl Zeiss, Inc. New York, New York									●	
Zip-a-Tone Para-Tone, Inc. La Grange, Illinois				●	●		●	●		

Index

238

240